OCEANSIDE PUBLIC LIBRARY
615 FOURTH STREET
OCEANSIDE, CALIF. 92054

D1042337

OCEANSIDE PUBLIC LIBRARY

3 1232 00237 0726

The
Oxford Book of English
Traditional Verse

821.08
OXF

The
Oxford Book of English
Traditional Verse

Chosen and edited by
Frederick Woods

OXFORD   NEW YORK
OXFORD UNIVERSITY PRESS
1983

OCEANSIDE PUBLIC LIBRARY
615 FOURTH STREET
OCEANSIDE, CALIF. 92054

Oxford University Press, Walton Street, Oxford OX2 6DP

London Glasgow New York Toronto
Delhi Bombay Calcutta Madras Karachi
Kuala Lumpur Singapore Hong Kong Tokyo
Nairobi Dar es Salaam Cape Town
Melbourne Auckland
and associates in
Beirut Berlin Ibadan Mexico City Nicosia

Introduction, Notes, and compilation © Frederick Woods 1983

All rights reserved. No part of this publication may be reproduced,
stored in a retrieval system, or transmitted, in any form or by any means,
electronic, mechanical, photocopying, recording, or otherwise, without
the prior permission of Oxford University Press

British Library Cataloguing in Publication Data
The Oxford book of English traditional verse.
1. Folk poetry, English
I. Woods, Frederick
821'.008 PR977
ISBN 0-19-214132-5

Library of Congress Cataloging in Publication Data
The Oxford book of English traditional verse.
Includes index.
1. Folk poetry, English. 2. Folk-songs,
English—Texts. 3. Ballads, English—texts.
I. Woods, Frederick.
PR977.09 1983 398.2'0941 82-14442
ISBN 0-19-214132-5

Set by Wyvern Typesetting Ltd
Printed in Great Britain by
Richard Clay (The Chaucer Press) Ltd,
Bungay, Suffolk

JUL 2 0 1986

INTRODUCTION

THIS is an anthology of English traditional verse—in other words, the literary constituent of traditional or folk-song, a genre that ranges from the high drama of the classic ballads to the more unassuming but revealing minor songs.[1]

Over the centuries these songs have been created—largely by the working-class communities—and handed down the generations, honed and polished by continual alteration as either individual memories faltered or the chance of intentional improvement presented itself. Initially they were transmitted orally but, with the spread of literacy, the printed word also became a method of dissemination and perpetuation, mainly through the thousands of broadsides that were written and printed in most of the larger towns.

Although around the beginning of this century and later a few singers claimed authorship when singing to collectors, the vast majority of the songs had become anonymous; but with the increasing development of print, names like John Freeth and Tommy Armstrong began to appear on songs which, in spite of the fact that they made their first appearance in print, were quickly absorbed into the oral tradition. Henceforward there were two parallel strands of transmission. While in general terms the earlier rural songs concerned themselves with more timeless matters, the broadsides dealt largely with immediacies: new crazes, recent events, murders and executions, sports, political controversies of the moment. It has been frequently said that they were the newspapers of their time; in their heyday they could command enormous sales, partly due to a highly organized system of regional syndication.[2] Many of these broadside texts found their way into the oral tradition and are still being sung; others, not so popular and presumably not so singable, fell into oblivion and have been rescued by antiquarians.

Later influences on the traditional repertoire came from the

---

[1] I have preferred the word 'traditional' to the perhaps more common 'folk'. The phrase 'folk-song' would be quite acceptable but as I am solely concerned with literary texts a linguistic quirk makes the unavoidable corollary 'folk-verse' misleading, since that term would include material that is not traditional in any sense, e.g. the Dorsetshire poetry of William Barnes, the monologues of Marriott Edgar and much of the homespun dialect poetry written by 'Sunday poets'.

[2] Murder ballads were particularly popular. The following sales figures are quoted in Charles Hindley's *Curiosities of Street Literature* (1871): Rush (1849)—2,500,000; The Mannings (1849)—2,500,000; Courvoisier (1840)—1,666,000; Greenacre (1840)—1,650,000; William Corder (1828)—1,166,000.

music-hall songs of the Victorian era and—though here we enter the Debatable Lands—some of the popular music of the twentieth century. Victorian and Edwardian collectors often declined to listen when traditional singers offered to sing them material that was clearly not traditional in the full sense, and thereby missed an essential aspect of the singer's repertoire and social function. The traditional singer was more omnivorous than they wished to think; if a song suited him he would sing it, at least for a while. He has always sung new songs: at the beginning of the nineteenth century he sang songs about Napoleon, Wellington, and Nelson; and, as murder succeeded murder, he sang the resultant broadside text (an existing melody was often suggested on broadsides of the time).

In more recent days, the Sussex folk-singer Jim Copper (1882–1954) kept two manuscript books of words; one held all his traditional material, but in the other he copied the words to songs popularized by singers like Bing Crosby, Al Bowlly, and Louis Armstrong. The separation shows clearly enough the distinction he made between the two types of material, but he kept them both and he sang them both.

More recently still the post-war regeneration of interest in traditional song, exemplified by the widespread existence of folk-song clubs and still somewhat misleadingly called the Folk Revival, has added what its participants apparently think to be a new dimension, the 'contemporary folk-song'. This has stimulated a great deal of controversy as to its suitability and relevance in the context of a revival of traditional music, a controversy that arises solely from a failure to appreciate the true nature of traditional song. As I have indicated, there has always been a place for contemporary song in the old singer's repertoire, at least for a certain period while its quality was tested. If it had that necessary permanence of appeal, it survived; if not, not.

From these various strands, then, I have gathered together this anthology. In selecting the verses, I have endeavoured to use those that have come down to us in the mainstream of the English folk-song tradition, and that are still in active use. Some of the broadside material is probably not being currently sung, but a large proportion of these lyrics, in one version or another, can be heard at clubs and festivals throughout the country, and many have been recorded. In a few places, one can still hear them sung by traditional singers in a traditional setting.

Recently scholarly attitudes towards traditional material have tended to emphasize the excellence of the musical qualities at the expense of the literary. In this context Professor Bertrand Bronson's famous question 'When is a ballad not a ballad?' (answer: 'When it has no tune') is an essentially twentieth-century attitude. But to imply that the text of a ballad—and therefore, by inescapable extension, the text of any traditional song—is invalid by itself is extraordinarily sweeping, to say the least. Fortunately, appreciation of the towering literary qualities of the major ballads has remained constant, as is shown by the existence of such collections as James Kinsley's *Oxford Book of Ballads* and Geoffrey Grigson's *Penguin Book of Ballads*, but virtually no significant study or collection of the 'lesser' lyrics has appeared since the 1950s, which saw the publication of Pinto and Rodway's *The Common Muse* and James Reeves's *The Idiom of the People* and *The Everlasting Circle*; these books, however, concerned themselves only with limited areas of the field.

Until the last quarter of the nineteenth century, scholarly interest was centred almost entirely on the *words* of folk-songs, on traditional verse. Sir Philip Sidney's well-known reference to 'the old song of Piercy and Douglas' is one of the very few to mention the music even in passing. Collectors such as John Selden, Anthony à Wood, Samuel Pepys, the Duke of Roxburghe, and Bishop Percy were interested in the literary aspects of the tradition, and its musical qualities received little or no serious attention until Revd Sabine Baring-Gould and his contemporaries started their work in the 1880s.[1] Since then, through the intensive work of Cecil Sharp, Ralph Vaughan Williams, Percy Grainger and others up to the present day, the lion's share of scholarly concentration has been given to the melodies.

It must be admitted that the earlier literary predilection led to an appalling ignorance of the many glories of British traditional song. It was, in fact, widely believed that England in particular had no traditional music. As Dr Burney put it: 'Though the natives of Scotland, Ireland and Wales can boast of national tunes ... the English have not a melody which they can call their own except the hornpipe and the Cheshire round.' To which one can add the wryly pithy statement that 'if there were any English folk-songs, they were Irish'. Clearly, therefore, a serious imbalance had been reached, and it was only to be expected that the wave of Victorian collectors who rode or pedalled through the English countryside would attempt to restore a more balanced view.

---

[1] John Clare was a notable exception, collectiong not only texts but also songs and dance tunes. The extent of his work in this field has only recently come to light, thanks to research by George Deacon (*John Clare and the Folk Tradition*, Archway Books, 1983).

Perhaps, though, they and subsequent collectors went too far in the other direction. In *English Folk Song: Some Conclusions* (1907) Cecil Sharp wrote: 'It is greatly to be deplored that the literature of the ballad has in the past attracted so much more attention than the music. Properly speaking the two elements should never be dissociated: the music and the text are one and indivisible and to sever one from the other is to remove the jewel from its setting.' But words and melodies are *not* 'one and indivisible' and probably never have been. Tunes have always been interchangeable, and to imply that a folk-song has one exclusive melody is as inapt as to describe any folk text or melody as definitive. Further, if readers have found satisfaction in the texts alone for several hundred years, it would seem self-evident that the words can be detached without damage. Not to know the music was indeed a loss for those readers, but no destruction was involved in the separation, and it is perhaps a situation for sympathy rather than condemnation. In any case, how many transient broadsides would have been lost without the pioneering work of Selden, Pepys and the others? As many, probably, as the songs that might have been lost had the later collectors not gone into the country lanes and meadows.

If the Victorian and Edwardian collectors insisted on indivisibility, the Folk Revival of the post-war years has gone even further, and shown itself little interested in literary qualities. But then that movement, in its practical aspects, has always preferred simple entertainment first and foremost; it is, after all, a minor branch of show business, however much it has managed to remain relatively uncontaminated by commercial pressures.

In the face of all this, however, it is salutory to remember that, for the old traditional singer, the text—the story—was the important thing, and the music was largely a mnemonic.[1] From the earliest minstrels on, the story has always taken precedence in the singer's set of priorities. Even with light-hearted songs such as 'Johnny Sands', the audience response centres entirely on the denouement of the plot, not on the melody, however attractive that may be. And in the big ballads it is again the tale that holds the attention; provided the tune is compatible with the story it is pretty much irrelevant which one is used.

Finally in this context, it is significant that the music of British

---

[1] How far this is still true is perhaps open to doubt. The majority of living traditional singers have been affected by the demands of the largely middle-class Folk Revival, to such an extent that some at least are learning songs from recordings of professional Revivalist singers—one of the several forms of subtle distortion imposed on traditional song by the Revival.

traditional song has had only a limited effect on our formal music. Individual songs were used during the eighteenth-century vogue for ballad operas, and modern composers such as Vaughan Williams, Delius, Butterworth, and Grainger have produced fine orchestral arrangements; but, these apart, folk-song has had little inspirational impact.

In literary terms, however, there is clear evidence of a continuing influence. There was, for a start, a definite stylistic and atmospheric similarity between the early rural texts and the writings of such pastoral poets as Nicholas Breton and Bartholomew Young. If Thomas and Sally are there translated into Strephon and Stella, and if the classical allusions are more frequent, there is none the less strong indication of a more than casual acquaintance with traditional lyrics on the part of the formal poets. If a distinction is to be made in this respect, then the traditional verses are naïve, whereas their poetic counterparts, in searching for that quality, achieve only *faux-naïveté*.

But even if this similarity is dismissed as merely an accidental parallel, the influence of the tradition made itself undeniably and permanently felt with the appearance in 1765 of Percy's *Reliques of Ancient English Poetry*. To a European audience already seduced by the spurious legends of Ossian, the old ballads, with their unique blend of history and fable, of realism and the supernatural, came as something fresh and, above all, genuine. Apart from thus stimulating an interest in the medieval, Percy's *Reliques* led directly to the revival of the ballad form in the hands of such practitioners as Scott and Coleridge. The subsequent collections by Scott and Motherwell, and the publication of the *Roxburghe Ballads* continued the process; while the five volumes of Child's *English and Scottish Popular Ballads* (1882–98) gave final recognition not only to the high literary quality of the verses but also to the universality of their themes. In the twentieth century the ballad has continued to demonstrate its vitality in the work of Kipling, Auden, and Causley, among others.

There was another aspect to this influence as well, perhaps more tenuous and less direct, but still unmistakable. By the time Percy published his volumes, England was beginning to see the first ripples of the Romantic tide. In Europe the movement was already associated in its widest sense with revolutionary philosophies, notably from Rousseau and Herder, that concerned themselves with the common man: the French Revolution was only a handful of years away. To such philosophies, the naturalness and genuineness of the traditional language were a beacon. In England the literary crests of the movement included Wordsworth's contributions to *Lyrical*

INTRODUCTION

Ballads and Coleridge's 'The Rime of the Ancient Mariner', all deeply concerned with the form and language of traditional verse. And in the revised (1800) edition of *Lyrical Ballads*, Wordsworth added a preface advocating that poetry should adopt the language of everyday life; it is difficult to find a better description of the language of traditional verse.

So, though some few may see this anthology as retrogression, there are in fact ample precedents and reasons for it. The words of traditional songs and ballads are more than capable of standing on their own. Those who wish to read them for pleasure can do so without fear of damaging the literary-musical entirety, just as one can read the lyrics of the Elizabethan lutenist songwriters.

Much can be learned from traditional verse of the minutiae of history, particularly of social history. The earlier songs were predominantly rural[1] and, generally speaking, couched in terms of contentment. Doubtless life was not as carefree and idyllic as the verses suggest, but the sheer weight of evidence does at least indicate that what they say should be taken seriously. These were, after all, the expressions of the multitude, of the ordinary working men and women; no external attitudes were imposed on them and there was no question of simulating happiness just to impress the squire. When conditions changed, the attitudes changed quickly enough. As the state of agriculture in England declined, as enclosures spread, as more and more farmers lost touch with their land and became (in their own eyes, at least) gentlemen, so gradually a tone of alienation began to creep in. By the beginning of the nineteenth century discontent was clearly apparent in the country songs, which became for the first time overtly agitatory.

Here in Britain we escaped open revolution—but by a narrower margin than many people think. Britain fought off the threat of domination by Napoleon, but the loyalty of the country was at the same time being severely tested. The naval mutinies of the period arose from the same sense of injustice that stimulated the farm worker and the factory hand, and to many Englishmen the prospect of invasion by the French meant not so much defeat and occupation as the possibility of freedom. The working classes were beginning to band together and to fight actively for what they regarded as basic rights. The Luddites, the followers of Captain Swing and others, physically opposed the use of mechanization as a means of increasing

[1] Inevitably so. In 1801 the rural population of England accounted for 75 per cent of the whole. This figure had dropped to 50 per cent by 1851, and it now (1981 census) stands at approximately 20 per cent.

profits at their expense; farm labourers, miners, factory hands began to form the first unions. Revolution was not *that* far distant, and the groundswell was clearly discernible to anyone who cared to listen to the singers of the day.

In the event, of course, few cared to listen. It was easier in the nineteenth century (and to a large extent in this century also) to repress rather than attempt to reform; and the establishment preferred to call out the troops and use the full harshness of the law.[1]

One can trace all this in the material that we now have. Sharp and his contemporaries missed much of it, for they believed traditional song to be an exclusively rural activity, and therefore only collected in the villages and smaller market towns. But subsequent collectors such as A. L. Lloyd and Ewan MacColl gathered the rich harvest of industrial song that burst into life as the Industrial Revolution proceeded on its frequently inhuman way. The progression through the centuries is clear, and it mirrors a steady decline in happiness, in trust and in honesty. From contentment and pride in one's work, we see attitudes deteriorate into bitterness, hatred, and envy. However later historians might theorize regarding the rights and wrongs of a given situation, these verses reflect what the people knew and believed *at the time*; they are indeed the raw material of history. For those who still think that traditional song is only about mollocking in the hay and dancing around the maypole, the later pages of this book may come as an unpleasant shock, for here lie the germs of many of the troubles that bedevil us to this day.

But what is it about a simple little lyric that has ensured its survival over several hundred years by word-of-mouth transmission alone? What is it that gives that remarkable permanance of appeal? Even today, in an age characterized by great technical sophistication and considerable moral cynicism, the perennial freshness of the old songs can still hold an audience spellbound.

George Sampson pinpointed some of these qualities accurately. He was writing specifically of the ballads, but his words apply equally to the lesser verse as well. '[They] are as little primitive as *Beowulf* or *The Iliad*; but they give a primitive and unspoiled poetic sensation, for they speak not only the language of tradition, but also with the voice of the multitude. From one vice of modern literature they are entirely free: they have no "thinking about thinking", no "feeling about feeling". They can tell a good tale. They are fresh with the open air; wind and sunshine play through them. And the distinction, old as

---

[1] After the Captain Swing disturbances, 644 men were hanged and about 500 transported.

criticism itself, which assigns them to nature rather than to art, though it was overworked by the romantic school and will always be liable to abuse, is practical and sound.'[1]

One can go further. The language they use is stripped-down, with an economy and directness that does not pall. Plain and down to earth, it is vivid as country phrases are vivid: never sentimental. It is the emphasis on strong narrative told in clean, uncluttered lines that makes traditional verse timeless, and which preserves the excitement and the satisfaction even for a modern audience. If there is no tiresome 'feeling about feeling', there is equally no imagery for its own sake, no padding, no self-indulgence.

The themes, too, are timeless. Love and death, the seasons, work, war—all these are as relevant now as they were in the twelfth century, from which the earliest verses in this collection date. Attitudes to them can change, but the themes themselves are the bedrock of existence; one can identify with the participants across the years with little or no loss of immediacy. And, of course—though this applies mainly to the rural songs—there is a constant, never-changing nostalgia for better times, simpler times.

One must be careful not to make too large claims for traditional verse. I have throughout carefully avoided using the word 'poetry', for it is rarely that in the accepted sense of the word. But it has its own qualities, which more formal poetry often lacks; and it is these qualities that have kept it fresh and vital through the ages, full of its own charm, spontaneity, and bite.

The English tradition—indeed, any healthy tradition—is essentially a continuing, re-creating thing. In Vaughan Williams's words, 'A folk song is like a tree, whose stem dates back to immemorial times, but which continually puts out new shoots . . . In one aspect a folk song is as old as time itself; in another aspect it is no older than the singer who sang it.' In spite of the Victorian belief that the tradition in England was dead, it is still very much alive, and 'new' traditional singers are still being discovered, some even with previously unrecorded songs in their repertoires.

By the same token, songs are still being written that appear to be at least *potential* folk-songs, and it is always possible that some of these will be accepted one day as representing an aspect of traditional art. In recognition of this fact I have included a final section of contemporary (i.e. post-war) verse by writers working within the framework of the Folk Revival, and generally accepted as writing 'contemporary folk-songs'. One or two of the names included are

[1] *Concise Cambridge History of English Literature* (CUP, 1970).

well known in the world of commercial pop music, but they are still accepted in the Folk Revival while others, apparently similar in style and quality, are not. It is very much a melting pot at the moment; the section is offered as an indication of a possible future, no more.

FREDERICK WOODS

CONTENTS

CONTENTS

THE JOYS OF LOVE

CONTENTS

SEDUCTION AND BETRAYAL

CONTENTS

SOLDIERS AND SAILORS

CONTENTS

CRIME AND PUNISHMENT

CONTENTS

CHRISTIAN AND OTHER FESTIVALS

CONTENTS

THE COUNTRY YEAR

CONTENTS

THE RISE OF INDUSTRY

CONTENTS

TRADITION IN THE MAKING

CONTENTS

NOTE ON THE TEXTS

THIS collection is not intended to be a representative cross-section of the whole of the tradition. Some categories, for example shanties, have little literary value, and I have therefore made a selection of texts which seem to me to have the highest literary quality in the field: these will not necessarily be the best-known versions; and, indeed, there is no reason why they should be, for the greater use implies the greater chance of corruption.

Since the folk tradition has always been—and still is—a constantly self-renewing process, there is clearly no virtue in retaining archaic spellings such as one often meets in editions of the old ballads. Indeed, as many generations of singers were illiterate or, at best, only partly literate, it would have been positively pretentious to retain old forms, since the singers themselves would have been entirely unaware of them. All texts, therefore, are given in the language in which they are used today.

Further, the often arbitrary techniques of Victorian and Edwardian collectors—to say nothing of the cavalier approach of still earlier scholars—has meant that it has been necessary to impose some sort of uniform punctuation and usage. To not a few collectors, gibberish, if in the mouth of a traditional singer, was apparently sacrosanct and faithfully transcribed. I have therefore endeavoured to clarify such corrupt readings, wherever possible by reference to other extant versions.

Where necessary, elucidations of obscure or unusual words have been given at the foot of the page; general background notes appear separately at the end, together with information regarding provenance.

It is essential to remember that there is, in fact, no such thing as *the* text of a traditional song, but only differing versions thereof. Broadsides frequently had variants, in spite of the fact that they were printed; and even in the case of a song that has only been collected once (e.g. 'The Queen of Hearts'), this must be taken as only one version among a theoretical number. For this reason I have occasionally included variant texts where more than one version has come down to us, for comparison and interest.

Although the title of this book specifies 'English', there has been a great deal of intertwining over the centuries between the Irish, Scottish, and English cultures. Baring-Gould, Sharp, and the other earlier collectors found English country people singing songs that were clearly of Celtic extraction, and in the post-war period this process has been accelerated. So while I have largely kept to the implicit limitations of that word 'English', I have occasionally included Scottish or Irish material. In such cases it may be taken that the verse in question has been firmly absorbed into the English tradition.

History for the People

1. Queen Eleanor's Confession

Queen Eleanor was a sick woman,
And afraid that she should die;
Then she sent for two friars of France,
For to speak with them speedily.

The King called down his nobles all,
By one, by two, and by three,
And sent away for Earl Marshal,
For to speak with him speedily.

When that he came before the King,
He fell on his bended knee;
'A boon, a boon, our gracious King,
That you sent so hastily.'

'I'll pawn my living and my lands,
My sceptre and my crown,
That whatever Queen Eleanor says,
I will not write it down.

'Do you put on one friar's coat,
And I'll put on another,
And we will to Queen Eleanor go,
One friar like another.'

Thus both attired then they did go;
When they came to Whitehall,
The bells they did ring, and the choristers sing,
And the torches did light them all.

When that they came before the Queen,
They fell on their bended knee:
'A boon, a boon, our gracious Queen,
That you sent so hastily.'

'Are you two friars of France?' she said,
'Which I suppose you be;
But if you are two English friars,
Then hangèd shall you be.'

'We are two friars of France,' they said,
'As you suppose we be;
We have not been at any mass
Since we came from the sea.'

'The first vile thing that e'er I did
I will to you unfold;
Earl Marshal had my maidenhead,
Underneath this cloth of gold.'

'That is a vile sin,' then said the King,
'God may forgive it thee!'
'Amen, amen,' quoth Earl Marshal,
With a heavy heart then spoke he.

'The next vile thing that e'er I did
To you I'll not deny;
I made a box of poison strong
To poison King Henry.'

'That is a vile sin,' then said the King,
'God may forgive it thee!'
'Amen, amen,' quoth Earl Marshal,
'And I wish it so may be.'

'The next vile thing that e'er I did
To you I will discover;
I poisoned fair Rosamund,
All in fair Woodstock bower.'

'That is a vile sin,' then said the King,
'God may forgive it thee!'
'Amen, amen,' quoth Earl Marshal,
'And I wish it so may be.'

'Do you see yonder little boy,
A-tossing of that ball?
That is Earl Marshal's eldest son,
And I love him best of all.

'Do you see yonder little boy,
A-catching of the ball?
That is King Henry's son,' she said,
'And I love him worst of all.'

'His head is like unto a bull,
His nose is like a boar.'
'No matter for that,' King Henry said,
'I love him the better therefore.'

The king pulled off his friar's coat,
And appeared all in red;
She shrieked and she cried, she wrung her hands,
She said she was betrayed.

The King looked over his left shoulder,
And a grim look lookèd he,
And said, 'Earl Marshal, but for my oath,
Then hangèd shouldst thou be.'

2. *Robin Hood's Progress to Nottingham*

Robin Hood he was a tall young man
   Derry derry down
And fifteen winters old,
And Robin Hood he was a proper young man,
Of courage stout and bold.
   Hey down derry derry down.

Robin Hood he would and to fair Nottingham,
With the general for to dine;
There he was ware of fifteen foresters,
And a-drinking beer, ale and wine.

'What news, what news?' said bold Robin Hood.
'What news fain wouldst thou know?
Our king hath provided a shooting-match.'
'And I'm ready with my bow.'

'We hold it in scorn,' then said the foresters,
'That ever a boy so young
Should bear a bow before our king,
That's not able to draw one string.'

'I'll hold you twenty marks,' said bold Robin Hood,
'By the leave of Our Lady,
That I'll hit a mark a hundred rod,
And I'll cause a hart to die.'

'We'll hold you twenty marks,' then said the foresters,
'By the leave of Our Lady,
Thou hitst not the mark a hundred rod,
Nor causest a hart to die.'

Robin Hood he bent up a noble bow,
And a broad arrow he let fly,
He hit the mark a hundred rod,
And he caused a hart to die.

Some said he brake ribs one or two,
And some said he brake three;
The arrow within the hart would not abide,
But it glanced in two or three.

The hart did skip, the hart did leap,
And the hart lay on the ground;
'The wager is mine,' said bold Robin Hood,
'If 'twere for a thousand pound.'

'The wager's none of thine,' then said the foresters,
'Although thou beest in haste;
Take up thy bow, and get thee hence,
Lest we thy sides do baste.'

Robin Hood he took up his noble bow,
And his broad arrows all amain,
And Robin Hood he laughed, and begun to smile,
As he went over the plain.

Then Robin Hood he bent his noble bow,
And his broad arrows he let fly,
Till fourteen of these fifteen foresters
Upon the ground did lie.

He that did this quarrel first begin
Went tripping over the plain;
But Robin he bent his noble bow,
And he fetched him back again.

'You said I was no archer,' said Robin Hood,
'But say so now again;'
With that he sent another arrow
That split his head in twain.

'You have found me an archer,' saith Robin Hood,
'Which will make your wives for to wring,
And wish that you had never spoke the word,
That I could not draw one string.'

The people that lived in fair Nottingham,
Came running out amain,
Supposing to have taken bold Robin Hood,
With the foresters that were slain.

Some lost legs, and some lost arms,
And some did lose their bleed,
But Robin Hood he took up his noble bow,
And is gone to the merry green wood.

They carried these foresters into fair Nottingham,
As many there did know;
They digged them graves in their churchyard,
And they buried them all in a row.

3. *Robin Hood's Death*

When Robin Hood and Little John
 Down a down a down a down
Went o'er yon bank of broom,
Said Robin Hood to Little John,
'We have shot for many a pound,
 Hey down a derry a derry down

'But I am not able to shoot one shot more,
My broad arrows will not flee;
But I have a cousin lives down below,
Please God, she will bleed me.'

Now Robin he is to fair Kirkly gone,
As fast as he can win;
But before he came there, as we do hear,
He was taken very ill.

And when he came to fair Kirkly Hall,
He knocked all at the ring,
But none was so ready as his cousin herself
For to let bold Robin in.

'Will you please to sit down, cousin Robin,' she said,
'And drink some beer with me?'
'No, I will neither eat nor drink
Till I am blooded by thee.'

'Well, I have a room, cousin Robin,' she said,
'Which you did never see,
And if you please to walk therein,
You blooded by me shall be.'

She took him by the lily-white hand,
And led him to a private room;
Then did he bleed all the livelong day,
Until the next day at noon.

He then bethought him of a casement there,
Thinking for to get down;
But was so weak he could not leap,
He could not get him down.

He then bethought him of his bugle-horn,
Which hung low to his knee;
He set his horn unto his mouth,
And blew out weak blasts three.

Then Little John, when hearing him,
As he sat under a tree,
'I fear my master is now near dead,
He blows so wearily.'

Then Little John to fair Kirkly is gone,
As fast as he can dree;
But when he came to Kirkly Hall,
He broke locks two or three.

Until he came bold Robin to see,
Then he fell on his knee:
'A boon, a boon,' cries Little John,
'Master, I beg of thee.'

'What is that boon?' quoth Robin Hood,
'Little John, thou begs of me?'
'It is to burn fair Kirkly Hall,
And all their nunnery.'

'Now nay, now nay,' quoth Robin Hood,
'That boon I'll not grant thee;
I never hurt woman in all my life,
Nor men in women's company.

'I never hurt fair maid in all my time,
Nor at mine end shall it be;
But give me my bent bow in my hand,
And a broad arrow I'll let flee;
And where this arrow is taken up,
There shall my grave digged be.

'Lay me a green sod under my head,
And another at my feet;
And lay my bent bow at my side,
Which was my music sweet;
And make my grave of gravel and green,
Which is most right and meet.

'Let me have length and breadth enough,
With a green sod under my head;
That they may say, when I am dead,
Here lies bold Robin Hood.'

These words they readily granted him,
Which did bold Robin please;
And there they buried bold Robin Hood,
Within the fair Kirkleys.

4. *Chevy Chase*

God prosper long our noble king,
Our lives and safeties all!
A woeful hunting once there did
In Chevy Chase befall.

To drive the deer with hound and horn
Earl Percy took the way:
The child may rue that is unborn
The hunting of that day!

The stout Earl of Northumberland
A vow to God did make
His pleasure in the Scottish woods
Three summer's days to take,

The chiefest harts in Chevy Chase
To kill and bear away;
These tidings to Earl Douglas came
In Scotland where he lay.

Who sent Earl Percy present word
He would prevent his sport;
The English earl, not fearing that,
Did to the woods resort,

With fifteen hundred bowmen bold,
All chosen men of might,
Who knew full well in time of need
To aim their shafts aright.

The gallant greyhounds swiftly ran
To chase the fallow deer;
On Monday they began to hunt
Ere daylight did appear.

And long before high noon they had
A hundred fat bucks slain;
Then having dined, the drovers went
To rouse the deer again.

The bowmen mustered on the hills,
Well able to endure;
Their backsides all with special care
That day were guarded sure.

The hounds ran swiftly through the woods
The nimble deer to take,
That with their cries the hills and dales
An echo shrill did make.

Lord Percy to the quarry went
To view the tender deer;
Quoth he, 'Earl Douglas promised once
This day to meet me here;

'But if I thought he would not come,
No longer would I stay.'
With that a brave young gentleman
Thus to the Earl did say:

'Lo, yonder doth Earl Douglas come,
His men in armour bright;
Full twenty hundred Scottish spears
All marching in our sight.'

'All men of pleasant Tivydale,
Fast by the river Tweed,
Oh cease your sports,' Earl Percy said,
'And take your bows with speed.

'And now with me, my countrymen,
Your courage forth advance,
For there was never champion yet
In Scotland nor in France,

'That ever did on horseback come,
But if my hap it were,
I durst encounter man for man,
With him to break a spear.'

Earl Douglas on his milk-white steed,
Most like a baron bold,
Rode foremost of his company,
Whose armour shone like gold.

'Show me,' said he, 'whose men you be
That hunt so boldly here,
That without my consent do chase
And kill my fallow deer.'

The first man that did answer make
Was noble Percy he,
Who said, 'We list not to declare
Nor show whose men we be;

'Yet we will spend our dearest blood
The chiefest harts to slay.'
Then Douglas swore a solemn oath,
And this in rage did say:

'Ere thus I will outbraved be,
One of us two shall die;
I know thee well, an earl thou art;
Lord Percy, so am I.

'But trust me, Percy, pity it were,
And great offence, to kill
Then any of these our guiltless men,
For they have done no ill.

'Let thou and I the battle try,
And set our men aside.'
'Accursed be he,' Earl Percy said,
'By whom it is denied.'

Then stepped a gallant squire forth—
Witherington was his name—
Who said, 'I would not have it told
To Henry our king, for shame,

'That ere my captain fought on foot,
And I stand looking on.
Ye be two earls,' quoth Witherington,
'And I a squire alone;

'I'll do the best that do I may,
While I have power to stand;
While I have power to wield my sword,
I'll fight with heart and hand.'

Our English archers bent their bows,
Their hearts were good and true;
At the first flight of arrows sent,
Full four score Scots they slew.

To drive the deer with hound and horn,
Douglas bade on the bent;
Two captains moved with mickle might,
Their spears to shivers went.

bade on the bent] stayed on the field

They closed full fast on every side,
No slackness was there found,
But many a gallant gentleman
Lay gasping on the ground.

O Christ! it was great grief to see
How each man chose his spear,
And how the blood out of their breasts
Did gush like water clear.

At last these two stout earls did meet,
Like captains of great might;
Like lions wood they laid on lode,
They made a cruel fight.

They fought until they both did sweat,
With swords of tempered steel,
Till blood down their cheeks like rain
The trickling down did feel.

'Oh yield thee, Percy,' Douglas said,
'And in faith I will thee bring
Where thou shall high advancèd be
By James our Scottish king.

'Thy ransom I will freely give,
And this report of thee,
Thou art the most courageous knight
That ever I did see.'

'No, Douglas,' quoth Earl Percy then,
'Thy proffer I do scorn;
I will not yield to any Scot
That ever yet was born.'

With that there came an arrow keen,
Out of an English bow,
Which struck Earl Douglas on the breast
A deep and deadly blow.

Who never said more words than these:
'Fight on, my merry men all!
For why, my life is at an end,
Lord Percy sees my fall.'

wood] maddened   laid on lode] gave heavy blows

II

Then leaving life, Earl Percy took
The dead man by the hand;
Who said, 'Earl Douglas, for thy life
Would I have lost my hand;

'O Christ! my very heart doth bleed
For sorrow for thy sake,
For sure, a more redoubted knight
Mischance could never take.'

A knight among the Scots there was
Which saw Earl Douglas die,
Who straight in heart did vow revenge
Upon the Lord Percy.

Sir Hugh Montgomery was he called,
Who, with a spear full bright,
Well-mounted on a gallant steed
Ran fiercely through the fight,

And past the English archers all,
Without all dread or fear,
And through Earl Percy's body then
He thrust his hateful spear.

With such a vehement force and might
His body he did gore,
The staff ran through the other side
A large clothyard or more.

Thus did both those nobles die,
Whose courage none could stain;
An English archer then perceived
The noble earl was slain.

He had a good bow in his hand,
Made of a trusty tree;
An arrow of a clothyard long
To the hard head haled he.

Against Sir Hugh Montgomery
His shaft full right he set;
The grey goose wing that was thereon
In his heart's blood was wet.

This fight from break of day did last
Till setting of the sun,
For when they ring the evening bell
The battle scarce was done.

With stout Earl Percy there was slain
Sir John of Egerton,
Sir Robert Harcliffe and Sir William,
Sir James, that bold baron.

And with Sir George and Sir James,
Both knights of good account,
Good Sir Ralph Rebbye there was slain,
Whose prowess did surmount.

For Witherington needs must I wail
As one in doleful dumps,
For when his legs were smitten off,
He fought upon his stumps.

And with Earl Douglas there was slain
Sir Hugh Montgomery,
And Sir Charles Morrell, that from field
One foot would never flee;

Sir Roger Hever of Harcliffe too,
His sister's son was he;
Sir David Lambwell, well esteemed,
But saved he could not be.

And the Lord Maxwell, in like case,
With Douglas he did die;
Of twenty hundred Scottish spears,
Scarce fifty-five did fly.

Of fifteen hundred Englishmen
Went home but fifty-three;
The rest in Chevy Chase were slain,
Under the greenwood tree.

Next day did many widows come
Their husbands to bewail;
They washed their wounds in brinish tears,
But all would not prevail.

Their bodies, bathed in purple blood,
They bore with them away;
They kissed them dead a thousand times
Ere they were clad in clay.

The news was brought to Edinburgh
Where Scotland's king did reign,
That brave Earl Douglas suddenly
Was with an arrow slain.

'Oh heavy news,' King James gan say,
'Scotland may witness be
I have not any captain more
Of such account as he.'

Like tidings to King Henry came,
Within as short a space,
That Percy of Northumberland
Was slain in Chevy Chase.

'Now God be with him,' said our king,
'Sith it will no better be;
I trust I have within my realm
Five hundred as good as he.

'Yet shall not Scots nor Scotland say
But I will vengeance take,
And be revengèd on them all
For brave Earl Percy's sake.'

This vow the king did well perform
After on Humbledown;
In one day fifty knights were slain,
With lords of great renown.

And of the rest of small account,
Did many hundreds die;
Thus endeth the hunting in Chevy Chase,
Made by the Earl Percy.

God save our king, and bless this land
With plenty, joy and peace,
And grant henceforth that foul debate
Twixt noble men may cease.

5. *Henry V's Conquest of France*

As our king lay musing on his bed,
He bethought himself upon a time
Of a tribute that was due from France,
Had not been paid for so long a time.
    Fal la la la la

He callèd for his lovely page,
His lovely page then callèd he,
Saying, 'You must go to the King of France,
To the King of France, sir, ride speedily.'

Oh then went away this lovely page,
This lovely page then away went he;
And when he came to the King of France,
Low he fell down on his bended knee.

'My master greets you, worthy sir;
Ten ton of gold that is due to he,
That you will send him his tribute home,
Or in French land you soon will him see.'

'Your master's young and of tender years,
Nor fit to come into my degree,
And I will send him three tennis balls,
That with them he may learn to play.'

Oh then returned this lovely page,
This lovely page then returnèd he,
And when he came to our gracious king,
Low he fell down on his bended knee.

'What news, what news, my trusty page,
What is the news you have brought to me?'
'I have brought such news from the King of France
That you and he will never agree.

'He says you're young and of tender years,
Not fit to come into his degree,
And he will send you three tennis balls,
That with them you may learn to play.'

'Recruit me Cheshire and Lancashire,
And Derby hills that are so free;
No married man nor no widow's son,
For no widow's curse shall go with me.'

They recruited Cheshire and Lancashire,
And Derby hills that are so free;
No married man nor no widow's son,
Yet there was a jovial bold company.

Oh then we marched into the French land,
With drums and trumpets so merrily;
And then bespoke the King of France,
'Lo, yonder comes proud King Henry.'

The first shot that the Frenchmen gave,
They killed our Englishmen so free;
We killed ten thousand of the French,
And the rest of them they ran away.

And then we marched to Paris gates,
With drums and trumpets so merrily:
Oh then bespoke the King of France,
'The Lord have mercy on my men and me.

'Oh I will send him his tribute home,
Ten ton of gold that is due to he,
And the finest flower that is in all France,
To the Rose of England I will give free.'

6. *The Agincourt Carol*

Our king went forth to Normandy,
With grace and might of chivalry,
The God for him wrought marvellously,
Wherefore England may call and cry
    Deo gratias, Deo gratias Anglia
    Redde pro victoria.

He set a siege, sooth for to say,
To Harfleur town with royal array.
That town he won and made a fray
That France shall rue till doomsday.

Then went our king with all his host
Through France, for all the Frenchman's boast,
Nor spared for dread of least or most
Until he came to Agincourt coast.

Then for sooth that knight comely
In Agincourt field he fought manly.
Through grace of God most mighty
He had both field and victory.

Their dukes and earls, lord and baron,
Were ta'en and slain, and that well soon,
And some were led into London
With joy and mirth and great renown.

Now gracious God may save our king,
His people and all his well willing.
Give him good life and good ending,
That we with mirth may safely sing
    Deo gratias, Deo gratias Anglia
    Redde pro victoria.

7. 'Six dukes went a-fishing'

Six dukes went a-fishing
Down by yon seaside.
One of them spied a dead body
Lain by the waterside.

The one said to the other,
These words I heard them say:
'It's the royal Duke of Grantham
That the tide has washed away.'

They took him up to Portsmouth,
To a place where he was known;
From there up to London,
To the place where he was born.

They took out his bowels,
And stretchèd out his feet,
And they balmèd his body
With roses so sweet.

Six dukes stood before him,
Twelve raised him from the ground,
Nine lords followed after him
In their black mourning gown.

Black was their mourning
And white were the wands,
And so yellow the flamboys
That they carried in their hands.

He now lies betwixt two towers,
He now lies in cold clay,
And the royal Queen of Grantham
Went weeping away.

8. *The Death of Queen Jane*

Queen Jane lay in labour full nine days or more,
Till the women were so tired, they could stay no longer there.

'Good women, good women, good women as ye be,
Do open my right side, and find my baby.'

'Oh no,' said the women, 'that never may be,
We will send for King Henry and hear what he say.'

King Henry was sent for, King Henry did come:
'What do ail you, my lady, your eyes look so dim?'

'King Henry, King Henry, will you do one thing for me?
That's to open my right side, and find my baby.'

'Oh no,' said King Henry, 'that's a thing I'll never do.
If I lose the flower of England, I shall lose the branch too.'

King Henry went mourning, and so did his men,
And so did the dear baby, for Queen Jane did die then.

And how deep was the mourning, how black were the bands,
How yellow, yellow were the flamboys they carried in their hands.

There was fiddling, aye, and dancing on the day the babe was born,
But poor Queen Jane belovèd lay cold as a stone.

9. *The Young Earl of Essex's Victory over the Emperor of Germany*

Come, sound up your trumpets and beat up your drums,
And let's go to sea with a valiant good cheer,
In search of a mighty vast navy of ships,
The like has not been for these fifty long year.

> *Raderer two, tandaro te,*
> *Raderer, tandorer, tan do re*

The Queen she provided a navy of ships,
With sweet flying streamers, so glorious to see,
Rich top and topgallants, captains and lieutenants,
Some forty, some fifty, brass-pieces and three.

They had not sailed past a week on the seas,
Not passing a week and days two or three,
But they were aware of the proud Emperor,
Both him and all his proud company.

When he beheld our powerful fleet,
Sailing along in the glory and pride,
He was amazed at their valour and fame,
Then to his warlike commanders he cried.

These were the words of the old Emperor,
'Pray who is this that is sailing to me?
If he be king that weareth a crown,
Yet I am a better man than he.'

'It is not a king, nor lord of a crown,
Which now to the seas with his navy is come,
But the young Earl of Essex, the Queen's lieutenant,
Who fears no foe in Christendom.'

'Oh, is that lord then come to the seas?
Let us tack about and be steering away.
I have heard so much of his father before
That I will not fight with young Essex today.'

Oh then bespoke the Emperor's son,
As they were tacking and steering away:
'Give me, royal father, this navy of ships,
And I will go fight with Essex today.'

'Take them with all my heart, loving son,
Most of them are of a capital size;
But should he do as his father has done,
Farewell thine honour and mine likewise.'

With cannons hot and thundering shot,
These two gallants fought on the main,
And as it was young Essex's lot,
The Emperor's son by him was ta'en.

'Give me my son,' the Emperor cried,
'Who you this day have taken from me,
And I'll give to thee three keys of gold,
The one shall be of High Germany.'

'I care not for thy three keys of gold,
Which thou hast proffered to set him free,
But thy son he shall to England sail,
And go before the Queen with me.'

'Then have I fifty good ships of the best,
As good as ever were sent to the sea,
And e'er my son into England sail,
They shall go all for good company.'

They had not fought this famous battle,
They had not fought it hours three,
But some lost legs, and some lost arms,
And some lay tumbling in the sea.

Essex he got this battle likewise,
Though 'twas the hottest that ever was seen;
Home he returned with a wonderful prize,
And brought the Emperor's son to the Queen.

Oh then bespoke the prentices all,
Living in London, both proper and tall,
In a kind letter, sent straight to the Queen,
For Essex's sake they would fight all.

10. *Captain Ward and the* Rainbow

Strike up, you lusty gallants, with music and sound of drum,
For I have descried a rover, upon the sea is come;
His name is Captain Ward, right well it doth appear,
There has not been such a rover found out this thousand year.

For he hath sent unto our King, the sixth of January,
Desiring that he might come in, with all his company:
'And if your King will let me come till I my tale have told,
I will bestow for my ransom full thirty ton of gold.'

'Oh nay, oh nay,' then said our King, 'Oh nay, this may not be,
To yield to such a rover my self will not agree;
He hath deceived the Frenchman, likewise the King of Spain,
And how can he be true to me that hath been false to twain?'

With that our King provided a ship of worthy fame,
Rainbow she is called, if you would know her name;
Now the gallant *Rainbow* she rows upon the sea,
Five hundred gallant seamen to bear her company.

The Dutchman and the Spaniard she made them for to fly,
Also the bonny Frenchman, as she met him on the sea;
When as this gallant *Rainbow* did come where Ward did lie,
'Where is the captain of this ship?' this gallant *Rainbow* did cry.

'Oh that am I,' says Captain Ward, 'there's no man bids me lie,
And if thou art the King's fair ship, thou art welcome unto me.'
'I'll tell thee what,' says *Rainbow*, 'our King is in great grief
That thou shouldst lie upon the sea and play the arrant thief,

'And will not let our merchant ships pass as they did before;
Such tidings to our King is come, which grieves his heart full sore.'
With this the gallant *Rainbow* she shot, out of her pride,
Full fifty gallant brass pieces, charged on every side.

And yet these gallant shooters prevailèd not a pin,
Though they were brass on the outside, brave Ward was steel within;
'Shoot on, shoot on,' says Captain Ward, 'your sport well pleaseth
     me,
And he that first gives over shall yield unto the sea.

'I never wronged an English ship, but Turk and King of Spain,
For and the jovial Dutchman as I met on the main.
If I had known your King but one two years before,
I would have saved brave Essex' life, whose death did grieve me sore.

'Go tell the King of England, go tell him thus from me,
If he reign king of all the land, I will reign king at sea.'
With that the gallant *Rainbow* shot, and shot, and shot in vain,
And left the rover's company, and returnèd home again.

'O royal King of England, your ship's returned again,
For Ward's ship is so strong it never will be ta'en.'
'Oh everlasting!' says the King, 'I have lost jewels three,
Which would have gone unto the seas and brought proud Ward to
  me.

'The first was Lord Clifford, Earl of Cumberland;
The second was the Lord Mountjoy, as you shall understand;
The third was brave Essex, from field would never flee,
Which would a gone into the seas and brought proud Ward to me.'

11. *George Ridler's Oven*

The stwuns, the stwuns, the stwuns, the stwuns, the stwuns . . .

The stwuns that built Gaarge Ridler's oven,
And they quem from the Bleakeney's Quaar;
And Gaarge he wur a jolly ould mon,
And his yead it graw'd above his yare.

One thing of Gaarge Ridler's I must commend,
And that wur vor a notable theng;
He mead his braags avoore he died,
Wi' any dree brothers his zons zshould zeng.

There's Dick the treble and John the mean
(Let every mon zeng in his auwn pleace)
And Gaarge he wur the elder brother,
And therevoore he should zeng the beass.

stwuns] stones	quem] came	Quaar] quarry	yare] hair
	braags] brags	zeng] sing	

Mine hostess's moid (and her neaum 'twur Nell),
A pretty wench, and I lov'd her well;
I lov'd her well—good reauzon why—
Because zshe lov'd my dog and I.

My dog has gotten zitch a trick,
To visit moids when thauy be zick;
When thauy be zick and like to die,
Oh, thether gwoes my dog and I.

My dog is good to catch a hen,
A duck and goose is voor vor men;
And where good company I spy,
Oh, thether gwoes my dog and I.

Droo aal the world ould Gaarge would bwoast,
Commend me to merry ould England mwoast;
While vools gwoes scramblin' vur and nigh,
We bides at whoam, my dog and I.

Ov their furrin tongues let travellers brag,
Wi' their fifteen names vor a puddin' bag;
Two tongues I knows ne'er told a lie,
And their wearers be my dog and I.

My mother told me when I wur young,
If I did vollow the strong beer pwoot,
That drenk would pruv my auverdrow,
And meauk me wear a threadbare cwoat.

When I have dree zixpences under my thumb,
O then I be welcome wherever I quem;
But when I have none, oh then I pass by;
'Tis poverty pearts good company.

When I gwoes dead, as it may hap,
My greauve shall be under the good yeal tap,
In vouled earms there wool us lie,
Cheek by jowl, my dog and I.

furrin] foreign   pwoot] pewter   auverdrow] overthrow
          yeal] ale   vouled earms] folded arms

12. *The Duke of Marlborough*

You generals all and champions bold
That take delight in fields,
That knock down palaces and castle walls,
But now to death must yield,
We must go and face our daring foes
And with the sword and shield;
I often fought with my merry men
But now to death must yield.

I am an Englishman by birth,
Lord Marlborough is my name.
In Devonshire I first drew breath,
That country of great fame.
I was well beloved by all my men,
By kings and princes likewise,
And in every town that we rode through
We took them by surprise.

King Charles the Second did I serve
To face our foes in France,
And at the battle of Ramillies
We boldly did advance.
That very day my horse was shot,
'Twas by a musket ball,
And as I mounted up again
My aide-de-camp did fall.

The sun went down, the earth did shake,
So loudly did I cry,
'Fight on, brave boys, for England's sake,
We'll conquer or we'll die.'
But now we've gained the victory
And bravely left the field.
We took great numbers of prisoners
And forced them all to yield.

Now I on a bed of sickness lie,
I am resigned to die.
You generals all and champions bold
Stand true, as well as I.

Let every man be true to his guns,
And fight with courage bold,
For I led my men through fire and smoke
And ne'er was bribed by gold.

13. *Bold General Wolfe*

On Monday morning as we set sail,
The wind did blow a most pleasant gale,
For to fight the French it was our intent,
Through smoke and fire, through smoke and fire,
And into the gloomy night we went.

Now the French were camped up on mountains high,
And we, poor hearts, at the foot did lie.
'Never mind, my lads,' General Wolfe did say,
'Brave lads of honour, brave lads of honour,
Old England shall win the day.'

Bold General Wolfe unto his men did say,
'Come, come, my lads, and follow me
Up yonder mountain that looks so high,
All for the honour, all for the honour
Of George the King and your country.'

Then the very first volley that the French gave us
Wounded our General in his right breast.
Then out of his breast living blood did flow,
Like any fountain, like any fountain,
Till all his men were filled with woe.

'Here's a hundred guineas all in bright gold,
Take it and part it for my blood runs cold.
Take it and part it,' General Wolfe did say,
'For you lads of honour, you lads of honour,
Have shown the French such gallant play.

'When to old England you shall return,
Tell all my friends I am dead and gone,
Tell my poor mother and my sweetheart dear
That I am dead, oh that I am dead,
And them I'll never see no more.

'At eighteen years old I did begin
All for the honour of George my King,
So use your soldiers as I've done my own,
Your soldiers own, your soldiers own,
And they will fight for evermore.'

14. *Under the Rose*

As Mars and Minerva were viewing of some implements
Bellona stepped forward and asked the news.
Were they for repairing those warlike instruments
That's now growing rusty for want to be used?
The money is withdrawn and our trade is diminishing,
Mechanics are wandering without shoes or hose.
Come, stir up the wars and our trade will be flourishing.
This grand conversation was under the rose.

See how they transact in the States of America,
Renowned independence sits on the throne.
They are not misguided by schemes of a ministry
That would extract the marrow from the centre of a bone.
Had we enlarged that hero who set the world a-trembling,
Whose name was a terror to his imperial foes
Although the day he lost it, it was brought by dissembling.
This grand conversation was under the rose.

He was a fine statesman, likewise a noble general,
His equal in France was never seen before;
His abilities were as bright as the diamond or the mineral,
Which thousands might verify that lay in their gore.
It was thought he was guided by the hand of providence
Until his gallant army he did wildly expose,
And when fortune did slight him it proved a bitter consequence.
This grand conversation was under the rose.

But Britannia of late has erected a grand residence
Embellished with a hall and an emblem of peace,
And his majesty is crowned with the greatest of opulence,
But her sportsmen are idle and they have no game to chase.

Her anchor's in harbour, her hearty tars they want their grog,
The broom at the masthead shows the daring foes
That she'll sweep the main ocean when again she bravely heaves the
    log.
This grand conversation was under the rose.

15. *Grand Conversation on Brave Nelson*

As some heroes bold, I will unfold, together were conversing,
It was in the praise of Nelson, as you shall quickly hear;
Said one unto the other, if we could behold another
In old England like Nelson, we proudly would him cheer.
From Norfolk it is known he came, he was a man of noted fame,
He struggled hard for liberty, as every Briton knows,
In battle he would loudly cry, 'I'll gain the victory or die.'
This grand conversation on brave Nelson arose.

Now at Copenhagen and the Nile, he gave command with a smile,
He said, 'Stand firm, British tars, the enemy to meet;
Prepare each gun—all terror shun, but never do surrender!'
The champion of the briny waves was Nelson and his fleet;
When Captain Hardy, you may see, who always done his duty free,
Brave Collingwood the enemy undaunted would oppose,
He caused some thousands to be slain while fighting on the raging
    main.
This grand conversation on brave Nelson arose.

Many a youth, I'll tell the truth, in action have been wounded,
Some left their friends and lovers in despair upon their native shore.
Others never returned again, but died upon the raging main,
Causing many a one to cry 'My son', and widows to deplore.
When war was raging, it is said, men for their labours were paid,
Commerce and trade flourishing, but now it ebbs and flows,
And poverty it does increase, though Britons say we live in peace.
This grand conversation on brave Nelson arose.

Some hardy tars they did survive, in Greenwich College now alive,
Will tell the deeds of Nelson and the battles that he won.
He never feared a cannon ball, till at Trafalgar he did fall,
No flinching from the enemy—no action did he shun.

He many powers did defeat, and never was that hero beat,
Neither would he surrender till he had thrashed his daring foes,
Although he lost an eye and wing, he was loyal and true to his king.
This grand conversation on brave Nelson arose.

Trafalgar I will mention, if you will give attention,
It long has been recorded where brave Nelson fell and bled,
The officers around him, all human aid was found,
But were affected to the heart to find that he was dead.
The gallant tars were grievèd sore to find Lord Nelson was no
    more,
All was in confusion in the midst of dying woes.
In rum they put him, it is said, and then to England him conveyed.
This grand conversation on brave Nelson arose.

Now in memory of that hero's loss, we understand at Charing Cross,
A monument of Nelson has been erected there.
An ancient building was pulled down, and an open space of ground
To commemorate the battle, it is called Trafalgar Square.
You British tars as do pass by, look up aloft and you will spy
The visage of that hero respected as it shows,
Though his remains are in decay, grim Death in action won the day.
This grand conversation on brave Nelson arose.

16. *Nelson's Death*

Old England's long-expected heavy news from our fleet—
It was commanded by Lord Nelson the French for to meet—
The news it came over, through the country was spread,
That the French were defeated but Lord Nelson was dead.

> *Rule Britannia, Britannia rules the waves,*
> *Britons never never never shall be slaves.*

Not only Lord Nelson but thousands were slain,
A-fighting the French on the watery main,
To protect our own country, both honour and wealth,
But the French they would not yield until they yield unto death.

The merchants of Yarmouth when they heard so
Said, 'Come, brother sailor, to church let us go;
And there we will build a most beautiful pile
In remembrance of Nelson, the hero of the Nile.'

'Your plans,' said Britannia, 'are excellent and good,
A monument for Lord Nelson and a sword for Collingwood.
Let it be of good marble and 'petuate his name:
Letters in bright gold wrote "He died for England's fame." '

Our soldiers and sailors, as I have been told,
Keep themselves in readiness their rights for to hold;
Their rights to maintain, the cause to expose,
If in an invasion to save British ports.

Our soldiers and sailors many brave deeds have done,
While fighting in foreign many battles have won.
If the Nile could but speak or did Trafalgar declare,
All the world with Lord Nelson they would not compare.

17. *Lamentation on the Death of the Duke of Wellington*

Britannia now lament for our hero that is dead,
That son of Mars, brave Wellington, alas, his spirit's fled.
That general of a hundred fights, to death he had to yield,
Who braved the cannons' frightful blaze upon the battle field.

Britannia weep and mourn, his loss all may deplore,
That conquering hero Wellington, alas, he is no more.

The destructive wars of Europe does not disturb him now,
Great laurels of bright victory sit smiling on his brow,
For the burning sands of India he traced with valour bright,
And against the daring Tippoo Saib so valiant did he fight.

Where cannons loud did rattle, spread death and sad dismay,
The Duke was always ready with his men to lead the way.
Fortified cities he laid low, that general of renown,
Intrenchments and their batteries he quickly levelled down.

Through Portugal and Spain his enemy did pursue,
With the veteran sons of Britain he marched to Waterloo,
And there he made a noble stand upon that blood-stained day,
And fought the French so manfully and made them run away.

On the plains of Waterloo where thousands they lay dead,
The iron balls in showers flew round his martial head,
While his valiant men and generals lay bleeding in their gore,
The laurels from the French that day brave Wellington he tore.

Napoleon was as brave a man as ever took the field,
And with the warlike sons of France he said he would not yield;
But the reverse of fortune that day did on him frown,
By Wellington and his army his eagles were pulled down.

Now let him rest in peace, and none upbraid his name,
On his military glory there never was a stain;
The steel-clad cuirassiers of France that day at Waterloo,
He quickly made them face about and cut their armour through.

Brave Ponsonby and Picton they fell upon that day,
And many a valiant soldier brave in peace their ashes lay,
And that brave Duke that led them on, his spirit's took its flight;
To see him laid down in his tomb will be a solemn sight.

18. *Balaclava*

Six hundred stalwart warriors of England's pride the best
Did grasp the lance and sabre on Balaclava's crest,
And with their trusty leader, Earl Cardigan the brave,
Dashed through the Russian valley to glory or a grave.
Their foemen stood in thousands, a dark and awful mass,
Beneath their famous strongholds resolved to guard the pass.
Their guns with fierce defiance belched thunders up the vale
Where sat our English horsemen firm beneath their iron gale.

It was a famous story
Proclaim it far and wide
And let your children's children
Re-echo it with pride
How Cardigan the fearless
His name immortal made
When he crossed the Russian valley
With his famous Light Brigade.

Brave Nolan brought the order. 'O God, can it be true?'
Said Cardigan the fearless, 'and my brigade so few.
To take those awful cannon from yonder teeming mass,
It's madness, sir, where shall we charge,
What guns bring from the pass?'

The messenger with hauteur looked once upon the earl,
Then pointing to the enemy, his lip began to curl.
'There, there, my lord, there are your guns
And there your foemen too.'
Then he turned his charger's head away
And bade the earl adieu.

And there were but six hundred 'gainst two score thousand foes,
Hemmed in with furious cannon and crushed with savage blows,
Yet fought they there like heroes for our noble England's fame,
Oh glorious charge, heroic deed, what honour crowns thy name.

Four hundred of those soldiers fell fighting where they stood,
And thus that fatal death vale they enriched with English blood.
Four hundred of those soldiers bequeathed their lives away
For the England they had fought for on that wild October day.

19. *Grace Darling*

'Twas on a longstone lighthouse there dwelt an English maid,
Pure as the air around her, of danger ne'er afraid.
One morning just at daybreak a storm-tossed wreck she spied:
Although to try seemed madness, 'I'll save the crew!' she cried.

> *And she pulled away o'er the rolling seas*
> *Over the waters wide*
> *'Help, help' she could hear the cry of the shipwrecked crew.*
> *But Grace had an English heart*
> *The raging storm she braved*
> *She pulled away mid the dashing spray*
> *And the crew she saved.*

They to the rocks were clinging, a crew of nine all told,
Between them and the lighthouse the seas like mountains rolled.
Said Grace, 'Come help me, father,
We'll launch the boat,' said she.
''Tis madness,' said her father, 'to face that raging sea.'

One murmured prayer, heaven guard us,
And then they were afloat,
Between them and destruction the planks of that frail boat.
Then said the maiden's father, 'Turn back or doomed are we.'
Then up spoke brave Grace Darling,
'Alone I'll brave the sea.'

They rode the angry billows and reached the rock at length.
They saved the shipwrecked sailors,
In heaven alone their strength.
Go tell the wide world over what English pluck can do
And sing of brave Grace Darling, who nobly saved the crew.

The Pain of Love

20. *Lady Maisry*

Oh she called to her little page boy,
Who was her mother's son,
She told him as quick as he could go
To bring the lord safe home.

Now the first mile he would walk,
And the second he would run,
And when he came to a broken, broken bridge
He would bend his breast and swim.

When he came to the new castle,
The lord was sat to meat.
'If you knew as much as me
How little would you eat.'

'Is my bower falling, falling down,
Or is my tower down,
Or is my gay lady put to bed
With a daughter or a son?'

'Oh no, your bower is not a-falling down
Neither your tower down,
Neither is your gay lady put to bed
With a daughter or a son.

'Oh no, your bower is not falling down,
Neither your tower down,
But we are afraid before you return
Your lady will be dead and gone.'

'Come saddle, saddle my milk-white steed,
Come saddle my pony too,
That I may neither eat nor drink
Till I come to the new castle.'

Now when he came to the new castle
He heard a big bell toll
And there he saw eight noble, noble men
A-bearing of a pall.

'Lay down, lay down that gentle, gentle corpse
As it lies fast asleep
That I may kiss her red ruby lips
Which I used to kiss so sweet.'

Six times he kissed her red ruby lips,
Nine times he kissed her chin,
Ten times he kissed her snowy white breast
Which love did enter in.

The lady was buried on that Sunday
Before the prayer was end,
And the lord he died on Sunday next
Before the prayer begun.

21. *Child Waters*

Child Waters in his stable stood,
And stroked his milk-white steed;
To him came a fair young lady
As ere did wear women's weed.

Says, 'Christ you save, good Child Waters!'
Says, 'Christ you save and see!
My girdle of gold which was too long
Is now too short for me.

'And all is with one child of yours
I feel stir at my side;
My gown of green, it is too straight,
Before it was too wide.'

'If the child be mine, fair Ellen,' he said,
'Be mine, as you tell me,
Take you Cheshire and Lancashire both,
Take them your own to be.

'If the child is mine, fair Ellen,' he said,
'Be mine, as you do swear,
Take you Cheshire and Lancashire both,
And make that child your heir.'

She says, 'I would rather have one kiss,
Child Waters, of thy mouth,
Than I would have Cheshire and Lancashire both,
That lies by north and south.

'And I had rather have a twinkling,
Child Waters, of your eye,
Than I would have Cheshire and Lancashire both,
To take them mine own to be.'

'Tomorrow, Ellen, I must forth ride
So far into the north country;
The fairest lady that I can find,
Ellen, must go with me.'
'And ever I pray you, Child Waters,
Your foot-page let me be.'

'If you will my foot-page be, Ellen,
As you do tell it me,
Then you must cut your gown of green
An inch above your knee.

'So must you do your yellow locks,
Another inch above your eye;
You must tell no man what is my name;
My foot-page you then shall be.'

All this long day Child Waters rode,
She ran barefoot by his side;
Yet he was never so courteous a knight
To say, 'Ellen, will you ride?'

But all this day Child Waters rode,
She ran barefoot through the broom;
Yet he was never so courteous a knight
To say, 'Ellen, put on your shoon.'

'Ride softly,' she said, 'Child Waters,
Why do you ride so fast?
The child which is no man's but yours
My body it will burst.'

He says, 'Seest thou yonder water, Ellen,
That flows from bank to brim?'
'I trust to God, Child Waters,' she said,
'You will never see me swim.'

But when she came to the waters wide,
She sailèd to the chin;
'Except the lord of heaven be my speed,
Now must I learn to swim.'

The salt waters bare up Ellen's clothes,
Our Lady bare up her chin,
And Child Waters was a woe man, good Lord,
To see fair Ellen swim.

And when she over the water was,
She then came to his knee:
He said, 'Come hither, fair Ellen,
Lo, yonder what I see!

'Seest thou not yonder hall, Ellen?
Of red gold shines the gates;
There's four and twenty fair ladies,
The fairest is my worldly make.

'Seest thou not yonder hall, Ellen;
Of red gold shineth the tower;
There is four and twenty fair ladies,
The fairest is my paramour.'

'I do see the hall now, Child Waters,
That of red gold shineth the gates;
God give good then of your self,
And of your worldly make:

                    make] mate

36

THE PAIN OF LOVE

'I do see the hall now, Child Waters,
That of red gold shineth the tower;
God give you good then of your self,
And of your paramour!'

There were four and twenty ladies,
Were playing at the ball,
And Ellen, she was the fairest lady,
Must bring his steed to the stall.

There were four and twenty fair ladies,
Were playing at the chess;
And Ellen, she was the fairest lady,
Must bring his horse to grass.

And then bespake Child Waters' sister,
And these were the words said she:
'You have the prettiest foot-page, brother,
That ever I saw with mine eye;

'But that his belly is so big,
His girdle goes wondrous high;
And ever I pray you, Child Waters,
Let him go into the chamber with me.'

'It is more meet for a little foot-page,
That has run through moss and mire,
To take his supper upon his knee
And sit down by the kitchen fire,
Than to go into the chamber with any lady
That wears so rich attire.'

But when they had supped every one,
To bed they took the way;
He said, 'Come hither, my little foot-page,
Hearken what I do say.

'And go thee down into yonder town,
And low into the street;
The fairest lady that thou can find,
Hire her in my arms to sleep,
And take her up in thine arms two,
For filing of her feet.'

for filing of] to avoid dirtying

Ellen is gone into the town,
And low into the street;
The fairest lady that she could find
She hired in his arms to sleep,
And took her in her arms two,
For filing of her feet.

'I pray you now, good Child Waters,
That I may creep in at your bed's feet;
For there is no place about his house
Where I may say a sleep.'

This night and it drove on afterward
Till it was near the day;
He said, 'Rise up, my little foot-page,
And give my steed corn and hay;
And so do thou the good black oats,
That he may carry me the better away.'

And up then rose fair Ellen,
And gave his steed corn and hay,
And so she did and the good black oats,
That he might carry him the better away.

She leaned her back to the manger side,
And grievously did groan;
And that beheard his mother dear,
And heard her make her moan.

She said, 'Rise up, thou Child Waters,
I think you are a curset man;
For yonder is a ghost in thy stable,
That grievously doth groan,
Or else some woman labours of child,
She is so woe-begone.'

But up then rose Child Waters,
And did on his shirt of silk;
Then he put on his other clothes
On his body as white as milk.

say] try

And when he came to the stable door,
Full still that he did stand,
That he might hear now fair Ellen,
How she made her monand.

She said, 'Lullaby, my own dear child,
Lullaby, dear child, dear!
I would thy father were a king,
Thy mother laid on a bier.'

'Peace now,' he said, 'good fair Ellen,
And be of good cheer, I thee pray,
And the bridal and the churching both,
They shall be upon one day.'

22. *Lord Thomas and Fair Ellinor*

Lord Thomas he was a gay forester
And a keeper of our king's deer;
Fair Ellinor she was a gay lady
And Lord Thomas he loved her dear.

'Now riddle my riddle, dear mother,' said he,
'And riddle it all in one;
Whether I shall marry the brown girl
Or bring fair Ellinor home.'

'The brown girl she has both houses and land,
Fair Ellinor she has none;
Wherefore I charge you upon my blessing
To bring the brown girl home.'

He dressed himself in gallant attire
His merry men all in white;
And every town that he passèd through
He was taken to be some knight.

And when he arrived at fair Ellinor's bower
He knocked loudly at the ring,
And who so ready as fair Ellinor
To let Lord Thomas in.

monand] moaning

'What news, what news, what news,' she cried,
'What news hast thou brought unto me?'
'I am come to bid thee to my wedding
Beneath the sycamore tree.'

'Oh God forbid that any such thing
Should ever pass by my side.
I thought that thou wouldst have been my bridegroom
And I should have been thy bride.

'Now riddle my riddle, dear mother,' said she,
'And riddle it all in one:
Whether I shall go to Lord Thomas's wedding
Or tarry with you at home.'

'Oh hundreds are your friends, dear daughter,
And thousands are your foes.
Therefore I charge you upon my blessing
To Lord Thomas's wedding don't go.'

She dressed herself in gallant attire,
Her merry men all in green;
And every town that she passèd through
She was taken to be some queen.

And when she arrived at Lord Thomas's bower
She knocked loudly at the ring,
And who so ready as Lord Thomas
To let fair Ellinor in.

He took her by the lily-white hand
And led her through the hall.
There were four and twenty gay ladies
But she was the fairest of them all.

'Is this your bride, Lord Thomas?' said she,
'Methinks she looks wondrous brown.
You might have chosen as fair a lady
As ever trod English ground.'

'Oh scorn her not, fair Ellen,' said he,
'Oh scorn her not unto me.
For better I love your little finger
Than the brown girl's whole body.'

The brown girl she had a knife in her hand,
It was both long and sharp;
Between the short ribs and the long
She pierced fair Ellinor's heart.

'Oh what is the matter, fair Ellen?' he said,
'Methinks you look wondrous wan.
You used to have as fair colour
As ever the sun shone on.'

'Oh are you blind, Lord Thomas?' she said,
'Or cannot you very well see?
For well I feel my own heart's blood
Come trickling down my knee.'

Lord Thomas he had a sword by his side,
It was both sharp and small.
He cut off the head of the brown girl
And he dashed it against the wall.

He put the hilt unto the ground,
The point into his heart.
Sure never three lovers so soon did meet
And never so soon did part.

Lord Thomas was buried in the church,
Fair Ellinor in the choir;
And out from her bosom there grew a red rose
And out of Lord Thomas a briar.

It grew till it reached the church tip top,
When it could grow no higher,
And there it entwined like a true love's knot
For all true loves to admire.

23. *The Gypsy Countess*

There came an earl a-riding by,
A gypsy maid espièd he.
'O nut-brown maid,' to her he said,
'I prithee come away with me.

'I'll take you up, I'll carry you home,
I'll put a safeguard over you,
Your shoes shall be of the Spanish leather,
And silken stockings all of blue.'

'My brothers three no more I'll see
If that I went along with you.
I'd rather be torn by thistle and thorn
With my bare feet all in the dew.'

'I'll lock you up in a castle tall,
I'll bar you up in a room so high,
Thou gypsy maid from greenwood glade,
That ne'er a gypsy shall come by.

'Thou shalt no more be set in stocks
And trudge about from town to town,
But thou shalt ride in pomp and pride
In velvet red and broidered gown.'

'I'll pawn my hat, I'll pawn my gown,
I'll pawn my ribbons, stockings blue.
I'll pawn my petticoat next my shift
To follow along with the gypsies O!'

'All night you lie 'neath the starry sky,
In rain and snow you walk all day,
But ne'er thy head shall have feather bed
And in thy arms no husband lay.'

'I love to lie 'neath a starry sky,
I do not heed the rain and snow,
And I will away, come night come day,
To follow along with my gypsies O!'

'I will thee wed, sweet maid,' he said,
'I will thee wed with a golden ring,
Then you shalt dance and merry, merry be
And I'll make thee a gay wedding.'

'I will not wed, kind sir,' she said,
'I will not wed with a golden ring,
For fickle as wind I fear I'll find
The man that would make my wedding.'

THE PAIN OF LOVE

Three gypsies stood at the castle gate,
They sang so high, they sang so low.
The lady sat in her chamber late,
Her heart it melted away as snow.

They sang so sweet, they sang so shrill
That fast her tears began to flow
And she laid down her golden gown,
Her golden rings and all her show.

And she put off her silken shoes
That were of Spanish leather O,
All forth for to go in the rain and snow,
All forth in the stormy weather,
And down the stair came the lady fair
To go away with the gypsies O.

At past midnight her lord came home
And where his lady was would know.
All servants replied on every side,
'She's gone away with the gypsies O.'

'Come saddle my horse, come saddle my mare,
And hang my sword to the saddle bow,
That I may ride for to seek my bride
That is gone away with the gypsies O.'

They saddled his horse, they saddled his mare
And hung his sword on his saddle bow
That he might ride for to seek his bride
That was gone away with the gypsies O.

Then he rode high, and he rode low,
He rode through hills and valleys O,
He rode till he spied his own fair bride
Following along with the gypsies O.

'What makes you leave both house and lands,
What makes you leave your money O,
What takes you abroad from your wedded lord
To follow along with the gypsies O?'

'Oh I want none of your house and lands
And I want none of your money O,
Neither care I for my wedded lord,
I will follow along with the gypsies O'

'Last night you slept in a feather bed
Rolled in the arms of your husband O,
And now you must sleep on the cold, cold ground
And walk along in the rain and snow.'

'I care not to sleep in a feather bed
Rolled in the arms of a husband O.
Far rather I'd sleep on the cold, cold ground
And walk along in the rain and snow.'

'Nay, that shall not be, I swear,' said he.
He drew his sword from his saddle bow,
And once he smote on her lily-white throat
And then her red blood down did flow.

24. *Fair Margaret and Sweet William*

Sweet William he would a-wooing ride,
His steed was lovely brown;
A fairer creature than Lady Margaret
Sweet William could not find.

Sweet William came to Lady Margaret's bower,
And knockèd at the ring,
And who so ready as Lady Margaret
To rise and let him in.

Down then came her father dear,
Clothèd all in blue:
'I pray, Sweet William, tell to me
What love's between my daughter and you?'

'I know none by her,' he said,
'And she knows none by me;
Before tomorrow at this time
Another bride you shall see.'

THE PAIN OF LOVE

Lady Margaret at her bower window,
Combing of her hair,
She saw Sweet William and his brown bride
Unto the church repair.

Down she cast her iv'ry comb,
And up she tossed her hair,
She went out of her bower alive,
But never no more came there.

When day was gone, and night was come,
All people were asleep,
In glided Margaret's grimly ghost,
And stood at William's feet.

'How d'ye like your bed, Sweet William?
How d'ye like your sheet?
And how d'ye like that brown lady
That lies in your arms asleep?'

'Well I like my bed, Lady Margaret,
And well I like my sheet;
But better I like that fair lady
That stands at my bed's feet.'

When night was gone, and day was come,
All people were awake,
The lady waked out of her sleep,
And thus to her lord she spake.

'I dreamed a dream, my wedded lord,
That seldom comes to good;
I dreamed that our bower was lin'd with white swine,
And our bride-chamber full of blood.'

He called up his merry men all,
By one, by two, by three:
'We will go to Lady Margaret's bower,
With the leave of my wedded lady.'

When he came to Lady Margaret's bower,
He knockèd at the ring,
And none were so ready as her brethren
To rise and let him in.

'Oh is she in the parlour,' he said,
'Or is she in the hall?
Or is she in the long chamber,
Amongst her merry maids all?'

'She's not in the parlour,' they said,
'Nor is she in the hall;
But she is in the long chamber
Laid out against the wall.'

'Open the winding sheet,' he cried,
'That I may kiss the dead;
That I may kiss her pale and wan
Whose lips used to look so red.'

Lady Margaret died on the over night,
Sweet William died on the morrow;
Lady Margaret died for pure, pure love,
Sweet William died for sorrow.

On Margaret's grave there grew a rose,
On Sweet William's grew a briar;
They grew till they joined in a true lover's knot,
And then they died both together.

25. *The Brown Girl*

I am as brown as brown can be,
And my eyes as black as sloe;
I am as brisk as brisk can be,
And wild as forest doe.

My love he was so high and proud,
His fortune too so high,
He for another fair pretty maid
Me left and passed me by.

Me did he send a love-letter,
He sent it from the town,
Saying no more he loved me,
For that I was so brown.

THE PAIN OF LOVE

I sent his letter back again,
Saying his love I valued not,
Whether that he would fancy me,
Whether that he would not.

When that six months were overpassed,
Were overpassed and gone,
Then did my lover, once so bold,
Lie on his bed and groan.

When that six months were overpassed,
Were gone and overpassed,
Oh then my lover, once so bold,
With love was sick at last.

First sent he for the doctor-man:
'You, doctor, must me cure;
The pains that now do torture me
I cannot long endure.'

Next did he send from out of town
Oh next did send for me;
He sent for me, the brown, brown girl
Who once his wife should be.

Oh ne'er a bit the doctor-man
His sufferings could relieve;
Oh never a one but the brown, brown girl
Who could his life reprieve.

Now you shall hear what love she had
For this poor lovesick man,
How all one day, a summer's day,
She walked and never ran.

When that she came to his bedside,
Where he lay sick and weak,
Oh then for laughing she could not stand
Upright upon her feet.

'You flouted me, you scouted me,
And many another one;
Now the reward is come at last,
For all that you have done.'

The rings she took off from her hands,
The rings by two and three:
'Oh take, oh take these golden rings,
By them remember me.'

She had a white wand in her hand,
She strake him on the breast:
'My faith and troth I give back to thee,
So may thy soul have rest.'

'Prithee,' said he, 'forget, forget,
Prithee, forget, forgive;
Oh grant me yet a little space,
That I may be well and live.'

'Oh never will I forget, forgive,
So long as I have breath;
I'll dance above your green, green grave
Where you do lie beneath.'

26. 'The trees they do grow high'

The trees they do grow high, the leaves they do grow green,
The time is long past, love, you and I have seen.
It's a cold winter's night when you and I must bide alone,
Though my bonny lad is young he's a-growing, growing,
Though my bonny lad is young he's a-growing.

'O father, dear father, you've done me much wrong;
You've married me to a boy who I fear is much too young.'
'O daughter, O daughter, if you stay at home with me,
A lady you shall be while he's growing, growing,
A lady you shall be while he's growing.'

'We'll send him to college for one year or two.'
'Perhaps then my love to a man he will grow.'
'I'll buy you white ribbons to tie round his bonny waist,
So the ladies shall know that he's married, married,
So the ladies shall know that he's married.'

At the age of sixteen he was a married man,
At seventeen the father of a son;
At the age of eighteen, his grave was a-growing green,
So she saw the end of his growing, growing,
So she saw the end of his growing.

I made my love a shroud of the holland, oh so fine,
And every stitch I put in it the tears came trickling down;
And I'll mourn his fate until the day I die,
But I'll watch o'er his child while it's growing, growing,
But I'll watch o'er his child while it's growing.

Now my love is dead, in his grave he doth lie;
The grass that's all o'er him it groweth so high.
Once I had a sweetheart but now I've never a one;
Fare you well, my own true love, for growing, growing,
Fare you well, my own true love, for growing.

27. *Let the Wind Blow High or Low*

One night when I was walking
Down by the riverside,
Gazing all around me,
When an Irish girl I spied.
Red and rosy were her cheeks,
Lovely coal black was her hair,
Costly were those lovely robes
This Irish girl did wear.

Her shoes were black,
Her stockings white,
All sprinkled with dew;
She wrung her hands and tore her hair,
Crying: 'Alas, what shall I do?
I'm going home, I'm going home,
I am going home,' said she.
'Oh would you go a-roving
To slight your own Polly?

'The very last time I saw my love
He seemed to be in pain,
With heartfelt grief and chilling woe
His heart it seemed near broke in twain.
There's many a man more true than he,
So why should I e'er complain?
Love it is a killing thing
Did you ever feel the pain.'

I wish I were a butterfly,
I would fly to my true love's breast;
I wish I were a linnet,
I would sing my love to rest;
I wish I were a nightingale,
I would sing to the morning clear;
I'll sit and sing for you, Polly,
The girl I love so dear.

I wish my love were red rosebud
Who in the garden grew,
And I to be the gardener
To her I ever would prove true.
There's not a month in all the year
But my love I would renew,
The lilies I would garnish,
Sweet William, thyme and rue.

I wish I were in Manchester
A-sitting on the grass
With a bottle of whisky in my hand
And upon my knee a lass.
I'd call for liquor merrily
And I would pay before I go,
I'll roll my lass all in the grass,
Let the wind blow high or low.

28. *My Johnny*

He's gone, I am now sad and lonely,
He's left me to cross the deep sea.
I know that he thinks of me only
And will soon be returning to me.

My eyes they are filled with devotion
For my husband he said he would be.
Blow gently the winds on the ocean
And send back my Johnny to me.

Each night as I lie on my pillow,
My bosom it heaves with a sigh.
I think of each angry billow
And I'm watching the clouds in the sky.
Some say that my love is returning
To his own native country and me,
So blow gently the winds on the ocean
And send back my Johnny to me.

He's gone for his fortune to better,
I know that he's gone for my sake.
I'll soon be receiving a letter
Or else my poor heart it will break.
Some say that my love is returning
To his own native country and me,
So blow gently the winds on the ocean
And send back my Johnny to me.

29. *The Grey Cock*

I must be going, no longer staying,
The burning Thames I have to cross.
Oh I must be guided without a stumble
Into the arms of my dear lass.

When he came to his true love's window,
He knelt down gently on a stone,
And it's a through a pane he whispered slowly,
'My dear girl, are you alone?'

She rose her head from her down-soft pillow,
And snowy were her milk-white breasts,
Saying, 'Who's there, who's there at my bedroom window,
Disturbing me from my long night's rest?'

'Oh I'm your lover, don't discover.
I pray you rise, love, and let me in,
For I am fatigued out of my long night's journey;
Besides I am wet into the skin.'

Now this young girl rose and put on her clothing,
Till she quickly let her true love in.
Oh they kissed, shook hands and embraced each other
Till that long night was near at an end.

'Willie dear, O dearest Willie,
Where is that colour you'd some time ago?'
'O Mary dear, the cold clay has changed me,
I am but the ghost of your Willie O.'

'Then cock, O cock, O handsome cockerel,
I pray you not crow until it is day;
For your wings I'll make of the very best beaten gold,
And your comb I will make of the silver ray.'

But the cock it crew and it crew so fully,
It crew three hours before it was day,
And before it was day my love had to go away,
Not by the light of the moon nor the light of day.

When she saw her love disappearing,
The tears down her pale cheeks in streams did flow.
He said, 'Weep no more for me, dear Mary,
I am no more your Willie O.'

'Then it's Willie dear, O dearest Willie,
Whenever shall I see you again?'
'When the fish they fly, love, and the sea runs dry, love,
And the rocks they melt by the heat of the sun.'

30. *The Unquiet Grave*

Cold blows the wind tonight, sweetheart,
Cold are the drops of rain.
The very first love that ever I had
In greenwood he was slain.

I'll do as much for my true love
As any young woman may.
I'll sit and mourn above his grave
A twelvemonth and a day.

A twelvemonth and a day being up
The ghost began to speak.
'Why sit you here by my graveside,
And will not let me sleep?

'O think upon the garden, love,
Where you and I did walk.
The fairest flower that blossomed there
Is withered on the stalk.

'The stalk will bear no leaves, sweetheart,
The flowers will never return,
And my true love is dead, is dead,
And I do nought but mourn.'

'What is it that you want of me
And will not let me sleep?
Your salten tears they trickle down
And wet my winding sheet.'

'What is it that I want of thee,
Oh what of thee in thy grave?
A kiss from off thy clay-cold lips
And that is all I crave.'

'Cold are my lips in death, sweetheart,
My breath is earthy strong.
If you do touch my clay-cold lips
Your time will not be long.'

'Cold though your lips in death, sweetheart,
One kiss is all I crave.
I care not, if I kiss but thee,
That I should share thy grave.'

'Go fetch me a light from dungeon deep,
Wring water from a stone,
And likewise milk from a maiden's breast
Which never babe had none.'

She stroke a light from out a flint,
An ice-bell pressed she,
She pressed the milk from a Johnnis wort
And so she did all three.

'Now if you were not true in word
As now I know you be
I'd tear you as the withered leaves
Are torn from off the tree.

'Now I have mourned upon his grave
A twelvemonth and a day,
I'll set my sail before the wind
To waft me far away.'

31. *Picking Lilies*

Down in a meadow fresh and gay,
Picking lilies all the day;
Picking lilies both red and blue,
I little thought what love could do.

Where love is planted there it grows,
It buds and blossoms like any rose,
It has so sweet and a pleasant smell,
No flowers on earth can it excel.

There's thousands, thousands in a room,
My love she carries the brightest bloom;
Surely she is the chosen one,
I will have her and I will have none.

I saw a ship sailing on the sea,
Loaded as deep as she could be;
But not so deep as in love I am,
I care not whether I sink or swim.

I leant my back unto an oak,
Thinking it was some trusty tree;
But first it bowed and then it brake,
And so did my true love to me.

Johnnis wort] St John's Wort

I put my hand into the bush
Thinking the sweetest rose to find,
I pricked my finger into the bone,
But left the sweetest rose behind.

If roses be such a prickly flower,
They ought to be gathered while they are green
And he that loves an unkind lover,
I am sure he striveth against the stream.

When my love and I is gone to rest,
I'll think on her whom I love best,
I'll wrap her in the linen strong,
And I'll think on her when she's dead and gone.

32. *I Live Not Where I Love*

Come all you maids that live at a distance
Many a mile from off your swain,
Come and assist me this very moment
For to pass some time away,
Singing sweetly and completely
Songs of pleasure and of love.
My heart is with you altogether
Though I live not where I love.

Oh when I sleeps I dreams about you,
When I wake I take no rest,
For every instant thinking on you
My heart e'er fixed in your breast.
Oh this cold absence seems at a distance
And many a mile from my true love,
But my heart is with her altogether
Though I live not where I love.

So farewell lads and farewell lassies,
Now I think I've got my choice.
I will away to yonder mountains
Where I think I hear his voice.

And if he holloa I will follow
Around the world that is so wide,
For young Thomas he did promise
I shall be his lawful bride.

Now if all the world was one religion,
Every living thing should die,
Or if I prove false unto my jewel
Or any way my love deny,
The world shall change and be most strange
If e'er I my mind remove.
My heart is with her altogether
Though I live not where I love.

33. *The Willow Tree*

As I passed by a willow tree
That willow leaf blew down on me.
I picked it up, it would not break,
I passed my love, he would not speak.

Oh speak, young man, and don't be shy,
I'm not a girl can pass you by,
For friends we met and friends we'll part,
Just take my hand and not my heart.

I wish your bosom was of glass,
That I could view it through and through,
Just view those secrets of your heart,
If I love one I can't love two.

Then give me back to the one I love,
Oh give, oh give him back to me,
If I only had that one I love,
How happy, happy should I be.

My love he is a sailor boy,
He sails the ocean through and through,
And when he gets so far away,
He hardly thinks of me no more.

Now give me back to the one I love,
Oh give, oh give him back to me.
If I only had that one I love,
How happy, happy should I be.

34. *Cupid the Ploughboy*

As I walked out one May morning
When may was white in bloom,
I walked into a tillage field
To breathe the sweet perfume.
I walked into a tillage field
And leaned upon a stile,
When there I saw a ploughing boy
Who did my heart beguile.

'Twas Cupid was this ploughing boy,
His furrows deep did plough,
He brake the clods that hard he found,
The seeds that he might sow.
I wish that pretty ploughing boy
My eyes had never seen.
Oh Cupid was that ploughing boy
With coulter sharp and keen.

If I should write a letter,
My inmost heart unfold,
Perhaps he would be scornful
And say that I was bold.
I would, I would that ploughing boy
My heart would yield again.
Oh Cupid was that ploughing boy
Who caused me all my pain.

35. *Ellen Taylor*

All round the room I waltzed with Ellen Taylor,
All round the room I waltzed till break of day;
And ever since that time I've done nothing but bewail her,
For she's gone to Manchester the summer months to stay.

'Twas at a ball at Islington I first did chance to meet her,
She really looked so nice I could not keep my eyes away;
I thought that all my life I never saw so sweet a creature,
She danced with me three hours, and then she fainted quite away.

For seven long years I'm bound apprentice to the city,
Four of them are gone, and I've only three to stay;
But if she'll not have me then I'll go and ask her father,
I'll go and ask her father and I don't think he'll say nay.

All round the room I waltzed with Ellen Taylor,
All round the room I waltzed till break of day;
And ever since that time I've done nothing but bewail her,
For she's gone to Manchester the summer months to stay.

36. *Molly of the North Country*

My love she was born in the north country wide,
Where's lofty hills and mountains all round on every side;
She's one of the fairest creatures that ever my eyes did see,
She exceeds all the maids in the north country.

My parents separated me and my dear,
Which caused me to weep and shed many a tear;
Asleep I do mourn, and awake I do cry,
And 'tis all for the sake of my darling I die.

Come saddle my horse that I may go ride
In search of my true love, let what will betide.
O'er lofty hills and mountains I'll wander and I'll rove
In quest of my Molly, my own constant love.

My hand is scarce able my pen for to hold,
To write my love's praises in letters of gold;
She's teeth as white as ivory, and eyes as black as sloes,
And she's wounded my poor heart wherever she goes.

Had I all the riches of the African shore,
Or had I all the gold that the misers have in store,
Or had I all the riches that e'er my eyes did see,
I'd part with it all for my love's company.

My love she's as near as the bark to a tree,
My love's she's as sweet as the cinnamon tree;
The top it will wither and the root will decay,
And a pretty maid's beauty it will soon fade away.

37. *The Lamenting Maid*

The yellow leaves do fly from the trees so high,
Upon the ground I see they do fall.
The man that I adore has lately left the shore,
Which grieves my poor heart worse than all.

The winter's gone and past, and the summer's come at last,
And the small birds are on every tree;
The hearts of those are glad while mine is very sad,
Since my true love is absent from me.

Farewell, my dearest dear, until another year,
Till the sweet spring I hope I shall see.
The linnet and the thrush will charm in the bush,
And the cuckoo will charm in the tree.

I'll put on my cap and black fringe all around my neck,
Rings on my fingers then I will wear.
Straightway I will repair to the county of Kildare,
And there I shall have tidings of him.

My father he was great in a plentiful estate,
He has forced my true love from me.
How cruel could he be to force my love to sea,
I'm afraid I shall never see him no more.

The livery I will wear and comb down my hair,
Then I dress in my velvet so green.
Straightway I will repair to the county of Kildare,
'Tis there I shall have tidings of him.

With patience I did wait till they'd run for the plate,
And thinking young Johnson for to see,
Fortune proved unkind to this sweetheart of mine,
Now he's gone to the lowlands from me.

Farewell my joy and heart, since you and I must part,
You are the fairest that ever I did see,
I never did design to alter my mind,
Though you are below my degree.

In the merry month of June if my jewel will return,
Garlands of flowers then I'll have,
Lilies, pinks and roses, a garland I'll prepare,
And I'll wear it for my dear Johnson's sake.

38. *Arise, Arise*

'Arise, arise, you pretty maiden,
Arise, arise, it is almost day,
And come unto your bedroom window
And hear what your true love do say.'

'Begone, begone, you'll awake my father,
My mother she can quickly hear;
Go and tell your tales unto some other
And whisper softly in their ear.'

'I won't begone for I love no other,
You are the girl that I adore;
It's I, my dear, who love you dearly,
It's the pains of love that have brought me here.'

Then the old man heard the couple talking,
He so nimbly stepped out of bed,
Putting his head out of the window,
Johnny dear was quickly fled.

'Now daughter dear, tell me the reason
You will not let me take my silent rest.
I'll have you confined to your bedchamber
And your true love to sea I will press.'

plate] the reference is to horse-racing

'Now father dear, pay down my fortune,
It's full five hundred pounds, you know,
That I may cross the briny ocean
Where the stormy winds do blow.'

'Now daughter dear, you may ease your mind
'Tis for your sweet sake that I say so:
If you cross the briny ocean
Without your fortune you must go.'

39. *Whistle, Daughter, Whistle*

'O mother, I longs to get married,
I longs to be a bride.
I longs to lay with that young man
And close to by his side.
Close to by his side,
Oh happy should I be,
For I'm young and merry and almost weary
Of my virginity.'

'O daughter, I was twenty
Before that I was wed
And many a long and lonesome mile
I carried my maidenhead.'
'O mother, that may be,
It's not the case by me,
For I'm young and merry and almost weary
Of my virginity.'

'Daughter, daughter, whistle,
And you shall have a sheep.'
'I cannot whistle, mother,
But I can sadly weep.
My maidenhead does grieve me,
That fills my heart with fear.
It is a burden, a heavy burden,
It's more than I can bear.'

'Daughter, daughter, whistle,
And you shall have a cow.'
'I cannot whistle, mother,
For 'deed I don't know how.

61

My maidenhead does grieve me,
That fills my heart with fear.
It is a burden, a heavy burden,
It's more than I can bear.'

'Daughter, daughter, whistle,
And you shall have a man.'
        (whistles)
'You see very well I can.'
'You nasty, impudent Jane,
I'll pull your courage down.
Take off your silks and satins,
Put on your working gown.
I'll send you to the fields,
A-tossing of the hay
With your fork and rake the hay to make
And then hear what you say.'

'Mother, don't be so cruel
To send me to the fields
Where young men may entice me
And to them I may yield.
For mother, it's quite well known
I am not too young grown,
For it is a pity a maid so pretty
As I should lay alone.'

40. *The Seeds of Love*

I sowed the seeds of love,
'Twas early in the spring,
In April and May, and in June likewise,
The small birds they do sing.

My garden is well planted
With flowers everywhere,
But I had not the liberty to choose for myself
Of the flowers that I lovèd dear.

My gardener he stood by,
I asked him to choose for me;
He chose me the violet, the lily and the pink,
But these I refused all three.

THE PAIN OF LOVE

The violet I forsook
Because it fades so soon.
The lily and the pink I did overlook
And I vowed I'd stay till June.

For in June there's a red rosebud,
And that's the flower for me,
So I pulled and I plucked at the red rosebud
Till I gained the willow tree.

For the willow tree will twist
And the willow tree will twine,
I wish I was in a young man's arms
That once had this heart of mine.

My gardener he stood by,
And told me to take good care,
For in the middle of the red rosebud
There grew a sharp thorn there.

I told him I'd take no care
Until I felt the smart.
I pulled and I plucked at the red rosebud
Till it pierced me to the heart.

I lockèd up my garden gate,
Resolving to keep the key,
But a young man he came a-courting me,
And he stole my heart away.

My garden is over-run,
No flowers in it grew,
For the beds that was once covered with sweet thyme
They are now over-run with rue.

Come, all you false young men
That leave me here to complain,
For the grass that is now trodden underfoot
In time it will rise again.

41. *A Brisk Young Widow*

In Chester town there lived
A brisk young widow,
For beauty and fine clothes
None could excel her.
She was proper, stout and tall,
Her fingers long and small,
She's a comely dame withal,
She's a brisk young widow.

At length of all there came
A brisk young farmer
With his hat turned up all round
Thinking to gain her.
Saying 'O madam, 'tis for you
This wide world I'll go through,
If that you'll prove true,
If you'll wed a farmer.'

She says, 'I'm not for you
Nor no such fellow.
I am for a lively lad
That hath got riches.
It's not your hogs nor yows
Can maintain furbelows,
Besides all my fine clothes
That's all my glory.'

'O madam, don't be coy
In all your glory,
For fear of another day
And another story.
If the world on you should frown,
Your topknot must come down
To a linsey wolsey gown
In all your glory.'

At last of all there came
A sooty collier,
With his hat bent down all round
He soon did gain her.

Which made the farmer swear,
'The widow's mazed, I'm sure.
I'll never go no more
Courting a widow.'

42. *The Wandering Shepherdess*

In the county of Essex there lived a squire,
And he had a daughter most beautiful and fair,
But she loved a shepherd below her degree,
Which caused her ruin and sad misery.

When her father came to know of it his passion grew hot,
And with a loaded pistol the shepherd he shot,
And as he lay bleeding this lady came by,
Which caused her to weep and to cry bitterly.

'Oh cursed be the gold, my true love lies slain,
My joys are transported to sorrow and pain.'
'Alas,' said the shepherd, 'no-one can my life save,
But a wonder you'll see when I'm laid in my grave.'

She took up his crook, his cloak and his plaid,
And like a true shepherd through the valley she strode,
When she got to the hill all the sheep to her came,
Bleating and entreating her true love to obtain.

The old ram she called Andrew, with Sally his dam,
Both Johnny and Charlotte they both knew their own name.
If she wanted them to stay on any green plain,
She said, 'You stay there until I come again.'

With humble submission they always do so,
When she stays away long they all bleating do go,
With humble submission they bleat in her face,
There's no such a token in the whole human race.

She wandered through England, to Scotland she came,
Ye true true love controllers, I'll tell you her doom.
Her shepherd's no more and her father soon died,
For the loss of a daughter and a murder beside.

'If I could return to my father's bright halls,
I might live in splendour, but that I ne'er shall.
I wander alone till death ends the strife,
And lament for my shepherd all the days of my life.'

43. *The Betrayed Maiden*

Of a brazier's daughter who lived near,
A pretty story you shall hear;
And she would up to London go,
To seek a service you shall know.

Her master had one only son,
Sweet Betsy's heart was fairly won,
For Betsy being so very fair
She drew his heart in a fatal snare.

One Sunday night he took his time,
Unto sweet Betsy he told his mind.
Swearing by all the powers above,
''Tis you, sweet Betsy, 'tis you I love.'

His mother happening for to hear,
Which threw her in a fatal snare,
For soon she contrived sweet Betsy away
For a slave in the province of Virginia.

'Betsy, Betsy, pack up your clothes,
For I must see what the country shows;
You must go with me a day or two,
Some of our relations there to view.'

They rode till they came to a sea town
Where ships were sailing in the Down.
Quickly a captain there was found,
Unto Virginia they were bound.

Both hired a boat, alongside they went,
Sweet Betsy rode in sad discontent,
For now sweet Betsy's upon the salt wave,
Sweet Betsy's gone for an arrant slave.

A few days after she returned again,
'You are welcome, mother,' says the son,
'But where is Betsy, tell me I pray,
That she behind so long doth stay?'

'O son, O son, I plainly see
How great your love is for pretty Betsy;
Of all such thoughts you must refrain,
Since Betsy's sailing over the watery main.

'We would rather see our son lie dead
Than with a servant girl to wed.'
His father spoke most scornfully,
'It would bring disgrace to our family.'

Four days after the son fell bad,
No kind of music could make him glad,
He sighed and slumbered, and often cried,
''Tis for you, sweet Betsy, for you I died.'

A few days after the son was dead,
They wrung their hands and shook each head,
Saying, 'Would our son but rise again,
We would send for Betsy over the main.'

44. *The Blacksmith*

A blacksmith courted me, nine months and better.
He fairly won my heart, wrote me a letter.
With his hammer in his hand, he looked so clever,
And if I was with my love, I'd live for ever.

And where is my love gone, with his cheek like roses,
And his good black billycock on, decked with primroses?
I'm afraid the scorching sun will shine and burn his beauty,
And if I was with my love, I'd do my duty.

Strange news is come to town, strange news is carried,
Strange news flies up and down that my love is married.
I wish them both much joy, though they don't hear me,
And may God reward him well for slighting of me.

'What did you promise when you sat beside me?
You said you would marry me, and not deny me.'
'If I said I'd marry you, it was only for to try you,
So bring your witness, love, and I'll never deny you.'

'Oh witness have I none save God almighty,
And He'll reward you well for slighting of me.'
Her lips grew pale and white, it made her poor heart tremble
To think she loved one, and he proved deceitful.

45. *Love is Teasing*

I never thought that my love would leave me
Until one evening when he came in.
He sat him down and I sat beside him
And then our troubles did begin.

Oh love is teasing and love is pleasing,
And love's a pleasure when first it's new.
But as it grows older it waxes colder
And fades away like the morning dew.

There is a blackbird sits on yon tree,
Some say that he's blind and cannot see.
How I wish it had been the same by me
Before my false love I did see.

Oh I wish my father had never whistled,
And I wish my mother had never sung.
I wish the cradle had never rocked me
And I had died low when I was young.

46. *An Old Man He Courted Me*

'Tis oft I'm tired of an old man,
And now got caught at last.
I wish to God he had a-been dead
Before the night was past.

THE PAIN OF LOVE

I wish the death might seize him
And take him at one call,
So that I might have a young man,
I'd roll from wall to wall.

He comes to bed at midnight,
His feet are cold as clay,
His feet are cold as midnight,
As any corpse you say.
His joints are out of order,
His pipes are all of one tune.
I wish to God he had a-been dead
And a young man in his room.

It was my cruel parents
That caused me to trepan,
To marry such an old man
For the sake of money and land.
I'd rather have a young man
Without any money at all.
He would take me in his arms, my love,
And roll me from the wall.

'Tis hold your tongue, dear Polly;
When first you came to town,
I bought you a beaver bonnet,
Likewise a silken gown.
There's never a lady in this land
That you and I can compare.
I'll buy you a little lapdog
To follow you at the fair.

I values not your lapdog,
No not your gentle care;
To pity such an old man
Of beauty me ensnare.
My age is scarcely sixteen,
I am scarcely in my bloom.
You are my daily torment
Both morning, night and noon.

Some they do persuade me
To drown him in a well;
Others do persuade me
To grind him in a mill.
I'd rather take my own advice
And tie him to a stake
And then I'd hammer his old hide
Until his bones did break.

47. *An Ape, Lion, Fox and Ass*

An ape, a lion, a fox and an ass
Do show forth man's life as it were in a glass;
For apish we are till twenty-and-one,
And after that lions till forty be gone;
Then witty as foxes till threescore and ten,
And after that asses, and so no more men.

A dove, a sparrow, a parrot, a crow,
As plainly set forth how you women may know;
Harmless they are till thirteen be gone,
Then wanton as sparrows till forty draws on;
Then prating as parrots till threescore be o'er,
Then birds of ill omen, and women no more.

48. *'Come all you young ladies and gentlemen'*

Come all you young ladies and gentlemen, let me with your company
    mingle:
Once I was young like you, and then I was happy and single.
Till my mother advised me to wed, until seventeen I had tarried;
I went off to church in a trance one day, like a man to be married.

Oh I wish I were single again.

My wife she came home in a pet and she burned my new boots to a
    cinder,
And the cat she kicked under the grate and the table threw out of the
    winder;

And the bedclothes, kettle and broom, and the washing-tub off she
    has carried,
And she sold both the poker and tongs, so I wish I had never got
    married.

It's seldom we get a bit of meat—but once a month, or I'm generally
    mistaken;
Then it's old sheep's head and a pluck, and a small piece of liver and
    bacon.
She says bread and butter is dear, and business most shocking and
    horrid,
And I've often times wished I'd been dead before I ever got married.

Now I should be happy and jovial once more if I could once see all
    things right;
May Old Nick come and fetch her away some morning before it is
    daylight.
Come all you young men that are single of mind and pray don't you
    ever be hurried,
For if I were single again, I'd be cussed if I ever got married.

49. *The Shoemakker*

My mother sent us to the school
To learn to be a stocking knitter,
But Aa was young and played the fool
And married wi' a shoemakker.
Shoemakker, leather-cracker,
Wi' all his stinking dirty water,
Aa wish a thousand deaths Aa'd died,
Ere Aa'd wed a shoemakker.

His hands are like a cuddy's houghs,
His face is like the high-lowed leather.
His ears are like I don't know what,
His hair is like a bunch o' heather.
Shoemakker, leather-cracker,
Stinking kit and rotten leather.

pluck] offal   **49** cuddy's houghs] donkey's hocks

Aa wish a thousand deaths Aa'd died,
Ere Aa'd wed a shoemakker.

He sent me for a pint of wine,
And Aa brought him a pint of watter,
But he played me as good a trick,
He made my shoes o' rotten leather.
Shoemakker, leather-strapper,
Three rows of rotten leather,
Balls of wax and stinking watter,
Who would have a shoemakker?

50. *A Poor Man's Work is Never Done*

When I was a young man I lived rarely,
I spent my time in grief and woe
For the want of a young wife to lie by me,
When my trouble did run so.

With my whack fal lor, the diddle and the dido,
Whack fal lor, the diddle aye day.

Now I hired one for my constant service,
To milk my cows and brush my shoes;
Some women take delight in a deal of pleasure;
Poor man's labour is always abused.

When I come home in the morning early
To see my flocks that were astray,
My wife she lay abed till noon
On the shortest winter's day.

When I come home all wet and weary,
No dry clothes for me to put on,
It's enough to make a poor man crazy:
Poor man's labour is never done.

The very first year that I was married
I could not get one wink of sleep,
For all night long she kept on crying,
'Husband, do not go to sleep.'

She kicked my shins till the blood ran down 'em,
Crying, 'Husband, my dear, my dear.'
It's very well I knew her meaning:
A poor man's labour is never done.

The second year that I was married
I had a fine baby born.
She forsook it, I took to it,
Wrapped it up and kept it warm.

One night as I sat by the fire
She came in roaring like a gun;
In my face her fist came slapping:
A poor man's work is never done.

All you men who want to marry,
Take care how you choose a wife,
For if you meet with my wife's sister,
She'll be a devil all the days of her life.

So court them long before you marry:
Women seldom prove a friend.
Well now, away with my wife and welcome,
Then my troubles will have an end.

51. *The Fox and the Hare*

Six wives I've had and they're all dead,
But I'll wager I don't have another.
I'm single again and I mean to remain
And I'll go and live with mother.

> *Oh the fox and the hare*
> *And the badger and bear*
> *And the birds of the greenwood tree,*
> *The pretty little rabbits*
> *Are engaging in their habits,*
> *And they've all got a wife but me.*

Oh the first on the page was little Sally Gage,
She once was a lady's maid,
And she ran away on a very dark day,
With a fellow in the fried fish trade.

73

Oh the next to charm was a girl on our farm,
Well versed in harrows and ploughs,
She guarded on the rigs a lot of little pigs,
And she squeezed new milk from the cows.

Oh the next was a cook, a beauty with a hook,
I'll tell you the reason why,
For a leg she'd a stump, on her neck she'd a bump,
And a naughty little squintle in her eye.

She was eighteen stone, all muscle and bone,
And she looked with an awful leer,
She would have been mine, but she fell in decline,
Through swallowing the bellows in her beer.

Oh the next to claim was a right jolly dame,
With a purse as long as your arm,
All full o' yellow gold, such a sight to behold,
And a heart so amazingly warm.

A rowley scene was a love for Jean,
Which broke her hope to the wreck,
For she slipped with her heel on a piece of orange peel,
And she fell and broke a bone in her neck.

The last I had through drink went mad,
In vain I tried to stop her,
But sad to say it was my dismay,
She got slowly boiled to death in the copper.

52. *Household Remedies*

Most folks believe in doctors, but there's my old girl she don't,
And when I'm laid upon my bed send out for one she won't;
She says she's got enough to do without her paying fees,
And doctor me herself she does with household remedies.

No matter what the ailment is she knows a simple cure,
But whether it fits my complaint we're never certain sure.
For instance, when my aching hollow tooth upset my health,
That putty didn't answer though she pushed it in herself.

THE PAIN OF LOVE

She tried to stop the toothache with her gutta-percha sole,
A thing she said was never known to fail,
And to melt the pieces in held a light beneath my chin—
It's a wonder I'm alive to tell the tale.

I used to have the bilious bile through eating pork at night,
And someone said a black draught would be the thing to set me right.
We hadn't got no black draughts but we have some dominoes—
She vaselined the double six and down my neck it goes.

And when I had a face which swelled as big as Pilsdon Hill,
I had the earache awful and the gumboil took a chill,
She said she'd try her grandad's cure, a thing she knew by heart,
And a little sweet oil and feather seemed to play the leading part.

She tried to stop the earache with some sweetened paraffin,
You'd have thought I was a bedstead from a sale;
But that beastly low-flashed oil blew off my lovely boil—
It's a wonder I'm alive to tell the tale.

I wore a dandelion when my liver became bad,
And all the boys got shouting after me in Laddin's Lane,
And then I up and tells her 'tis medicine I need;
Instead of Carter's liver pills she gave me Carter's seeds.

And when my blood was very hot, well ninety in the shade,
She very nearly corpsed me with the cooling stuff she made.

She got some salts and senna and some raspberry ice-cream
And asked the man to cool it in his pail.
What I suffered no-one knows when the raspberry unfroze—
It's a wonder I'm alive to tell the tale.

The Joys of Love

53. Lord Bateman

Lord Bateman was a noble lord,
A noble lord of high degree,
He shipped himself on board a ship,
Some foreign countries to go and see.

He sailèd east, he sailèd west,
He sailèd into proud Turkey,
Where he was taken and put in prison
Until he of life was quite weary.

And in this prison there growed a tree,
It growed so stout, it growed so strong.
He was chained up all by the middle,
Until his life was almost done.

This Turk he had one only daughter,
The fairest creature that ever you see,
She stole the keys of her father's prison
And swore Lord Bateman she would set free.

'Have you got lands, have you got livings,
Or dost Northumberland belong to thee?
What will you give to a fair young lady
If out of prison she'll set you free?'

'Yes, I've got lands and I've got livings
And half Northumberland belongs to me,
And I'll give it all to a fair young lady
If out of prison she will set me free.'

She took him to her father's cellar
And give to him the best of wine,
And every health that she drinked unto him:
'I wish, Lord Bateman, that you were mine.

'Seven long years we will make a vow,
And seven long years we will keep it strong:
If you will wed with no other woman,
I will never wed with no other man.'

She took him to her father's harbour
And give to him a ship of fame.
'Farewell, farewell to you, Lord Bateman,
I'm afraid I never shall see you again.'

Now seven long years is a-gone and past,
And fourteen days well known to me.
She packed up all her gay clothing
And swore Lord Bateman she'd go and see.

And when she came to Lord Bateman's castle
So boldly how she did ring the bell.
'Who's there, who's there?' cried the proud young porter,
'Who's there, who's there? come quickly tell.'

'Oh is this called Lord Bateman's castle,
Oh is his lordship here within?'
'Oh yes, oh yes,' cries the proud young porter,
'He has just now taken his young bride in.'

'You tell him to send me a slice of bread
And a bottle of the best of the wine,
And not forgetting that fair young lady
That did release him when he was close confined.'

Away, away went this proud young porter,
Away, away, away went he,
Until he came to Lord Bateman's chamber,
Down on his bended knees he fell.

'What news, what news, my proud young porter,
What news, what news has thou brought to me?'
'There is the fairest of all young ladies
That ever my two eyes did see.

'She has got rings on every finger,
Round one of them she have got three.
She have gold enough around her middle
To buy Northumberland that belongs to thee.

78

'She tells you to send her a slice of bread
And a bottle of the best of wine
And not forgetting that fair young lady
That did release you when you were close confined.'

Lord Bateman then in a passion flew,
He broke his sword in splinters three,
Saying, 'I will give you all my father's riches
And if Sophia have a-crossed the sea.'

Oh then up spoke this young bride's mother
Who was never heard to speak so free,
Saying, 'You'll not forget my only daughter
For if Sophia have a-crossed the sea.'

'I only made a bride of your daughter,
She's neither the better nor worse for me.
She came to me on a horse and saddle,
She may go back in a coach and three.'

Lord Bateman prepared for another marriage,
So both their hearts so full of glee.
'I will range no more to foreign countries
Now since Sophia have a-crossed the sea.'

54. *The Famous Flower of Serving-Men*

You beauteous ladies, great and small,
I write unto you one and all,
Whereby that you may understand
What I have suffered in this land.

I was by birth a lady fair,
My father's chief and only heir,
But when my good old father died,
Then I was made a young knight's bride.

And then my love built me a bower,
Bedecked with many a fragrant flower;
A braver bower you never did see
Than my true love did build for me.

But there came thieves late in the night,
They robbed my bower, and slew my knight,
And after that my knight was slain,
I could no longer there remain.

My servants all from me did fly
In the midst of my extremity,
And left me there by myself alone,
With a heart more cold than any stone.

Yet, though my heart was full of care,
Heaven would not suffer me to despair;
Wherefore in haste I changed my name
From Fair Elise to Sweet William.

And therewithal I cut my hair,
And dressed myself in man's attire,
My doublet, hose, and beaver-hat,
And a golden band about my neck.

With a silver rapier at my side,
So like a gallant I did ride;
The thing that I delighted on
Was for to be a serving-man.

Thus in my sumptuous man's array,
I bravely rode along the way;
And at the last it chancèd so
That I unto the king's court did go.

Then unto the king I bowed full low,
My love and duty for to show,
And so much favour I did crave
That I a serving-man's place might have.

'Stand up, brave youth,' the king replied,
'Thy service shall not be denied;
But tell me first what thou canst do;
Thou shalt be fitted thereunto.

'Wilst thou be usher of my hall,
To wait upon my nobles all?
Or wilt thou be taster of my wine,
To wait on me when I shall dine?

'Or wilt thou be my chamberlain,
To make my bed both soft and fine?
Or wilt thou be one of my guard?
And I shall give thee thy reward.'

Sweet William, with a smiling face,
Said unto the king, 'If't please your grace
To show such favour unto me,
Your chamberlain I fain would be.'

The king then did the nobles call,
To ask the counsel of them all,
Who gave consent Sweet William he
The king's own chamberlain should be.

Now mark what strange things came to pass:
As the king one day a-hunting was,
With all his lords and noble train,
Sweet William did at home remain.

Sweet William had no company then
With him at home but an old man;
And when he saw the coast was clear,
He took a lute which he had there.

Upon the lute Sweet William played,
And to the same he sung and said,
With a pleasant and most noble voice,
Which made the old man to rejoice:

'My father was as brave a lord
As ever Europe did afford;
My mother was a lady bright,
My husband was a valiant knight.

'And I myself a lady gay,
Bedecked with gorgeous rich array;
The bravest lady in the land
Had not more pleasure to command.

'I had my music every day,
Harmonious lessons for to play;
I had my virgins fair and free,
Continually to wait on me.

'But now, alas! my husband's dead,
And all my friends are from me fled;
My former joys are past and gone,
For now I am a serving-man.'

At last the king from hunting came,
And presently upon the same
He callèd for the good old man,
And thus to speak the king began:

'What news, what news, old man?' quod he,
'What news hast thou to tell to me?'
'Brave news,' the old man did say,
'Sweet William is a lady gay.'

'If this be true thou tellest me
I'll make thee a lord of high degree;
But if thy words do prove a lie,
Thou shalt be hanged up presently.'

But when the kind truth had been found,
His joys did more and more abound;
According as the old man did say,
Sweet William was a lady gay.

Therefore the king without delay
Put on her glorious rich array,
And upon her head a crown of gold,
Which was most famous to behold.

And then for fear of further strife,
He took Sweet William for his wife;
The like before was never seen,
A serving-man to be a queen.

55. *Searching for Lambs*

As I walked out one May morning,
One May morning betimes,
I overlooked a handsome lass
Just as the sun was rise.

'What makes you rise so soon, my dear,
Your journey to pursue?
Your pretty little feet they tread so sweet,
Strike off the morning dew.'

'I am going to feed my father's flock,
It's young and tender lambs,
It's over hills and over dales
Lay waiting for their dams.

'How glorious like the sun do shine,
How pleasant across the mead;
But I'd rather be in my true love's arms
Than any other where.

'For I am thine and thou art mine,
No man shall uncomfort me.
We'll join our hands in a wedded band
And a-married we will be.'

56. *The Banks of Claudy*

As I walked out one morning
All in the month of May,
Down through some flowery gardens
I carelessly did stray.
I overheard a damsel
In sorrow to complain
Now for her absent lover
That ploughs the raging main.

I stepped up to this fair maid,
I put her in surprise,
I own she did not know me,
I being dressed in disguise.
Says I: 'My lovely maiden,
My joy and heart's delight,
How far have you to wander
This dark and dreary night?'

'All the way, kind sir, to Claudy,
If you will please to show
Pity a poor girl distracted,
It's there I have to go.
I'm in search of a faithless young man
And Johnny is his name,
And on the banks of Claudy
I'm told he does remain.

'If my Johnny he was here this night
He'd keep me from all harm,
But he's in the field of battle
All in his uniform.
He's in the field of battle,
His foes he will destroy
Like a roving king of honour
He fought on the banks of Troy.'

'Oh 'tis six months and better
Since your Johnny left the shore,
He's a-cruising the wide oceans
Where foaming billows roar.
He's a-cruising the wide ocean
For honour and for gain.
The ship's been wrecked as I am told
All on the coast of Spain.'

As soon as she heard him say so
She fell into deep despair
By wringing of her milk-white hands
And tearing of her hair.
'If my Johnny he be drownded
No man on earth I'll take,
But through lonesome groves and villages
I will wander for his sake.'

As soon as he heard her say so
He could no longer stand,
But he fell into her arms
Saying: 'Bessie, I'm the man.
I am that faithless young man
Whom you thought was slain,
And once we've met on Claudy banks
We'll never part again.'

57. *The Only Daughter*

'Tis down in the valley my father does dwell—
See, Mary on yonder stile is leaning—
And all that the cottage produces I sell,
And earn him a little by gleaning.

Then I must away by the break of the day,
My basket to fill by the water,
To earn all I can for my father, poor man,
For I am his only daughter.

Besides, there is William has fetched from the valley
Three pretty cows from old Mary,
He'll soon want some one, for he told me he should,
A maid to look after his dairy.

So he asked me to go, and I could not say no,
For it's only just over the water;
So he asked me to go, and I could not say no,
For I am the only daughter.

58. *The Streams of Lovely Nancy*

Oh the streams of lovely Nancy are divided in three parts,
Where the young men and maidens they do meet their sweethearts.
It is drinking of good liquor caused my heart for to sing,
And the noise in yonder village made the rocks for to ring.

At the top of this mountain, there my love's castle stands.
It's all overbuilt with ivory on yonder black sand,
Fine arches, fine porches and diamonds so bright.
It's a pilot for a sailor on a dark winter's night.

On yonder high mountain, where the wild fowl do fly,
There is one amongst them that flies very high.
If I had her in my arms, love, near the diamond's black land,
How soon I'd secure her by the sleight of my hand.

At the bottom of this mountain there runs a river clear.
A ship from the Indies did once anchor there,
With her red flags a-flying and the beating of her drum,
Sweet instruments of music and the firing of her gun.

So come all you little streamers that walk the meadows gay,
I'll write unto my own true love, wherever she may be.
For her rosy lips entice me, with her tongue she tells me no,
And an angel might direct us right, and where shall we go?

59. *The Rifles*

Oh, the Rifles have stolen my dear jewel away,
And I in old England no longer can stay;
I will cross the wide ocean, all on my bare breast,
To find my own true love, whom I do love best.

And when I have found him, my own heart's delight,
I will prove to him kinder by day and by night,
I will prove to him kinder than the true turtle-dove,
I never will at any time prove false to my love.

And when we are married the bells they shall ring,
With many sweet changes our joys to begin;
The music shall play and the drums make a noise,
To welcome my true love with ten thousand bright joys.

60. *To Milk in the Valley Below*

'Oh, Nancy, my heart,
Don't you hear the sweet lark?
Don't you hear the sweet nightingale sing?
Don't you hear the fond tale
Of the sweet nightingale,
How she sings in the valley below,
How she sings in the valley below?

'Oh, Nancy, don't fail!
May I carry thy pail?
May I carry thy pail to the cow?'
But the maid she replied,
'I'll not walk by thy side,
To milk in the valley below,
To milk in the valley below.'

'Now sit yourself down
All on this cold ground,
I'll do you no harm, I avow.'
But the more she was afraid
For to walk by his side
Or to milk in the valley below,
Or to milk in the valley below.

This couple agreed,
They were married with speed,
They were married the very next day.
Now no more she's afraid
To walk by his side,
Or to milk in the valley below,
Or to milk in the valley below.

61. *New Garden Fields*

On the eighteenth of August, at the eighth month of the year,
Down by New Garden Fields there I first met my dear.
She appeared like some goddess or some one divine
And she came like some torment to trouble my mind.

'Oh I am no tormentor, young man,' she did say,
'I'm a-picking those flowers so fresh and gay,
'I'm a-picking those flowers that nature doth yield
For I takes great delight in the New Garden Fields.'

And I said, 'Lovely Nancy, dare I make so bold
Your lily-white hand one minute to hold?
It will give me more pleasure than all earthly store,
So grant me this favour and I'll ask you no more.'

And she turned and said, 'Young man, I fear you must jest.
If I thought you were in earnest I would think myself blest,
But my father is coming there now,' did she say,
'So fare you well, young man, it's I must away.'

So now she's gone and left me all in the bonds of love,
Kind Cupid, protect me, and you powers above,
Kind Cupid, protect me, and pray take my part,
For she's guilty of murder and quite broke my heart.

She turned and said, 'Young man, I pity your moan.
I'll leave you no longer to sigh all alone.
I will go along with you to some foreign part,
You are the first young man that has won my heart.

'We'll go to church on Sunday and married we'll be,
We'll join hands in wedlock and sweet unity.
We'll join hands in wedlock and vow to be true,
To father and mother we will bid adieu.'

62. *Grandma's Advice*

My grandmother lived in yonder little lane,
As nice an old lady as ever was seen.
She ofttimes cautioned me with care
Of false young men to be aware.

Timy i, timy i,
Timy umpy tumpy tee,
Of false young men to be aware.

These false young men they flatter and deceive,
But, love, you must not them believe.
They kiss you and court you, and get you in the snare,
Then away goes poor old grandma's care.

The first that came was little Johnny Green,
As nice a young fellow as ever was seen.
My grandmother's words came ringing in my head,
I could not hear one word he said.

The next that came was little Johnny Clove,
Then he came with a joyous love;
With a joyous love how could I be afraid?
And away went what poor old grandma said.

I said to myself, there must be some mistake,
Dear me, what a fuss these old folks make.
If all the lads and lasses they had been afraid,
Why, grandma herself would have died an old maid!

63. *Blackberry Fold*

It's of a rich squire in Bristol doth dwell,
There are ladies of honour that love him well,
But all was in vain, in vain was said,
For he was in love with a charming milkmaid.

As the squire and his sister did sit in the hall,
And as they were talking to one and to all,
And as they were singing each other a song,
Pretty Betsy, the milkmaid, came tripping alone.

'Do you want any milk,' pretty Betsy did say.
'Oh yes,' said the squire, 'step in, pretty maid.
It is you, fair body, that I do adore,
Was there ever a body so wounded before?'

'Oh hold your tongue, squire, and let me go free,
Do not make your game of my poverty.
There are ladies of honour more fitter for you,
Than I, a poor milkmaid, brought up from the cows.'

A ring from his finger he instantly drew,
And right in the middle he broke it in two,
And half he gave to her, as I have been told,
And they both went a-walking to Blackberry Fold.

'O Betsy, O Betsy, let me have my will,
So constant a squire I'll prove to you still;
And if you deny me, in this open field,
Why, the first time I'll force, and make you to yield.'

With hugging and struggling, poor Betsy got free,
Saying, 'You never shall have your will of me,
I'll protect my own virtue, as I would my life,'
And drew from her bosom a large dagger knife.

Then with her own weapon she run him quite through,
And home to her master like lightning she flew,
Saying, 'O dear master,' with tears in her eyes,
'I have wounded the squire, and I'm afraid dead he lies.'

The coach was got ready, the squire brought home,
The doctor was sent for to heal up the wound.
Poor Betsy was sent for, the gay maiden fair,
Who wounded the squire, drove his heart in a snare.

The parson was sent for, this couple to wed,
And she did enjoy the sweet marriage bed.
It's better to be honest if ever so poor,
For he's made her his lady instead of his whore.

64. *The Pride of Kildare*

When first from sea I landed I had a roving mind;
Undaunted I rambled, my true love to find,
When I met with pretty Susan in the street like a rose,
And her bosom was more fairer than the lily that grows.

Her keen eyes did glitter like the bright stars by night,
And the robe she was wearing was costly and bright,
And her bare neck was shaded by her long, ravening hair,
And they calls her pretty Susan, the Pride of Kildare.

Long time I courted her till I wasted all my store,
Her love turned to hate because I were poor.
She said, 'I will have another one whose fortune I'll share,
So begone from pretty Susan, the Pride of Kildare.'

'Twas early one morning as I lonely did stray,
There I spied Susan with her young lad so gay,
And I passed by them with my mind full of care,
Sighs for pretty Susan, the Pride of Kildare.

Once more on the ocean I'm resolved to go
And bound to West Indies with my heart full of woe.
There I beheld the ladies with jewels so rare,
There was none like pretty Susan, the Pride of Kildare.

Sometimes I am jovial, sometimes I am sad,
Since my love she's been courted by some other young lad.
But now I'm at a distance no more I'll despair,
But my blessings on Susan, the Pride of Kildare.

65. *My Man John*

'O madam, I will give to thee a new silk gown
With five and thirty flounces a-bobbing to the ground
If you'll be my bride, my joy and my dear,
If you'll go a-walking with me anywhere.'

'Indeed I won't accept of your new silken gown
With five and thirty flounces a-bobbing to the ground;
I won't be your bride, your joy or your dear,
I won't go a-walking with you anywhere.'

'Old man Jan, what can the matter be?
You see I love the lady and she won't love me.
She won't be my bride, my joy nor my dear,
She won't go walking with me anywhere.'

'You court her, court her, master, you court her, never fear,
For she'll be your bride, your joy and your dear.
Yes, she will be your bride, your joy and your dear
And she'll go walking with you anywhere.'

'O madam, I will give to you a cushion full of pins
For you to pin up your baby's mu-se-lins.
If you'll be my bride, my joy and my dear,
If you'll go a-walking with me anywhere.'

'Indeed I won't accept of your cushion full of pins
For to pin up my baby's mu-se-lins.
I won't be your bride, your joy or your dear,
I won't go a-walking with you anywhere.'

'Old man Jan, what can the matter be?
You see I love the lady and she won't love me.
She won't be my bride, my joy and my dear,
She won't go a-walking with me anywhere.'

'You court her, court her, master, you court her, never fear,
For she'll be your bride, your joy and your dear.
Yes, she will be your bride, your joy and your dear
And she'll go a-walking with you anywhere.'

'O madam, I will give to you a little greyhound,
If every hair upon its back is worth a thousand pound,
If you will be my bride, my joy and my dear,
If you will go a-walking with me anywhere.'

'Indeed, I won't accept of your little greyhound,
If every hair upon its back is worth a thousand pound,
I won't be your bride, your joy or your dear,
I won't go a-walking with you anywhere.'

'O madam, I will give to you a little set of bells
For to call up your servants where you are not well,
If you will be my bride, my joy and my dear,
If you will go a-walking with me anywhere.'

'Indeed, I won't accept your little set of bells
For to call up my servants when I am not well.
I won't be your bride, your joy or your dear,
I won't go a-walking with you anywhere.'

'Old man Jan, what can the matter be?
You see I love the lady and she won't love me.
She won't be my bride, my joy and my dear,
She won't go a-walking with me anywhere.'

'You court her, court her, master, you court her without fear,
For she'll be your bride, your joy and your dear.
Yes, she will be your bride, your joy and your dear,
And she'll go a-walking with you anywhere.'

'O madam, I will give to you the keys of my heart
For to lock it up for ever and never more to part,
If you will be my bride, my joy and my dear,
If you will go a-walking with me anywhere.'

'Indeed, I will accept of you the keys of your heart,
I'll lock it up for ever and never more to part.
And I will be your bride, your joy and your dear,
And I will go a-walking with you anywhere.'

66. *The Sign of the Bonny Blue Bell*

As I was a-walking one morning in the spring
To hear the birds whistle and the nightingale sing,
I heard a fair damsel, so sweetly sung she,
Saying, 'I will be married on Tuesday morning.'

I stepped up to her and thus I did say,
'Pray tell me your age and where you belong?'
'I belong to the sign of the Bonny Blue Bell,
My age is sixteen and you know very well.'

'Sixteen, pretty maid, you are young to be married.
I'll leave you another four years to be tarry.'
'You speak like a man without any skill,
Four years I have been single against my own will.

'On Monday night when I goes there
To powder my locks and to curdle my hair,
There was three pretty maidens awaiting for me,
Saying: I will be married on a Tuesday morning.

'On a Tuesday morning the bells they shall ring
And three pretty maidens so sweetly shall sing.
So neat and so gay is my golden ring,
Saying: I will be married on a Tuesday morning.

curdle] curl

93

'On Tuesday night when I goes to bed
With my precious jewel that I lately wed,
Farewell and adieu to my maidenhead.
Goodnight, pretty maidens, till Wednesday morning.'

67. *The Green Mossy Banks of the Lee*

When first in this country a stranger,
Curiosity caused me to roam
Through Europe to ramble all over,
So I left Philadelphia, my home.
To England I quickly sailed over
Where forms of great beauty did shine.
'Twas there I beheld a fair damsel
And wished in my heart she was mine.

Three steps and I steppèd up to her,
Her fair cheeks did blush like a rose.
I said, 'Now my charming fair creature,
Your guardian I'll be if you choose.'
'Kind sir, oh I ne'er want a guardian,
Young man, you're a stranger to me,
And yonder my father is coming
On the green mossy banks of the Lee.'

I waited till up came her father.
I plucked up my spirits once more.
I said, 'Kind sir, if this is your daughter,
Why she is the girl I adore.
Ten thousand a year is my fortune,
Your daughter a lady shall be.
She shall ride in her chariot and horses
On the green mossy banks of the Lee.'

Then they welcomed me home to their cottage
And soon we were in wedlock joined,
And there I erected a castle
In grandeur and splendour to shine.
So now this American stranger
All pleasure and pastime doth see
With the adorable gentle Matilda
On the green mossy banks of the Lee.

68(a). *The Foggy Dew*

When I was a bachelor young and gay
I followed the roving trade
And all the harm that ever I done,
I courted a pretty maid.
I courted her in the summer season
And part of the winter too,
And many a night I walked with her
All over foggy dew.

One night as I lay on my bed
As I lay fast asleep,
Then up comes this pretty fair maid
And most bitterly did weep.
She wept, she moaned, she tore her hair,
Crying, 'Alas, what shall I do?
This night I'm resolved to stay with you
For fear of the foggy dew.'

'Twas in the first part of the night
We passed our time away,
And in the latter part of the night,
For she stayed with me till day.
And when broad daylight did appear
She cried, 'I am undone.'
'Oh hold your tongue, you silly girl,
For the foggy dew has gone.

'Suppose that you should have a child,
What need have you to fear?
Suppose that you should have another,
What need have we to care?
And suppose that we should have another
And another and another too,
'Twould make you think of your foolish tricks
And about the foggy dew.'

I loved this girl most dearly
And I loved her as my life;
I took this girl and married her,
Made her my lawful wife.

And I never told her of her faults
And never intended to,
But every time she smiled at me
I think of the foggy dew.

68(b). *The Foggy Dew*

Once I was a little boy,
I went to learn my trade,
And all that my delight it was
In courting of a maid.

I courted her one midsummer day
And part of the winter too,
Until I gained this fair maid's heart,
She knew not what to do.

She wrung her hands and tore her hair,
Crying, asking, 'What shall I do?'
'Come into my bed, my fair pretty maid,
For fear of the foggy dew, dew, dew.'

So there they laid all that long night
Till daylight did appear.
'Come rise, pretty maid, and don't be afraid
For the foggy dew is gone.'

And when she rose and saw the light
She cries, 'I am undone.'
I said, 'Fair maid, be not afraid
For the foggy dew is done.'

'Oh when shall you come on, my dear,
Oh when shall you come on?'
'When oaken leaves fall off the trees
And greener ones come on.'

'Oh that will be too long, my dear,
Oh that will be too long.
My heart will burst and die I must
That is if you don't come on.'

The very next day I married her,
I married her for life,
And ever since I married her
I proved her for my wife.

'When we have a child, my dear,
Oh that will make you smile,
And when we have another
We will wait a little while.

'And when we have another, my dear,
And have another two,
Why we must leave off kissing
And think of the foggy dew.'

69. *Seventeen Come Sunday*

As I walked out one May morning,
One May morning early,
'Twas then I spied a pretty maid
So handsome and so clever.

    With my rue, rum, ray
    Fol the riddle ay
    Whack fa loora lido

Her shoes were black, her stockings white,
And her buckles shone like silver;
She had a dark and rolling eye,
And her hair hung down her shoulders.

'How old are you, my pretty fair maid,
How old are you, my honey?'
She answered me quite cheerfully,
'I am seventeen come Sunday.'

'Will you marry me, my pretty fair maid,
Will you marry me, my honey?'
She answered me quite cheerfully,
'I dare not for my mammy.

'If you come down to my mammy's house
When the moon is shining brightly,
Then I'll come down and let you in
And my mammy will not hear me.'

I went to her mammy's house
When the moon was brightly shining;
She came down and let me in
And I lay in her arms till morning.

'Oh soldier, will you marry me?
For now's your time or never.
Oh soldier, will you marry me?
Or I'm undone for ever.'

And now she is a soldier's wife
And sails across the brine O.
'The drum and fife is my delight
And a merry man is mine O.'

70. *'A farmer's son so sweet'*

A farmer's son so sweet
Was keeping of his sheep,
So careless fell asleep
While his lambs were playing.

A fair young lady gay
By chance she came that way,
Found him sleeping lay
Whom she loved so dear.

She kissed his lips so sweet
As he lay fast asleep.
'I'm afraid my heart will break
For you, my dear.'

She said, 'Awake, I pray,
Your flock will go astray,
Your flock will go astray
From you, my dear.'

He woke with great surprise
To behold her handsome eyes,
Like an angel from the skies
She did appear.

''Twas for your sweet sake alone
I wandered from my home.
My friends are dead and gone,
I am left alone.'

His flock he laid aside,
Made her his lawful bride.
In wedlock she was tied
To the farmer's son.

71. *William and Phyllis*

Says William to Phyllis, 'How came you here so soon?
You seem for to ramble all in the month of June.
The birds were singing cheerfully, you sit you down by me
And talk about the tales of love, likewise the greenwood tree.'

They both went together to sail the ocean wide,
William did his duty for Phyllis was his bride.
But mark the desolation, the winds began to blow,
The lightning flashed, the thunder roared, in flakes fell down the
    snow.

For three weeks on the ocean they were tossed up and down,
The ship has lost her anchor, the masts away were blown.
At length upon a dismal night they were cast upon the sands
In the coast of America, a kind and friendly land.

They met with kind assistance, it did their health restore,
Now they are united all on the peaceful shore.
They're happy in America all in prosperity,
The young Phyllis and William all from the greenwood tree.

72. *Locks and Bolts*

'Twas over hills and over dales
Through lonesome woods and valleys
When my true love was sent from me
All out of spite and malice.

I went unto my true love's house
Inquiring for my dearest,
But the answer that was give to me,
'I have no daughter near me.'

But hearing of her true love's voice
She looked out of the window,
Saying, 'I can't be in your sweet company
For locks and bolts doth prevent me.'

The locks he broke in pieces three
And the door he split asunder.
Soon as he entered his true love's room
So quickly did he gain her.

True love's for ever and I'll endure
And so will I for ever,
Till fatal death does destroy my breath
We'll live and die together.

True love's for ever and I'll endure
And so will I for ever.
Let every man be as true as me,
Take one and fight for the other.

73. *Young Barnswell*

Abroad as I was walking
All on a summer's day,
I heard two lovers talking,
These words to him did say.

'O true love, true love Samuel,
I'm come to break my vow.'
'O true love, true love Saro,
Don't tell me nothing so.'

'My friends and brother Barnswell
Are in such spite with thee,
Swearing that they will slay thee
All on the mountains high.'

'Your friends and brother, Saro,
Take me for such a man,
But not them do I care for,
I'll do the best I can.

'Give to me your hand, sweet Saro,
And stand you true by me,
And I will fight young Barnswell
All on the mountains high.'

'And when you're on the mountains,
You're by yourself alone;
You're far from town or city,
You're far from any home.

'You're far from town or city,
Where no-one will come by.
Pray use my brother kindly
All on the mountains high.'

Young Barnswell spoke to young Samuel,
Saying, ''Tis unto me draw nigh.
'Tis here I mean to slay thee
All on the mountains high.'

Young Samuel stood amazed,
Not knowing what to say,
And at last stepped up to him
And took his bow away.

His arrow he took from him,
His bow he slent in three.
'There,' he cried out, 'young Barnswell,
I have no shot for thee.'

slent] broke

And yonder he spied young Saro,
She's tripping all over the plain,
Thinking to meet her brother
And her true love being slain.

Young Barnswell he stepped up to her
And took her by the hand,
And gave her to young Samuel
In the place where they did stand.

'May God send you prosper both
All the days of your life.
I give you my dear sister
To be your wedded wife.

'I must confess that you
Were a better man than I.
It lay in your power to slay me
All on the mountains high.'

74. *Billy Boy*

'Is she fitting for your wife, Billy boy, Billy boy,
Is she fitted for your wife, Billy boy?'
'She is fitted for my wife
As the haft is to the knife,
She's my Nancy, please-my-fancy,
I'm her charming Billy boy.'

'Did she ask you to sit down, Billy boy, Billy boy,
Did she ask you to sit down, Billy boy?'
'Yes, she asked me to sit down
And she curtsied to the ground,
She's my Nancy, please-my-fancy,
I'm her charming Billy boy.'

'Did she light you up to bed, Billy boy, Billy boy,
Did she light you up to bed, Billy boy?'
'Yes, she lit me up to bed
With the bowing of her head,
She's my Nancy, please-my-fancy,
I'm her charming Billy boy.'

'Did she lay so close to you, Billy boy, Billy boy,
Did she lay so close to you, Billy boy?'
'Yes, she lay so close to me
As the rind upon the tree,
She's my Nancy, please-my-fancy,
I'm her charming Billy boy.'

75. *Oh no John*

On yonder hill there stands a creature,
Who she is I do not know.
I'll go and court her for her beauty,
She must answer yes or no.

  Oh no John, no John, no John, no.

On her bosom are bunches of posies,
On her breast where flowers grow,
If I should chance to touch that posy,
She must answer yes or no.

'Madam, I am come for to court you,
Whether your passions I can gain.
Come and set yourself down alongside of me,
Fear I should never see you again.'

'My husband he was a Spanish captain,
Went to sea but a month ago,
And the very last time we kissed and parted
He always bid me answer no.'

'Madam, in your face is beauty,
In your bosom flowers grow,
In your bedroom there is pleasure,
Shall I view it, yes or no?

'Madam, shall I tie your garter,
Tie it a little above your knee?
If my hand should slip a little farther,
Would you think it amiss of me?'

My love and I we went to bed together,
There we lay till the cocks did crow.
'Unclose your arms, my dearest jewel,
Unclose your arms and let me go.'

Oh no John, no John, no John, no.

76. *Arise and Pick a Posy*

Small birds and turtle doves
In every bush a-building,
The sun's just a-glimmering.
Arise, my dear.

Arise and pick a posy,
Sweet lily, pink and rosy;
It is the finest flower
That ever I did see.

Yes, I will pick a posy,
Sweet lily, pink and rosy,
But there's none so sweet a flower
As the lad that I adore.

77. *Polly Oliver's Rambles*

One night as Polly Oliver was lying in her bed,
A project very wondrous came into her head.
She'd go through the country disguisèd to rove
And so she would seek for her own dearest love.

So early next morning the fair maid arose.
She dressed herself up in a man's suit of clothes,
Coat, waistcoat and breeches and a sword by her side,
And her father's black gelding fair Polly would ride.

She rode till she came to a place of renown
And there she put up at the sign of the Crown.
She sat herself down with brown ale at the board
And the first that came in was an outlandish lord.

THE JOYS OF LOVE

The next that came in was fair Polly's true love.
She looked in his face and resolved him to prove.
Oh he was a captain, a captain so fine,
He sat at the board and he called for red wine.

'A letter, a letter that's come from a friend
Or else 'tis a letter your true love did send,
And under the seal will a guinea be found
For you and your soldiers to drink ale around.'

'Then what are your tidings, my little foot-page?
For you are a boy of the tenderest age
With locks that are curling and smooth is your chin,
A voice as a flute warbles softly and thin.'

'I am not a foot-page, a gelding I ride,
And I am a squire with a sword by my side.
The letter was given me, riding this way,
But who 'twas that gave it I never can say.'

The maid being drowsy, she hung down her head,
She called for a candle to light her to bed.
'My house it is full,' the landlady swore,
'My beds are engaged, let him lie on the floor.'

The captain he answered, 'I've a bed at my ease
And you may lie with me, young boy, if you please.'
'I thank you, sir captain,' fair Polly she said,
'I'll lie by the fire, on the saddle my head.

'To lie with a captain's a dangerous thing.
I'm a new-listed soldier to fight for the king.
Before the lark whistles I must ride away
And miles must make many before break of day.'

Then early next morning this fair maid arose
And dressed herself up in her own woman's clothes.
Down over the stair she so nimbly did run,
As he had proved constant to his loved one.

So now she is married and lives at her ease,
She goes where she wills and comes where she please.
She has left her old parents behind her to mourn,
And give hundreds of thousands for their daughter's return.

78. *Johnny Sands*

A man whose name was Johnny Sands
Had married Betty Haigh,
And though she brought him gold and lands,
She proved a terrible plague.
For, oh, she was a scolding wife,
Full of caprice and whim;
He said that he was tired of life,
And she was tired of him
And she was tired of him.

Says he, 'Then I will drown myself,
The river runs below.'
Says she, 'Pray do, you silly elf,
I wished it long ago.'
Says he, 'Upon the brink I'll stand,
Do you run down the hill
And push me in with all your might.'
Says she, 'My love, I will,'
Says she, 'My love, I will.'

'For fear that I should courage lack
And try to save my life,
Pray tie my hands behind my back.'
'I will,' replied his wife.
She tied them fast as you may think,
And when securely done,
'Now stand,' she says, 'upon the brink,
Now I'll prepare to run
Now I'll prepare to run.'

All down the hill his loving bride
Now ran with all her force
To push him in—he stepped aside
And she fell in of course.
Now splashing, dashing like a fish,
'Oh save me, Johnny Sands.'
'I can't, my dear, though much I wish
For you have tied my hands
For you have tied my hands.'

79. *The Shepherd and the Shepherdess*

My love is but a shepherd lad,
A shepherdess am I,
From morn till eve we tend our flocks
Beneath the bright blue sky.

He's going to take me to the church,
Some fine day in spring;
The hedges will be white with may,
The village bells will ring.

For he's as good as gold, he is,
Just as good as gold;
For I can see that he loves me,
And that's as good as gold.

The sound will linger in our ears,
Till we are both grown old;
And oh, how happy we shall be,
For he's as good as gold.

For he's as good as gold, he is,
Just as good as gold;
For I can see that he loves me,
And that's as good as gold.

Our cottage will be thatched with straw,
To keep out rain and cold;
And oh, how happy we shall be,
For he's as good as gold.

For he's as good as gold, he is,
Just as good as gold;
For I can see that he loves me,
And that's as good as gold.

80. *'I know where I'm going'*

I know where I'm going,
And I know who's going with me.
I know who I love,
But the dear knows who I'll marry.

I'll have stockings of silk,
Shoes of fine green leather,
Combs to buckle my hair
And a ring for every finger.

Feather beds are soft,
Painted rooms are bonny:
But I'd leave them all
To go with my love Johnny.

Some say he's dark,
But I say he's bonny,
He's the flower of them all,
My handsome, winsome Johnny.

I know where I'm going,
And I know who's going with me.
I know who I love,
But the dear knows who I'll marry.

81. *Old Brown's Daughter*

There's an ancient party
At the other end of town,
They keep a little chandler's shop,
Their ancient names are Brown.
They're such a jolly party,
Such a party I never saw,
But by jingo, I would like to be
That old chap's son-in-law.

Old Brown's daughter
She's a proper sort of girl,
Old Brown's daughter
She's as fair as any pearl.

I wish I were a Lord Mayor,
A marquis or an earl,
I'm blowed if I wouldn't marry
Old Brown's girl.

Old Brown keeps a shop,
Sells anything you please—
Treacle, wood, buns and soap,
Lollipops and cheese.
Miss Brown she minds the shop,
It's a treat to see her serve;
I'd like to run away with her,
But I haven't got the nerve.

Old Brown is often troubled with the gout,
He grumbles in his little parlour
When he can't get out.
Miss Brown she smiles so sweetly
When she hands me the change,
She makes me feel so galvanised
I feel so very strange.

Miss Brown she smiles so sweetly
When I say a tender word.
Old Brown says she'll marry
A marquis or a lord.
I don't suppose that ever
One of those swells I shall be,
But, by jingo, next election
I shall put up as MP.

82. *The Bailiff's Daughter of Islington*

There was a youth, and a well-belovèd youth,
And he was an esquire's son,
He loved the bailiff's daughter dear,
That lived in Islington.

She was coy, and she would not believe
That he did love her so,
No, nor at any time she would
Any countenance to him show.

But when his friends did understand
His fond and foolish mind,
They sent him up to fair London,
An apprentice for to bind.

And he had been seven long years,
And his love he had not seen.
'Many a tear have I shed for her sake,
When she little thought of me.'

All the maids of Islington
Went forth to sport and play;
All but the bailiff's daughter dear,
She secretly stole away.

She put off her gown of grey,
And put on her puggish attire;
She's up to fair London gone,
Her true love to require.

As she went along the road,
The weather being hot and dry,
There was she aware of her true love,
At length came riding by.

She stepped to him, as red as any rose,
And took him by the bridle-ring:
'I pray you, kind sir, give me one penny
To ease my weary limb.'

'I prithee, sweetheart, canst thou tell me
Where that thou wast born?'
'At Islington, kind sir,' said she,
'Where I have had many a scorn.'

'I prithee, sweetheart, canst thou tell me
Whether thou dost know
The bailiff's daughter of Islington?'
'She's dead, sir, long ago.'

puggish] as of a servant

'Then I will sell my goodly steed,
My saddle and my bow;
I will into some far country,
Where no man doth me know.'

'Oh stay, oh stay, thou goodly youth!
She's alive, she is not dead;
Here she standeth by thy side,
And is ready to be thy bride.'

'Oh farewell grief and welcome joy,
Ten thousand times and more!
For now I have seen my own true love,
That I thought I should have seen no more.'

83. *The Queen of Hearts*

To the Queen of Hearts is the Ace of Sorrow,
He's here today and he's gone tomorrow.
Young men are plenty but sweethearts few;
If my love leave me, what shall I do?

Had I the store in yonder mountain
Where gold and silver are had for counting,
I could not count for the thought of thee,
My eyes so full I cannot see.

My father left me both house and lands
And servants many at my command.
At my commandment they ne'er shall be,
I'll forsake them all and follow thee.

84. *The Three Ravens*

There were three ravens sat on a tree
  Down a down, hay down, hay down
There were three ravens sat on a tree
They were as black as they might be.
  With a down derry derry derry down down

Then one of them said to his make,
'Where shall we our breakfast take?'

'Down in yonder green field,
There lies a knight slain under his shield.

'His hounds they lie down at his feet,
So well they can their master keep.

'His hawks they fly so eagerly,
There's no fowl dare him come nigh.'

Down there comes a fallow doe,
As great with young as she might go.

She lifted up his bloody head,
And kissed his wounds that were so red.

She got him up upon her back,
And carried him to earthen lake.

She buried him before the prime,
She was dead herself ere evensong time.

God send every gentleman
Such hawks, such hounds, and such a leman.

85. *Spencer the Rover*

These words were composed by Spencer the Rover,
As have travelled most parts of Great Britain and Wales;
But being reduced has caused my confusion,
And that was the very reason I set off on trails.

But at Yorkshire, near Rotherham, where I first took my ramble,
Being weary of travelling I sat down to rest.
At the foot of yonder mountain where runs a clear fountain,
With bread and cold water myself to refresh.

But it tasted more sweet than the gold I had wasted,
More sweeter than honey, and gave more content;
But the thoughts of my babies lamenting their father
Brought tears in my eye, and caused me to lament.

But the fifth of November I have reason to remember,
When first I arrived to my family and wife;
She stood so surprised when she saw me arrived,
To see such a stranger once more in her sight.

Now my children come round me with their pretty, prattling stories,
With their pretty, prattling stories to drive dull care away;
So we'll unite together, like birds of one feather,
Like the bees in one hive contented we'll be.

But now I am placed in my cottage contented,
Where the roses and woodbines grow over my door;
As contented as those who have thousands of riches,
I'll stay at home with my wife and go rambling no more.

86. 'When Adam was first created'

When Adam was first created
And lord of the universe crowned,
His happiness was not completed
Until that a helpmate was found.
He had all things in food that were wanting
To keep and support him in life,
He'd horses and foxes for hunting,
Which some men love more than a wife.

He'd a garden so planted by nature
Man cannot produce in his life,
But yet the all-wise Creator
Still saw that he wanted a wife.
Then Adam he lay in a slumber,
And there he lost part of his side,
And when he awoke, with a wonder,
He beheld his most beautiful bride.

In transport he gazèd upon her,
His happiness now was complete;
He praised his most beautiful donor
Who had thus bestowed him a mate.
She was not took out of his head, sir,
To reign or to triumph o'er man;
Nor was she took out of his feet, sir,
By man to be trampled upon.

But she was took out of his side, sir,
His equal and partner to be,
But as they're united in one, sir,
The man is the top of the tree.
Then let not the fair be despisèd
By man, as she's part of himself,
For woman by Adam was prizèd
More than the whole world full of wealth.

Man without woman's a beggar,
Suppose the whole world he possessed;
And the beggar that's got a good woman
With more than the world is he blest.
When Adam was first created
And lord of the universe crowned,
His happiness was not completed
Until that a helpmate was found.

87. *The Jolly Shilling*

I have a jolly shilling, a lovely jolly shilling,
I love my jolly shilling as I do love my life;
I've a penny for to spend, another for to lend,
And a jolly, jolly tenpence to carry home to my wife.

There's neither pints nor quarts shall grieve me,
Nor this wide world shall deceive me,
But bring me to the girl that will keep me
While I go rambling about.

I have a jolly tenpence, a lovely jolly tenpence,
I love my jolly tenpence as I do love my life;
I've a penny for to spend, another for to lend,
And a jolly, jolly eightpence to carry home to my wife.

[*and so on, the amounts reducing until . . .*]

I have a jolly twopence, a lovely jolly twopence,
I love my jolly twopence as I do love my life;
I've a penny for to spend, another for to lend,
And nothing at all to carry home to my own dearest wife.

88. *Nine Times a Night*

A buxom young fellow from London came down
To set up his trade in Ramsbottom town;
They asked who he was and he answered them right,
'I belong to a family called "Nine times a night".'

A buxom young widow who still wore her weeds,
Whose husband had left her her riches and deeds,
Resolvèd she was by her conjugal right,
To fill up her chisum with nine times a night.

She ordered her waiting maids, Betty and Nan,
To keep a lookout for that wonderful man,
And whenever they saw him appear in their sight,
To bring her glad tidings of nine times a night.

Fortune favoured the joke on the very next day,
Those giggling girls saw him coming that way.
Then upstairs they ran with amorous delight,
'Upon my word, madam, here's nine times a night.'

From a chair she arose (what I say is true),
And down to the hall door like lightning they flew,
She viewed him all over and gave him a smack,
The bargain was struck and done in a crack.

The marriage being over, the bride tolled the bell,
He did six times and pleased her so well,
She vowed from her heart she was satisfied quite,
Still she gave him a hint of nine times a night.

He said, 'My dear bride, you mistook the wrong thing,
I said to that family I did belong.
Nine times a night is too much for a man,
I can't do it myself, but my sister, she can.'

89. 'My old wife's a good old cratur'

My old wife's a good old cratur,
My old wife's a good old soul,
Every morning for my breakfast
She gives me good toast and roll.

And at night, when work is over,
She brings me baccy and me beer;
So you see I live in clover,
Ain't a wife a good old dear?

And when matters run three-cornered,
She sidles up so droll and kind,
Gives me a buss and gently whispers,
'Did 'em vex 'e? Never mind!'

And, as now and then 'twill happen,
I get beery, even then
She never says a cross word to me,
But welcomes me with 'Well done, Ben.'

And next morning for my breakfast
She gives me good toast and roll.
My old wife's a good old cratur,
My old wife's a good old soul.

We have lived many years together,
We've seen ups and downs in life,
But through fine and stormy weather
She always proved a faithful wife.

Some folks live in larger houses,
Some folks live on daintier cheer,
But none of them have got such spouses,
No such baccy, no such beer.

90. *Wedding Song*

Now some people thinks it's jolly for to lead a single life,
But I believe in marriage and the comforts of a wife.
In fact you might have quarrels, just an odd one now and then,
It's worth your while a-falling out to make it up again.

Then it's get a little table, then a little chair,
And then a little house in the corner of a square,
Get a little teapot and save a little tin,
But don't forget the cradle for to rock the baby in.

Now a married man has comforts where a single man has not,
His clothes is always mended and his meals is always hot.
No matter what your trouble is your wife'll pull you through,
So if you think of marriage, lads, I'll tell you what to do.

A single man in lodgings can't have much delight,
For there's no-one to speak with him when he sits home at night,
Nothing to attract him or to pass his time away,
So he'll quickly find the difference if he listens what I say.

It's little use of asking a girl to marry you,
Unless you've got a little corner of the table too,
For a good wife loves to see you cosy, clean and nice,
So if you wish to marry, boys, I'll tell you what to do.

91. *'Dance to thee daddy'*

Dance to thee daddy, my little laddy,
Dance to thee daddy, my little man.
Thou shalt have a fish, thou shalt have a fin,
Thou shalt have a haddock when the boat comes in.
Thou shalt have a codlin boiled in a pan.
Dance to thee daddy, my little man.

Dance to thee daddy, my bonnie laddy,
Dance to thee daddy, my little lamb.
When thou art a woman fitter to be married,
Thou shalt have a penny for to buy a man.
Thou shalt have a penny, thou shalt have a penny,
Dance to thee daddy, my little lamb.

Seduction and Betrayal

92. *Little Musgrave and Lady Barnard*

As it fell one holy-day
   Hay down
As many be in the year,
When young men and maids together did go,
Their matins and mass to hear,

Little Musgrave came to the church-door;
The priest was at private mass;
But he had more minds of the fair women
Than he had of Our Lady's grace.

The one of them was clad in green,
Another was clad in pall,
And then came in my Lord Barnard's wife,
The fairest among them all.

She cast an eye on Little Musgrave,
As bright as the summer sun;
And then bethought this Little Musgrave,
This lady's heart have I won.

Quoth she, 'I have loved thee, Little Musgrave,
Full long and many a day.'
'So have I loved you, fair lady.
Yet never word durst I say.'

'I have a bower at Bucklesfordberry,
Full daintily it is dight;
If thou wilt wend thither, little Musgrave,
Thou'll lie in my arms all night.'

Quoth he, 'I thank ye, fair lady,
This kindness thou showest to me,
But whether it be to my weal or woe,
This night I will lie with thee.'

With that he heard, a little tiny page,
By my lady's coach as he ran:
'Although I am my lady's foot-page,
Yet I am Lord Barnard's man.

'Lord Barnard shall know of this,
Whether I sink or swim;'
And ever where the bridges were broke,
He laid him down to swim.

'Asleep or wake, thou Lord Barnard,
As thou art a man of life,
For Little Musgrave is at Bucklesfordberry,
Abed with thy own wedded wife.'

'If this be true, thou little tiny page,
This thing thou tellest to me,
Then all the land in Bucklesfordberry,
I freely will give to thee.

'But if it is a lie, thou little tiny page,
This thing thou tellest to me,
On the highest tree in Bucklesfordberry,
Then hangèd shalt thou be.'

He callèd up his merry men all:
'Come saddle me my steed;
This night must I go to Bucklesfordberry,
For I never had greater need.'

And some of them whistled, and some of them sung,
And some these words did say,
And ever when my Lord Barnard's horn blew:
'Away, Musgrave, away.'

'Methinks I hear the thressel-cock,
Methinks I hear the jay;
Methinks I hear my Lord Barnard,
And I would I were away.'

'Lie still, lie still, thou Little Musgrave,
And huggle me from the cold;
'Tis nothing but a shepherd's boy,
A-driving his sheep to the fold.

'Is not thy hawk upon a perch?
Thy steed eats oats and hay;
And thou a fair lady in thine arms,
And wouldst thou be away?'

With that my Lord Barnard came to the door,
And lit a stone upon;
He pluckèd out three silver keys,
And he opened the doors each one.

He lifted up the coverlet,
He lifted up the sheet.
'How now, how now, thou Little Musgrave,
Dost thou find my lady sweet?'

'I find her sweet,' quoth Little Musgrave,
'The more 'tis to my pain;
I would gladly give three hundred pounds
That I were on yonder plain.'

'Arise, arise, thou little Musgrave,
And put thy clothes on;
It shall ne'er be said in my country
I have killed a naked man.

'I have two swords in one scabbard,
Full dear they cost my purse;
And thou shalt have the best of them,
And I will have the worse.'

The first stroke that Little Musgrave stroke,
He hurt Lord Barnard sore;
The next stroke that Lord Barnard stroke,
Little Musgrave ne'er struck more.

With that bespake this fair lady,
In bed whereas she lay:
'Although thou'rt dead, thou Little Musgrave,
Yet I for thee will pray.

'And wish well to thy soul will I,
So long as I have life;
So will I not for thee, Barnard,
Although I am thy wedded wife.'

He cut the paps from off her breast;
Great pity it was to see
That some drops of this lady's heart's blood
Ran trickling down her knee.

'Woe worth you, woe worth, my merry men all,
You were ne'er born for my good;
Why did you not offer to stay my hand,
When you see me wax so wood?

'For I have slain the bravest knight
That ever rode on steed;
So have I done the fairest lady
That ever did woman's deed.

'A grave, a grave,' Lord Barnard cried,
'To put these lovers in;
But lay my lady on the upper hand,
For she came of the better kin.'

93. *Barbara Allen*

'Twas early in the month of May
When green leaves they were springing,
When a young man on his deathbed lay
For the love of Barbara Allen.

He sent to her his servant-man
To the place where she was dwelling,
Saying, 'Fair maid, you must come to my master
If your name is Barbara Allen.'

Slowly, slowly she walked along
And slowly she got to him,
And when she got to his bedside,
'Young man,' said she, 'You're dying.'

'Dying, dying? Oh don't say so!
One kiss from you will cure me.'
'One kiss from me you never shall have
If your poor heart is breaking.

wood] mad

'Don't you remember the other day
When in the city dwelling,
You gave kind words to the other girls
And none to Barbara Allen?'

As she was walking through the fields
She heard the bells a-ringing,
And as they rang they seemed to say
'Hard-hearted Barbara Allen.'

Hard-hearted creature sure was I
To him that loved me dearly.
I wish I had more kinder been
In time of life when he was near me.

As she was walking up the town
She saw the corpse a-coming.
'Put him down, put him down, you six young men,
And let me gaze upon him.'

The more she looked the more she laughed
And the further she got from him,
Till all her friends cried out, 'For shame,
Hard-hearted Barbara Allen!'

'Twas he that died on one good day
And she died on the morrow.
'Twas him that only died for love
And she that died for sorrow.

One was buried in the old chancel,
The other in the choir.
Out of him grew a red rosebud
And out of her a sweet briar.

It grew, it grew to the old church top
Where it could not grow any higher,
Tied himself in a true lovers' knot
For all false hearts to admire.

94. *The Carpenter's Wife*

'Well met, well met, my own true love,
Long time am I a-seeking of thee.
I'm lately come from the salt, salt sea
And all for the sake, sweet love, of thee.

'I might have had a king's daughter,
She fain would have a-married me,
But I naught did hold for her crown of gold
And for the sake, sweet love, of thee.'

'If you might have had a king's daughter
I think you were much to blame.
I would not 'twere found for a hundred pound
That my husband should know the same.

'For my husband he is a carpenter,
A carpenter good is he.
By him I have gotten a little son
Or else I would go, sweet love, with thee.

'But if I should leave my husband dear,
My fair sweet boy also,
Oh what have you got far far away
That along with thee I should go?'

'I have seven ships that sail on the sea,
It was one brought me to land.
I have mariners many to wait on thee,
To be, sweet love, at thy command.

'A pair of slippers thou shalt have,
They are made of beaten gold.
They're lined within with coney's fur
To keep thy feet from the cold.

'A gilded boat thou also shalt have,
The oars be gilded also,
And the mariners shall pipe and sing
As through the salt waves we go.'

124

SEDUCTION AND BETRAYAL

They had not rowed a bowshot off,
A bowshot on the main,
But o'er her shoulder she looked back:
'I would I were home again!'

They had not rowed a bowshot off,
A bowshot from the land,
But o'er her shoulder she looked and said,
'Set me back on the yellow sand,

'For I have a child in my little chamber
And I think I hear him cry.
I would not, I would not my babe should wake
And his mother not standing by.'

The captain he smiled and stroked his arms
And said, 'This may not be.
Behind is the shore and the sea is before
And thou must go, sweet love, with me.'

She had not been long upon the sea,
Not long upon the deep,
Before that she was wringing her hands
And loudly did wail and weep.

'Oh why do you wail and wherefore weep
And wring your hands?' said he.
'Do you weep for the gold that lies in the hold
Or do you weep for my fee?'

'I do not weep for your gold,' she said,
'Nor yet do I weep for your fee,
But by the mast-head is my baby dead
And I weep for my dead baby.'

She had not a-been upon the seas
The days they were three or four,
And never a word she spoke nor stirred
As she looked towards the shore.

She had not a-been upon the seas
But six days of the week
Before that she lay as cold as the clay
And never a word could speak.

They had not sailed upon the seas
Of weeks but three or four
But down to the bottom the ship did swim
And never was heard of more.

And when the news to England came
The carpenter's wife was drowned,
The carpenter rent his hair and wept
And then as dead he swound.

A curse be on all sea-captains
That lead such a godless life.
They will ruin a good ship-carpenter,
His little one and his wife.

95. *The Wanton Seed*

As I walked forth one morning fair,
To view the fields and take the air,
I espied a pretty maid making this complaint,
That she stood in need of the chiefest grain.

I stepped up to this fair maid
And unto her these words I said,
I said, 'My pretty fair maid, do you stand in need,
I've a grain that is called the wanton seed.'

'Oh yes, kind sir, I do stand in need
Of a grain that is called the wanton seed,
And if you are the man that can well do the deed,
Come and sow my meadow with your wanton seed.'

Then she sowed high and I sowed low,
And under her apron the seed did grow;
It sprung up so neatly without any weed,
And she always commended me well for my seed.

96. *Rosemary Lane*

I once was in service
Down Rosemary Lane,
I had a kind mistress
And master the same.

One day a young sailor
Came to our house to tea;
And this was the commencement
Of my misery.

When supper was over
He hung down his head,
Then he asked for a candle
To light him to bed.

I gave him a candle
As a maiden should do;
Then he vowed and declared
That I should go too.

Me like a silly girl
Was thinking no harm,
So I jumped into bed with him
To keep myself warm.

Early next morning
When the young sailor arose
He threw in my apron
Two handfuls of gold.

'Oh take it, oh take it,
For the wrong I have done;
I have left you a daughter
Or else a fine son.

'If it be a daughter
She shall wait upon me,
But if it's a sonny,
He shall cross the blue sea.

'He shall wear a blue jacket
And his cap lined with gold;
He shall cross the blue ocean
Like his young father bold.'

Now all you young lasses
Take a warning from me:
Never trust a young sailor
Whoe'er he may be.

They kiss you, they court you,
They swear they'll be true,
But the very next moment
They'll bid you adieu.

Like the flower in the garden
When its beauty's all done;
So you see what I've come to
Through loving that one.

No father, no mother,
No friend in the world,
So me and my baby
To the workhouse must go.

97. *As I Walked Through the Meadows*

Now the winter is gone and the summer is come,
And the meadows look pleasant and gay;
I met a young damsel, so sweetly sang she,
And her cheeks like the blossoms of may.

I says, 'Fair maiden, how came you here,
In the meadows this morning so soon?'
The maid she replied, 'For to gather some may
For the trees they are all in full bloom.'

I says, 'Fair maiden, shall I go with you
To the meadows to gather some may?'
Oh the maid she replied, 'Oh I must be excused
For i'm afeared you will lead me astray."

Then I took this fair maid by her lily-white hand
On the green mossy banks we sat down
And I placed a kiss on her sweet rosy lips
And the small birds were singing all round.

When we arose from the green mossy banks
To the meadows we wandered away;
I placed my love on a primrosy bank
And I plucked her a handful of may.

98. *I Wish, I Wish*

I wish, I wish, but it's all in vain,
I wish I were a maid again,
A maid again I never will be
Till apple grows on orange tree.

I wish my baby it was born
And smiling on its papa's knee,
And I to be in yon churchyard
With long green grass growing over me.

When my apron strings hung low
He followed me through frost and snow,
But now my apron's to my chin
He passes by and says nothing.

Oh grief, oh grief, I'll tell you why,
That girl has more gold than I,
More gold than I and beauty, fame,
But she will come like me again.

99. *The Broomfield Wager*

A squire, a squire, he lived in the woods,
He courted a lady gay;
A little while and he passed a joke
And a wager he did lay.

A wager, a wager, I'll lay to any man,
A thousand guineas to one
That a maid won't go to the merry green woods
And a maid return again.'

Oh when she came to the merry green woods
She found her love asleep
With a knife in his hand and a sword by his side
And a greyhound at his feet.

Three times she walked all round his head,
Three times all round his feet,
Three times she kissed his red rosy cheeks
As he lay fast asleep.

And when she had done all that she could
She walked softly away,
She hid herself in the merry green woods
To hear what her love did say.

When he waked out from his dream,
He looked up in the skies,
He looked round and round and down on the ground
And he wept most bitterly.

Up he called his serving-man
Whom he loved so dear:
'Why hasn't thou awakened me
When my true love was here?'

'And with my voice I holloaed, Master,
And with my bells I rung:
Awake, awake and awake, master,
Your true love's been and gone.'

'I wish I had my true love here
As free as I got my will
And every bird in the merry green wood
For they should have their fill.'

'Sleep more in the night, Master,
And wake more in the day,
And then you will see when your true love comes
And when she goes away.'

100. *Blow Away the Morning Dew*

'Twas of a shepherd's son,
Keeps sheep all in the hill,
And he went out one May morning
To see what he could kill.

And it's blow away the morning dew,
Blow the wind i-o,
Blow away the morning dew,
How sweet the winds do blow.

He lookèd high, he lookèd low,
He gave an under-look
And then he saw a pretty maid
A-swimming in the brook.

'Oh do not touch my mantle,
Pray leave my clothes alone,
But take me out of the water
And convey me to my home.'

As they were riding along the road
They came to some cocks of hay,
Saying, 'This is a pretty place
For men and maids to play.'

'My father keeps a bantam cock,
He would not tread the hen.
He flutters his wings and crows,
Saying: I think you're one of them.

'Oh take me to my father's house
And you may sit me down,
And you shall have my maidenhead
And fifteen hundred pound.'

When she got to her father's house
She stepped boldly in,
Saying: 'You are a fool without the gate
And I'm a maid within.'

So if you meet any pretty girl
And your father in the town,
Oh never mind her squalling
Or the rumpling of her gown.

101. *Early in the Springtime*

'Twas early in the springtime of the year,
When the sun did begin to shine;
Oh I had three branches, all for to choose but one,
And the first I chose was thyme.

Thyme, thyme, it is a precious thing,
It's a root that the sun shines on;
And time it will bring everything to an end,
And so our time goes on.

And while that I had my thyme all for my own,
It did flourish by night and day,
Till who came along but a jolly sailor lad,
And stole my thyme away.

And now my thyme is perished for me,
And I never shall plant it more,
Since into the place where my thyme did use to spring
Is grown a running rue.

Rue, rue, it is a running root,
And it runs all too fast for me;
I'll dig up the bed where thyme of old was laid
And plant there a brave oak tree.

Stand up, oh stand up, my jolly oak,
Stand you up, for you shall not die!
For I'll be so true to the one I love so dear
As the stars shine bright in the sky.

102. *The Buxom Young Dairy Maid*

I am a young dairy maid, buxom and tight,
In minding my dairy I take great delight,
In making of butter and cheese that is new,
And a young man to play with my how do you do.

> *With my gee ho Dobbin, drive on your waggon,*
> *Drive on your waggon, gee up and gee ho.*

The first was young Johnny, a pretty ploughboy,
He called me his honey delight and his joy,
He kissed me so sweetly, my cheeks gave a pat,
And he's welcome at all times to a share for all that.

The next was a young shepherd, a buxom young lad,
And many's the frolic together we've had,
He used me so kindly, he shoved it in tight,
And he played a sweet tune on his Tabarin pipe.

The waggoners they are all jolly blades,
They know very well how to please the young maids,
They are hearty and willing, good-natured and free,
And these are the boys that shall do it for me.

My mother she told me of men to beware,
Unless they should draw my poor heart in a snare,
But for all her advice I care not a fig,
The young men shall play with my hairy wig.

My snatch is my own, and the ground is the king's,
It is free for a young man that brings a good thing,
Let him be ever so strong and ever so stout,
I'll warrant I'll make him quickly give out.

103(a). *The Buck's Elegy*

As I was walking down Covent Garden,
Listen awhile and the truth I'll declare,
Who should I meet but my dearest comrade,
Wrapped up in flannel, so hard was his fate.

Tabarin pipe] tabor and pipe

Had I but known what his disorder was,
Had I but known it, and took it in time,
I'd took pila cotia, all sorts of white mercury,
But now I'm cut off in the height of my prime.

Doctors, take away your mercury bottles,
For I am going to draw my last breath,
And into my coffin throw handfuls of funeral fine,
Let them all see that I die a sad death.

When I am dead, wrap me up in funeral fine,
Pinks and fine roses adorning my head,
Come all gallows whores that do mourn after me,
Let them all follow me unto my grave.

There is Captain —— and likewise Captain Townsend,
These are the men that shall hold up my pall.
Come draw up your merry men, draw them in rank and file,
Let them fire over me when I lay low.

Come bumble your drums, bumble them with crapes of black,
Beat the dead march as we go along.
Come draw up your merry men, draw them in rank and file,
Let them fire over me when I lay low.

103(b). *The Sailor Cut Down in his Prime*

One day as I strolled down the Royal Albion
Dark was the morning, cold was the day,
Then who should I spy but one of my shipmates
Draped in a blanket far colder than clay.

He called for a candle to light him to bed,
Likewise an old flannel to wrap round his head.
His poor head was aching, his poor heart was breaking,
For he was a young sailor cut down in his prime.

We'll beat the drums loudly, play the pipes merrily,
Play the dead march as we carry him along,
Take him to a churchyard and fire three volleys over him;
There goes a young sailor cut down in his prime.

pila cotia, white mercury] treatments for syphilis

But now he is dead and laid in his coffin,
Six jolly sailor boys march on each side
And each of them carries a bunch of white roses
That no-one might smell him as we passed 'em by.

At the corner of the street there's two girls a-standing,
Each to the other does whistle and sing,
'Here comes a young fellow whose money we squandered,
Here comes a young sailor cut down in his prime.'

'Pon top of his tombstone you'll see these words written,
All you young fellows take a warning by me,
And never go courting these girls of the city
For these girls of the city were the ruin of me.

104. *Died of Love*

There was three worms on yonder hill,
They neither could not hear nor see.
I wish I'd been but one of them
When first I gained my liberty.

Then a brisk young lad came a-courting me,
He stole away my liberty.
He stole it away with a free good will,
He've a-got it now and he'll keep it still.

Oh for once I wore my apron strings low,
My love followed me through frost and snow,
But now they're almost up to my chin
My love passed by and say nothing.

Now there is an alehouse in this town
Where my false love go and sit himself down
And takes strange girls all on his knee
Because they have more gold than me.

So gold will waste and beauty pass
And she will come like me at last.
That mortal man when he served me so
When I was down where the daisies grow.

Now there is a flower I heard them say
Would ease my heart both night and day.
I wish to God that flower I could find
That would ease my heart and my troubled mind.

Then out in the mead the poor girl run
To cull those flowers fast as they sprung.
'Twas some she picked, some she pulled
Till at length she gained her apron full.

On these sweet flowers she made her bed,
A stony pillow for her head.
Then down she lay and never more spoke,
And now her tender heart is broke.

Now she is dead and her corpse is cold,
I met her false lover and him I told.
Come and walk after your heart's delight,
She will walk with you both day and night.

So dig her a grave long, wide and deep
And strow it over with flowers sweet.
Lay on her breast a turtle dove
That folks may see that she died for love.

105(a). *Down by the Riverside*

As I walked one May morning
Down by the river side,
I heard a couple discoursing
Which filled my heart with pride.

'Come sing to me another song
And my bride you shall be.'
'Kind sir,' she said, 'I'm yet too young
Your bride for to be.'

'The younger you are the better for me,
The fitter to be my bride,
And perhaps that I might say some day
I married my wife a maid.'

SEDUCTION AND BETRAYAL

He kissed her and he courted her
Till he gained the will of her,
And soon as he gained the will of her
He stole her maidenhead.

The grass was wet and slippery
And both her feet did slide,
They both fell down together
Down by the river side.

'Since you have had your will of me
Pray tell to me your name,
That when my pretty babe is born
I may call it the same.'

'My name is Captain Thunderbolt,
To you I'll never marry;
I'm wed to a glazier's daughter dear
Down by the river side.'

'This is not what you promised me
Down by the river side.
You promised that you'd marry me,
Make me your lawful bride.'

'If I promised that I'd marry you
'Tis more than I would do.
For I never intend to wed a girl
So easy found as you.'

'It's of the farmer's daughters
To market they may go,
While I poor girl must stop at home
And rock the cradle o'er.

'And rock the cradle o'er and o'er
And sing sweet lullaby.
Was there ever poor girl in all the town
So crossed in love as I?'

105(b). *'Abroad as I was walking'*

Abroad as I was walking,
Down by some green woodside,
I heard some young girl singing
I wish I was a bride.

'I thank you, pretty fair maid,
For singing of your song.
It's I myself shall marry you.'
'Kind sir, I am too young.'

'The younger the better,
More fitter for my bride,
That all the world may plainly see
I married my wife a maid.'

Nine times I kissed her ruby lips,
I viewed her sparkling eye,
I catched her by the lilywhite hand,
One night with her to lie.

All the fore part of that night
How we did sport and play,
And all the latter part of that night
I slept in her arms till day.

Till day, till day, till day,
Till daylight did appear.
The young man rose, put on his clothes,
Said: 'Fare you well, my dear.'

'What did you promise me last night
As I lay by your side;
You promised me you would marry me,
Make me your lawful bride.'

'What I did promise you last night
Was in a merry mood.
I vow, I swear, I do declare,
I'm not so very good.'

'Now my parents have brought me up
Like a small bird in a cage,
And now I am in child by you,
Not fourteen years of age.

'It's all the farmers' daughters
To the market they do go
But it's I, poor girl, must stay at home
And rock the cradle so.

'Rock the cradle, sing and sew,
Sing hushee lullaby.
Was there ever any poor young girl
So crossed in love as I?'

106. *Love it is Pleasing*

When I was young, love, and in full blossom
All young men then came surrounding me.
When I was young, love, and well-behaved,
A false young man came a-courting me.

So love it is pleasing, love it is teasing
And love is a treasure when first it's new,
But as it grows older it still grows colder
And fades away like the morning dew.

I left my father, I left my mother,
I left my brothers and sisters too,
I left my home and my kind relations,
Forsaked them all for the love of you.

So girls beware of your false young lovers,
Never mind what a young man say.
He's like a star on a foggy morning,
You think he's near when he's far away.

I never thought my love would leave me
Until one morning when he came in,
He drew a chair and sat down beside me
And then my troubles oh they did begin.

107. *The Mower*

As I walked out one morning on the fourteenth of July,
I met a maid, she asked my trade, I made her this reply:
'Oh, for my occupation I ramble up and down
With my taring scythe in order to mow the meadows down.'

She says, 'My handsome young man, if a mower that you be,
Come put your scythe in order and come along with me,
For I have a little meadow long time been kept in store,
And on the dew I can tell you true it never was cut before.'

He says, 'My canty dairymaid, what wages will you give?
For mowing is hard labour unless the scythe be good.'
'I'll give you a crown an acre, I solemnly declare,
I'll give you a crown an acre and plenty of strong beer.'

He says, 'My canty dairymaid, I like your wages well,
For my scythe it's in good order and we will have a spell,
For on your bonny countenance I never saw a frown,
My bonny lass, I'll cut your grass that ne'er was trampled down.'

Like a lion, he being undaunted, he entered in her field,
He said he'd mow her meadow down before that he would yield.
He wrought from six till breakfast time till it went beyond his skill,
He was forced to yield and quit the field for the grass was standing
  still.

He says, 'My canty dairymaid, oh do not on me frown,
For although I mow all summer I cannot mow it now.'
Then she put her hand in her pocket and paid us down a crown:
'Oh when you come this way again, inquire for Betsy Brown.

'All in my little meadow there is neither hill nor rock,
Oh when you come this way again the cradle you may rock.'
Come all you pretty fair maids wheresoever you may be,
Oh when you meet a ploughboy, oh treat him kind and free.
He ploughs the furrows deep and rambles up and down,
With his taring scythe in order to mow the meadows down.

canty] merry

108. *Strawberry Fair*

As I was a-going to Strawberry Fair,
 Ri toll ri toll, riddle tol de lido
I saw a fair maiden of beauty rare,
 Tol de dee.
I saw a young maiden go selling her ware
As she went on to Strawberry Fair,
 Ri tol, ri tol riddle tol de lido,
 Ri tol, ri tol, riddle tol de dee.

'O pretty fair maid, I prithee, tell,
My pretty fair maid, what do you sell?
Oh come tell my truly, my sweet damsel,
As you go on to Strawberry Fair.'

'Oh I have a lock that doth lack a key,
Oh I have a lock, sir,' she did say.
'If you have a key then come this way,
As we go on to Strawberry Fair.'

Between us I reckon that when we met
The key to the lock it was well set;
The key to the lock it well did fit,
As we went on to Strawberry Fair.

'Oh would that my lock had been a gun,
I'd shoot the locksmith for I'm undone;
And wares to carry I now have none
That I should go to Strawberry Fair.'

109(a). *The Cuckoo*

The cuckoo is a fine bird,
She sings as she flies;
She brings us good tidings
And tells us no lies.

She sucks those sweet flowers
To make her voice clear
And the more she sings cuckoo
The summer draws near.

So come all you fair maidens
Wherever you be,
Don't fix your minds on
The top of a tree.

For the leaves will soon wither
And the roots will soon die
And if I am forsaken
I know not for why.

109(b). *The Cuckoo*

A-walking and a-talking
And a-walking goes I
For to meet my sweet William,
He will come by and by.

For to meet him it's pleasure
And to part it's grief,
For a false-hearted young man
He's worse than a thief.

For a thief he will rob you
And take all you have,
When a false-hearted young man
Will bring you to the grave.

And the grave it will rot you
And turn you to dust.
There is not one in twenty
That a maiden can trust.

The cuckoo is a small bird,
He sings as he flies;
He bringeth us good tidings
And he tells us no lies.

He sucks the small birds' eggs
To make his voice clear
And then he sings cuckoo
Three months in the year.

So if he's gone, let him go,
Let him sink or let him swim,
For he's madly mistaken
If he thinks that I mourn.

110. *The Brickster*

'Twas of a young brickster a-going from his work,
A beautiful damsel appeared in his sight.
He said, 'My dearest, stay one moment or two
While I tell you what I dreamed of last night.'

Then she made a full stop with a smile on her cheek,
Then she made a full stop, saying 'No,
I'm going down for my cow, oh I cannot stay now,
So I pray you, young man, let me go.'

Then we both sat down together under the green shady tree
Where the green leaves are plain to be seen,
And what we did there I never will declare,
But this beautiful damsel she made out my dream.

And we both rose up together from the green shady tree
And so carelessly tripped over the plain.
Oh she said, 'My Jimmy sweet, oh next time that we do meet,
We will tell these dreams over again.'

111. *Gently Johnny my Jingalo*

I put my hand all on her toe
 Fair maid is a lily O
I put my hand all on her toe
She says to me, 'Do you want to go?'
 Come to me quietly,
 Do not do me injury,
 Gently Johnny my jingalo.

I put my hand all on her knee.
She says to me, 'Do you want to see?'

I put my hand all on her thigh.
She says to me, 'Do you want to try?'

I put my hand all on her billy.
She says to me 'Do you want to fill 'ee?'

I put my hand all on her breast.
She says to me, 'Do you want a kiss?'

I put my hand all on her head.
She says to me, 'Do you want my maidenhead?'

112. *Hares on the Mountain*

'O Sally my dear, shall I come up to see you?'
She laugh and reply, 'I'm afraid you'll undo me.'

    Sing fal the diddle ido
    Sing whack fal the diddle day

'O Sally my dear, why I will not undo you.'
She laugh and reply, 'You may come to bed to me.'

'O Sally my dear, I cannot undo my breeches.'
She laugh and reply, 'Take a knife and rip stitches.'

'O Sally my dear, I cannot undo them.'
She laugh and reply, 'There's a knife in the window.'

Now he took off his breeches and into bed trundled.
I leave you to guess how the gay couple fumbled.

If blackbirds was blackbirds as thrushes is thrushes,
How soon the young men would go beating the bushes.

Should young women be hares and race round the mountain,
Young men'd take guns and they'd soon go a-hunting.

Should young women be ducks and should swim round the ocean,
Young men would turn drakes and soon follow after.

113. *The False Bride*

I heard my love published in church,
I rose from my seat and went out in the porch.
I thought she was constant, as constant could be,
But now she is going to get married.

When I saw my love to the church go,
Bridesmen and bridemaidens they made a fine show.
Then I followed after with my heart full of woe,
For to see how my false love discarded.

When I saw my love in the church stand
With the glove putting off and the ring putting on,
Then I thought to myself that you ought to be mine,
But now she is tied to some other.

When I saw my love sat down to eat,
I sat by her side but nothing could eat.
I thought her sweet company better than mine,
Though now she is gone to some other.

When I saw my love in the bride-bed
With the curtains and valance around her sweet head,
I slipped in between them and kissed her dear lips
And felt I could be with her for ever.

You dig me a grave that is long, wide and deep
And cover it all over with flowers so sweet,
That I may lie down and take my long sleep
And adieu to my false love for ever.

114. *The Leicester Chambermaid*

It's of a brisk young butcher, as I have heard them say,
He started out of London town upon a certain day,
Says he, a frolic I will have, my fortune for to try,
I will go into Leicestershire some cattle for to buy.

When he arrived at Leicester town he went into an inn,
He called for an ostler, and boldly walkèd in;
He called for liquors of the best, he being a roving blade,
And quickly fixed his eyes upon the chambermaid.

The day it being over, the night it being come,
The butcher came to the inn, his buisness being done.
He called for his supper, reckoning being left unpaid,
Says he, 'This night I'll put a trick upon the chambermaid.'

She then took a candle to light him up to bed,
And when they came into the room, these words to her he said,
'One sovereign I will give to you all to enjoy your charms.'
This fair maid did sleep all night within the butcher's arms.

He rose up in the morning and prepared to go away.
The landlord said, 'Your reckoning, sir, you have forgot to pay.'
'Oh no,' the butcher did reply, 'pray do not think it strange,
I gave a sovereign to the maid, but did not get the change.'

He straightway called the chambermaid and charged her with the
     same,
The sovereign she did lay down, fearing to get the blame.
The butcher he went home, well pleased with what was passed,
For soon this pretty chambermaid grew thick about the waist.

'Twas in a twelvemonth after, he came to town again,
And then as he had done before, he stoppèd at the inn.
'Twas then the buxom chambermaid she chanced him to see,
She brought the babe just three months old, and placed it on his
     knee.

The butcher sat like one amazed, and at the child did stare,
But when the joke he did find out, how he did stamp and swear.
She said, 'Kind sir, it is your own, so do not think it strange,
One sovereign you gave to me, and I have brought the change.'

The company they laughed again, the joke went freely round,
And the tidings of the same was spread through Leicester town.
The butcher was to a justice brought, who happened to live near,
One hundred pounds he did lay down, before he could get clear.

So all you brisk and lively blades, I pray be ruled by me,
Look well into your bargains before you money pay,
Or soon, perhaps, your folly will give you cause to range,
For if you sport with pretty maids you are sure to have your change.

115. *In Oxford City*

In Oxford city there's a wealthy fair maid,
The truth to you, love, I'm going to tell.
She was strongly courting a handsome young man,
Who always told to her he loved her well.

He loved her dearly all at a distance,
While walking down by the shady strand;
And he often told her he'd never leave her,
While walking down by the shady strand.

It's to a dance house they were invited,
And to a dance house they both did go,
Till this other young man came between them
And cruel jealousy, love, run in his mind.

While she was dancing with this other young man,
Cruel jealousy, love, did run in his mind;
For to take the life of his own true lover,
This wicked young man had well inclined.

He went outside to prepare the poison
And mixed it with a glass of wine,
And he gave it all to his own true lover;
She drank it up with a willing smile.

It's not long after she had this taken,
'Oh take me home, O my love,' cries she.
'For the glass of wine you have lately gave me,
It makes me feel quite ill indeed.'

As they walked home, as they walked together,
As they went home by the shady strand,
For he says, 'My darling, I gave you poison,
To take your pretty young life away.

'The same myself, love, sure I have taken,
The same myself I give to thee.'
In each other's arms they died together,
So let me beware of cruel jealousy.

116. *The Posy of Thyme*

In Staffordshire I was born,
Near Newcastle-under-Lyme,
But the pretty maidens all laugh me to scorn
For my wearing of the posy of thyme.

It was in the time of the year
When the thyme it grew wild;
It was just at the height of my bloom
When my false love he got me with child.

But now he is gone to the sea,
He has blasted me just in my prime;
I never more shall him see,
So I'll wear the posy of thyme.

For the time will go swiftly along,
And time for no man will stay;
May the time and tide be his guide
And send my true love unto me.

If fortune proves to me severe,
And I should never see him no more,
I'll wear the sweet posy of thyme
For the false man whom I adore.

Young maidens take warning by me,
Lest ye are cropped in the height of your prime,
And are forced to sing lullaby
And like me wear the posy of thyme.

117. 'Saw you my father'

'Saw you my father,
Saw you my mother,
Saw you my true love John;
He told his only dear
That he would soon be here,
But he to another is gone.'

'I saw not your father,
I saw not your mother,
But I saw your true love John;
He has met with some delay
Which has caused him to stay,
But he will be here anon.'

Then John he up arose
And to the door he goes,
And he twirled, he twirled at the pin;
The lassie took the hint,
And to the door she went,
And she let her true love in.

Fly up, fly up,
My bonny grey cock,
And crow when it is day;
Your breast shall be
Of the beaming gold
And your wing of the silver grey.

The cock he proved false
And untrue he was,
For he crowed an hour too soon;
The lassie thought it day,
So she went her love away,
And it proved but the blink of the moon.

118. *Bushes and Briars*

Through bushes and through briars I lately took my way,
All for to hear the small birds sing one evening in May.
Oh I overheard my true love and her voice it was so clear:
'Long time I have been waiting for the coming of my dear.'

I drew myself up to a tree, a tree that did look green,
Where the green leaves shaded over me, I scarcely could be seen;
And as I listened to my love, my love began to mourn,
Crying: 'I'm of the opinion that my heart is not my own.

'Sometimes I am uneasy and a-troubled in my mind,
Sometimes I think I'll go to my love and tell to him my mind;
But if I should go unto my love, what would my love say then?
It would show to him my boldness and he'd ne'er love me again.

'Oh I cannot think the reason why young women love young men,
For they are so false-hearted, young women to trepan;
For they are so false-hearted, young women to trepan,
So the green grave shall ease me if I cannot have that man.'

119. *The Water is Wide*

The water is wide, I cannot get o'er,
And neither have I wings to fly.
Give me a boat that will carry two,
And both shall row, my love and I.

Down in the meadows the other day,
A-gathering flowers both fine and gay,
A-gathering flowers both red and blue
I little thought what love can do.

I leaned my back up against some oak,
Thinking that he was a trusty tree,
But first he bended and then he broke
And so did my false love to me.

I put my hand into the bush,
Thinking the fairest flower to find.
I pricked my finger to the bone,
But oh, I left the rose behind.

A ship there is and she sails the sea,
She's loaded deep as deep can be;
But not so deep as the love I'm in,
I know not if I sink or swim.

Love is handsome and love is kind,
And love's a jewel when she is new.
But when it is old, it groweth old
And fades away like the morning dew.

120. *The New Bury Loom*

As I walked between Bolton and Bury,
It was on a moonshiny night,
I met with a buxom young weaver
Whose company gave me delight.
She says, 'Young fellow, come tell me
If your level and rule are in tune.
Come give me an answer correct
Can you get up and square my new loom?'

I said, 'My dear lassie, believe me,
I am a good joiner by trade,
And many a good loom and shuttle
Before in my time have I made.
Your short lams and jacks and long frame,
I quickly can put them in tune,
My rule is now in good order
To get up and square a new loom.'

She took me and showed me her loom,
The down on her warp did appear,
The lamjacks and healds put in motion,
I levelled her loom to a hair.

My shuttle was well in her lathe,
My tread it worked up and down,
My level stood close to her breastbone,
The time I was reiving her loom.

The chords on my lamjacks and treadles
At length they began to give way.
The bobbin I had in my shuttle,
The weft in it no longer would stay.
Her lathe it went bang to and fro,
My main treadle it still kept in tune,
My pickers went nickety nack,
All the time I was squaring her loom.

My shuttle it still kept in motion,
Her lams she worked well up and down,
The weight in her rods they tremble,
She said she would weave a new gown.
My strength now began for to fail me,
I said, 'It's now right to a hair.'
She turned up her eyes and said, 'Tommy,
My loom you have got pretty square.'

Soldiers and Sailors

121. *The* Golden Vanity

'I have a ship in the north country,
And she goes by the name of the *Golden Vanity*;
I'm afraid she will be taken by some Turkish gallee,
As she sails upon the Low Lands Low.'

Then up starts our little cabin boy,
Saying, 'Master, what will you give me if I do them destroy?'
'I will give you gold, I will give you store,
You shall have my daughter when I return to shore,
If ye sink them in the Low Lands Low.'

The boy he bent his breast and away he swam back again,
He swam till he came to this Turkish gallee
As she laid on the Low Lands Low.

The boy he had an augur to bore holes two at twice;
While some were playing cards, and some were playing dice,
He let the water in, and it dazzled in their eyes,
And he sunk them in the Low Lands Low.

The boy he bent his breast and away he swam back again,
Saying, 'Master, take me up or I shall be slain,
For I have sunk them in the Low Lands Low.'

'I'll not take you up,' the master he cried,
'I'll not take you up,' the master replied,
'I will kill you, I will shoot you, I will send you with the tide,
I will sink you in the Low Lands Low.'

The boy he swam round all by the starboard side;
They laid him on the deck, and it's there he soon died.
Then they sewed him up in an old cow's hide,
And they threw him overboard, to go down with the tide,
And they sunk him in the Low Lands Low.

122. *The Female Sailor*

Good people give attention who now around me stand,
While I unfold a circumstance that does to love belong,
Concerning of a pretty maid who ventured, we are told,
All across the briny ocean as a female sailor bold.

Her name was Ann Jane Thornton, as presently you will hear,
And, as we are informed, she was born in Gloucestershire;
Her father lived in Ireland, respected well, we are told,
But never thought his daughter was a female sailor bold.

She was courted by a captain when scarce sixteen years of age,
And to be bound in wedlock this couple did engage;
But the captain had to leave this land, as I will now unfold,
Then she ventured o'er the ocean like a female sailor bold.

She dressed herself in sailor's clothes and, overcome with joy,
She with a captain did engage to serve as cabin boy;
And when New York in America this fair maid did behold,
She run to seek her lover true, did this female sailor bold.

She to her true love's father, she hastened there with speed,
And inquired for employment but—dreadful news indeed—
Her lover had sometime been dead, this pretty maid was told;
Then in agony and sorrow wept the female sailor bold.

Some thousands of miles she was from home, from parents far away;
She travelled seventy miles through woods in North America,
Bereft of friends and kindred, no parents to behold,
'My true love's gone,' in anguish cried the female sailor bold.

With pitch and tar her hands were hard, though once like velvet soft;
She weighed the anchor, heaved the lead and boldly went aloft;
Just one and thirty months she braved the tempest, we are told,
And always done her duty, did the female sailor bold.

In the month of February, eighteen hundred and thirty-five,
She to the port of London in the *Sarah* did arrive.
Her secret was then discovered and the secret did unfold,
And the captain gazed with wonder on the female sailor bold.

This female was examined of course by the Lord Mayor,
And in all the public papers the reasons did appear;
Why she left her father, her native land she sold,
To cross the briny ocean as a female sailor bold.

It was to seek her lover she sailed across the main;
Through love she did encounter storm, tempest, wind and rain.
It was love caused all her troubles and hardships, we are told:
May she rest at home contented now, the female sailor bold.

123. *Early, Early in the Spring*

Oh very early all in the spring
I went on board for to serve the king,
Leaving my dearest dear behind,
She oft-times told me her heart was mine.

Oh then I hugged her all in my arms,
I thought I got ten thousand charms,
For promise vows and kisses sweet
Promised to marry next time we meet.

Oh when I was sailing all on the raging seas
Taking of all opportunities,
Sending of letters to my dearest dear,
But one from her could not I hear.

Oh then I returned back to old England,
I went unto her father's house.
Her father axed me oh what I mean.
'My daughter married long time has been.'

So cursed be all gold and silver too
And all false women that don't prove true.
I'd sooner be where the bullets fly
Than be in a false woman's company.

124. 'Our captain cried all hands'

Our captain cried all hands
To sail tomorrow,
Leaves many a fair pretty maid
In grief and sorrow.
So dry those mountain tears
And leave off weeping.
How happy we shall be
At our next meeting.

How can you go away
Fighting for strangers?
You'd better stay at home
Free from all dangers.
I would roll you in my arms,
My dearest jewel,
So stay at home with me
And don't be cruel.

When I had gold in store
You did write me,
But now I'm low and poor
You seem to slight me.
You courted me awhile
Just to deceive me;
Now my poor heart you have won
You're going to leave me.

She fell upon the ground
Like one that was dying.
This house is full of grief,
Sighing and crying
There is no belief in man,
Not your own brother,
So girls if you must love,
Love one another.

Farewell, my dearest friends,
Father and mother,
I am your only child,
I have no brother.

It's in vain to weep for me
For I am going
Into everlasting joys
Where fountains are flowing.

125. *Adieu my Lovely Nancy*

Adieu, my lovely Nancy, ten thousand times adieu,
I'm going to cross the ocean to seek for something new.
Come change your ring with me, love, come change your ring with
    me;
It shall be a token of true love when I am on the sea.

When I am on the sea, dear love, you know not where I am,
Love letters I will write to you from every foreign land
With secrets of my heart, my dear, and the best of my goodwill.
Oh let my body be where it will, my heart is with you still.

Now see the storm arising, see how it's gathering round
While we poor jolly sailors are fighting for the crown.
Our officers commanded us and them we must obey,
Expecting every moment for to get cast away.

So now the storm is over and we are safe on shore
We'll drink to our wives and sweethearts and girls that we adore.
We'll call for liquor merrily and spend our money free
And when our money is all gone we'll boldly go to sea.

126. *Our Ship She Lies in Harbour*

Said the father to the daughter,
'What makes you so lament?
Isn't there men enough in this country
That can give your heart content?'

'There's men enough in this country
But there's never one for me.
You have pressed the only lad I love
And did me satisfy.'

Seven long years was gone and past,
Twelve long weary days,
When she saw a ship come dashing along the deep
And in it was her own.

He said, 'Yonder sits my angel
A-watching there for me.
Tomorrow to the church we'll go
And married we will be.'

As she went to get married
And a-turning home again,
She met her aged father
And seven armèd men.

'Here's fifty guineas in bright gold,
Dear girl, I'll give to thee,
If you'll forsake the lad you love
And come home with me.'

'But it's not your gold that glitters
And your silver does not shine.
I'm married to the lad I love
And I'm happy in my mind.'

127. *The Shepherdess and the Sailor*

It's of a little shepherdess who was keeping of her sheep
On the rocks that are near the seaside,
The weather being warm so she lay down to sleep
And by chance a young sailor came that way.

He kissed her sweet lips as she lay fast asleep,
Saying, 'O dear, you stole my heart away.'
Then she waked in surprise and she opened her eyes
And she saw the young sailor standing by.

'Young sailor,' then said she, 'how came you here by me?'
And with that she begins for to cry.
'I'm just come on shore from the ship that you see,
On these rocks I am landed alone.
So I hope, my dearest dear, I shall find some comfort here.
Or else I'm for ever undone.'

'Young sailor,' then said she, 'how can you fancy me?
I never can give consent.
For when you're on the seas I could never be at ease
But you leave me to sigh and lament.'

'Young shepherdess,' said he, 'if you can fancy me,
I have plenty of money in store,
And the sea I will forsake and promise to you I'll make,
I'll be true unto you evermore.'

Then she gave him her consent and to church they quickly went
And were married the very same day.
With joy, love and peace each to their hearts they did increase,
The young sailor his shepherdess adored.

Come all you jolly shepherdesses who are keeping of your sheep
On the rocks that are near the seaside,
Take a sailor for your life and he'll make you his wife
And the sailor your fortune he will make.

128. *Just as the Tide was A-Flowing*

One morning in the month of May,
Down by the rolling river,
A jolly sailor he did stray,
There he beheld some lover.
She scarcely along did stray
A-viewing of those daisies gay,
She sweetly sang a roundelay
Just as the tide was a-flowing.

And her dress it was as white as milk
And jewels did around her;
Her shoes were of the crimson silk
Just like some lady.
Her cheeks were red, her eyes were brown,
Her hair in ringlets hanging down;
Her lovely brow without a frown
Just as the tide was a-flowing.

I made a bow and said, 'Fair maid,
How come you here so early?
My heart by you it is betrayed
And I could love you dearly.
I am a sailor come from sea,
If you'll accept my company
For to walk and to view the fishes play
Just as the tide was a-flowing.'

No more was said, but on our way
We both did gang together.
The small birds sung and the lambs did play
And pleasant was the weather.
Oh we was weary, both sat down
Beneath a tree with branches round.
And what was done shall never be known
Just as the tide was a-flowing.

And as she laid all on the grass
Her colour it kept changing.
'Alas,' cried out my lovely lass,
'Never let your mind be changing.'
She gives me twenty pounds in store,
Saying, 'Meet me when you will, there's more,
For my jolly sailor I adore
Just as the tide was a-flowing.'

We both shook hands and off did steer.
Jack Tar loves rum and brandy
To keep his shipmates in full cheer,
For the lady's gold was handy.
With some other girls he then will go
To some public house where brandy flow.
Success to the girl that will do so
Just as the tide was a-flowing.

129. *Pleasant and Delightful*

It was pleasant and delightful on one midsummer's morn,
When the green fields and meadows they were covered in corn,
And the blackbirds and thrushes sang in every green tree,
And the larks they sang melodious at the dawning of the day.

As the sailor and his true love they walked out one day,
Said the sailor to his true love, 'I am bound far away,
I am bound for the East Indies where the loud cannon roar,
And I'm going to leave my Nancy, she's the girl that I adore.'

Three heavy sighs she gave and said, 'Jimmy my dear,
And are you a-going to leave me in despair?
And are you a-going to leave me in such pain,
Till you from the Indies return home again?'

Now a ring from her finger she instantly drew,
Saying, 'Take this, sweet Jimmy, and my heart will go too.'
And while he was embracing her, tears from her eyes fell,
Saying, 'May I go along with you?' 'Oh no, my love, farewell.'

Said the sailor to his true love, 'I can no longer stay,
For our tops'ls they are hoisted and her anchor is weighed.
Our big ship lies waiting for the next flowing tide,
And if ever I return again I will make you my bride.'

130. *William Taylor*

I'll sing you a song about two true lovers,
And from Lichfield town they came.
And this young man's name was William Taylor,
And this young woman's name was Sarah Jane.

William Taylor's a nice young sailor,
He went courting a lady fair,
And just as he was going to be married,
He was pressed and sent away.

She dressed herself in man's apparel,
Went to fight among the rest.
The winds did blow her jacket open,
There they saw her lily-white breast.

Then the captain stepped up to her,
Asking her what she did there.
'Oh I am come to seek my true love
Whom I lately loved so dear.'

'If you are come to seek your true love,
Pray tell me what his name may be.'
She cried, 'His name is William Taylor,
Who from the Irish ranks did come.'

'You've come to seek your own true lover
And he hath proved to you severe,
For he is married to a rich young lady,
He was married the other year.'

She rose early the very next morning,
She rose by the break of day.
There she saw her true love Billy
Walking with his lady gay.

And then she called for a brace of pistols,
A brace of pistols she did command.
So she bide and shoot her William Taylor
With his bride at his right hand.

Now this captain was well pleased,
Was well pleased with what she'd done.
So she soon came a beau-commander
On shipboard with all his men.

Then the captain was well pleased,
Was well pleased with all that passed.
It was only three weeks after
Sarah became the captain's wife.

131. *The Saucy Sailor*

'Come my own one, come my fond one,
Come my dearest unto me.
Will you wed with a jolly sailor lad
That's just returned from sea?'

'You are ragged, love, you are dirty, love,
And you smell so much of the tar.
So begone, you saucy sailor boy,
So begone, you Jack Tar.'

'If I'm ragged, love, if I'm dirty, love,
If I smell so much of the tar,
I got silver in my pocket, love,
And gold in bright store.'

So when she heard these words come from him,
On her bended knees she fell.
'To be sure I shall wed with Henry,
For I love a sailor well.'

'Do you think that I am foolish, love,
Do you think that I am mad;
For to wed with a poor country girl
Where no fortune is to be had?

'I'll cross the briny ocean
Where the meadows they grow green.
Since you refuse the offer,
Some other girl shall wear the ring.

'For I'm young, love, and I'm frolicsome,
Good-tempered, kind and free,
And I don't care a single straw, my love,
What the world says of me.'

132. *Sweet William*

A sailor's life is a merry life,
They'll rob young girls of their hearts' delight.
They'll go and leave them to sigh and moan,
No tongue can tell when they will return.

'Four and twenty sailors all in one row,
And my sweet William is the finest of all.
He's proper, tall and gentle withal,
And if I don't have him I'll have none at all.'

She had not sailed far upon the deep
Before a Queen's ship she chanced to meet.
'O all you jolly sailors, come tell me true,
Is my sweet William on board with you?'

'Oh no, fair lady, he is not here,
He is a-drownded, greatly is my fear.
On the islands high when the wind blew high
There we lost sight of your sailor boy.'

She sailed home and wrote a song,
She wrote it wide and she wrote it long.
And at every line, oh she shed a tear,
And at the end, 'I shall lose my dear.

'O father, father, come dig my grave,
Dig it wide, both long and deep,
And on my tombstone put two turtle doves
So the world might see that I died for love.'

She wrung her hands and tore her hair
Just like a lady in deep despair.
She flung her body down in the deep,
In her true love's arms she fell fast asleep.

133. *The* Flying Cloud

My name is Edward Hollander as you may understand,
I was born in the city of Waterford in Erin's lovely land.
When I was young an' in my prime an' beauty on me shone,
Me parents doted on me, 'cos I was their only son.

My father he rose up one morn an' with him I did go,
He bound me as a butcher boy to Kearney's of Wicklow;
I wore the bloody apron there for three long years or more,
Then I shipped aboard the *Erin's Queen*, the pride of old Tramore.

'Twas when we reached Bermuda's isle I met with Captain Moore,
The master of the *Flying Cloud*, the pride of Baltimore;
An' I undertook to sail with him on a slavin' voyage to go,
To the burnin' shores o' Africay, where the sugar-cane do grow.

Oh all went well until we came to Africay's sunny shore,
Five hundred o' them slaves, me boys, from their native lands we
    bore;
Oh each man loaded down with chains as we made 'em march below,
Just eighteen inches space, me boy, oh each man had to show.

The plague it came an' fever too, an' took 'em off like flies,
We had the niggers up on deck and hove 'em in the tide;
'Twas better for the rest o' them if they had died before,
Than to drag the chain an' feel the lash in Cuba for evermore.

An' now our money is all gone we must go to sea for more,
So each man stayed an' listened to the words o' Captain Moore:
'There's gold an' silver to be had, if with me you remain,
Let's hoist the pirate flag aloft an' sweep the Spanish Main.'

We sank an' plundered many a ship down on the Spanish Main,
Left many wife an' orphan child in sorrow to remain;
To them we gave no quarter but we gave them watery graves,
For a sayin' of our Captain was that dead men tell no tales.

Pursued were we by many a ship, by frigates and liners too,
Until a British man-o'-war, the *Dungemore*, hove in view;
A shot then killed our Captain Moore an' twenty of our men,
An' a bombshell set our ship on fire, we had to surrender then.

An' now to Newgate we must go bound down with iron chains,
For the sinkin' an' the plunderin' of ships on the Spanish Main;
The judge he found us guilty, an' we are condemned to die.
Young man, a warning by me take an' shun all piracy.

134. *The Indian Lass*

As I was a-walking on yon far distant shore,
I went into an alehouse for to spend an hour,
And as I sat smoking and taking my glass,
By chance there came by a young Indian lass.

This lovely sweet Indian and the place where she stood,
I viewed her sweet features and found they were good,
She was both tall and handsome, her age was sixteen,
She was born and brought up in the place New Orleans.

She sat down beside me and squeezed my hand,
'Kind sir, you're a stranger, not one of this land;
I have got fine lodgings if you with me will stay,
My portion you shall have without more delay.'

With a glass of good liquor she welcomed me in:
'Kind sir, you are welcome to have anything.'
And as I embraced her, this was her tune:
'Oh you're a poor sailor and far from home.'

There we tossed and we tumbled in each other's arms,
All night I stayed admiring her beautiful charms,
With sweetest enjoyments this time passed away,
And I did not leave her till nine the next day.

The day was appointed I was going away,
And on the wide ocean to leave her astray.
She said, 'When you are in your native land,
Remember the Indian who squeezed your hand.'

The day was appointed and I was going to sail,
This Indian lass on the beach did bewail.
I took out my handkerchief and wiped her eyes,
'Oh do not leave me, dear sailor,' she cried.

We weighed our anchor and away then we flew,
And a sweet pleasant breeze parted me from her view.
So now I am over and taking my glass,
Here's a health, a good health, to that Indian lass.

135. *The Greenland Whale Fishery*

We may no longer stay on shore
Since we are deep in debt,
So off to Greenland let us steer
Some money, boys, to get, brave boys,
So to Greenland bear away.

In eighteen hundred and twenty-four
On March the twenty-third,
We hoist our colours to the mast head
And for Greenland bore away, brave boys,
And for Greenland bore away.

John Paigent was our captain's name,
Our ship the *Lion* bold.
We weighed anchor at the bow
To face the storm and cold, brave boys,
And to Greenland bore away.

We were twelve gallant men on board
And to the north did steer.
Old England left we in our wake,
We sailors know not fear, brave boys,
And to Greenland bore away.

Our boatswain to the mast head went
With a spyglass in his hand.
He cries, 'A whale! a whale-fish blows,
She blows at every span, brave boys,'
And to Greenland bore away.

Our captain on the quarterdeck,
A violent man was he,
He swore the devil should take us all
If that fish were lost to we, brave boys,
And to Greenland bear away.

Our captain on the quarterdeck,
A violent man was he,
'O'erhaul, o'erhaul!' he loudly cried,
'And launch our boats to sea, brave boys,
And to Greenland bear away.'

Our boat being launched and all hands in ,
The whale was full in view.
Resolved was every seaman bold
To steer where the whale-fish blew, brave boys,
And to Greenland bear away.

The whale was struck, the line paid out,
She gave a flash with the tail.
The boat capsized, we lost five men
And never caught the whale, brave boys,
And to Greenland bear away.

Bad news we to the captain brought,
We'd lost five 'prentice boys.
Then down his colours he did haul
At hearing this sad news, brave boys,
And from Greenland bore away.

'The losing of the whale,' said he,
'Doth grieve my heart full sore.
But the losing of my five brave men
Doth grieve me ten times more, brave boys,'
And from Greenland bore away.

The winter star doth now appear,
So, boys, the anchor weigh.
'Tis time to leave the cold country
And for England bear away, brave boys,
And from Greenland bear away.

For Greenland is a barren place,
A land where grows no green,
But ice and snow where the whale-fish blow
And the daylight's seldom seen, brave boys,
So for England bear away.

136. *A British Man-of-War*

As I walked down yon meadow, I carelessly did stray,
There I beheld a lady fair with some young sailor gay.
He said, 'My lovely Susan, I soon must leave the shore
For to fight for England's glory in a British man-of-war.

'O Susan, lovely Susan, the truth to you I tell,
The British flag is insulted, old England knows it well.
It may be crowned with laurels, then like a jolly tar
I will face the wars in China in a British man-of-war.'

'O sailor, do not venture to face the proud Chinese
For they will prove as treacherous as any Portuguese,
And by some deadly dagger you may get a scar;
Then turn your inclination from a British man-of-war.'

'O Susan, lovely Susan, the time away will pass,
So come down to the Ferry House and take a parting glass.
My shipmates they are waiting to take me from the shore
For to cross the briny ocean in a British man-of-war.'

The sailor took his handkerchief and tore it fair in two,
Saying, 'Susan, keep one part for me and I'll do the same for you.'
The bullets they surrounded us and cannons loudly roared
And young Susan blessed her sailor on a British man-of-war.

Then a few more words together and her love let go her hand.
The noble crew did launch the boat so merrily from the land.
The sailor waved his handkerchief when he got far from shore
And young Susan loved her sailor on a British man-of-war.

137. *Blooming Sally*

I'm a young lad, Jack Rollins by name,
The briny ocean I rove;
My pursuit is with courage, for glory and fame,
King George and my country I love.

My trousers milk white, my shoes jetty black,
And buckles so clean and so smart,
A natty blue jacket set tight on my back,
Was always the pride of my heart.

When called to, I cheerfully go,
And see every order obeyed;
Though the billows run mountains, or hurricanes blow,
Bold Jack's not daunted or afraid.

And if that by chance we meet with our foes
And to fight them our order does run,
With cutlass and pistol to my station I'll go,
Stick firm to my duty and guns.

A good ten knots an hour I like for a grace
In pursuing an enemy ship,
While they send it away, we're giving them chase,
And boring our grog and our flip.

Thus o'er the rough billows, where driven along
On many strange coasts as I go,
The girls of each port, they give me a smile,
Their meanings I know very well.

Then find them a gig when lovers I call,
And left at my ease on return,
I laugh and joke, and talk with them,
But Sally's my only concern.

At —— this little rogue dwells,
Well known by her nice winning air,
That all other girls of the place she excels,
She is pretty Sally the fair.

We have both made a vow, should we get the stuff,
To marry, and so become one,
As others have done, for 'tis common enough,
And we'll set up a house of our own.

Then she'll be called Madam, and I'll be called Sir,
We'll stick up the sign of the Tar;
Amongst girls and their sailors, we'll bustle and stir,
While Sally shall attend to the bar.

138. *Jack Robinson*

The perils and the dangers of the voyage being past,
And the ship at Portsmouth arrived at last,
The sails all furled, and the anchor cast,
The happiest of the crew was Jack Robinson.
For his Poll he had trinkets and gold galore,
Besides prize money quite a store,
And along with the crew he went ashore,
As coxswain to the boat, Jack Robinson.

He met with a man and said, 'I say,
Perhaps you know one Polly Gray?
She lives somewhere hereabout;' the man said, 'Nay,
I do not, indeed,' to Jack Robinson.

So says Jack to him, 'I have left my ship,
And all my messmates, they gave me the slip,
Mayhap you'll partake of a good can of flip?
For you're a good sort of fellow,' says Jack Robinson.

In a public house then they both sat down,
And talked of admirals of high renown,
And drank as much grog as came to half a crown,
This here strange man, and Jack Robinson.
Then Jack called out the reckoning to pay,
The landlady came in, in fine array.
'My eyes and limbs, why here's Polly Gray!
Who'd have thought of meeting here?' says Jack Robinson.

The landlady staggered against the wall,
And said, at first, she didn't know him at all.
'Shiver me,' says Jack, 'why here's a pretty squall,
Damn me, don't you know me? I'm Jack Robinson!
Don't you remember this handkerchief you giv'd me?
'Twas three years ago, before I went to sea,
Every day I've looked at it, and then I thought of thee,
Upon my soul, I have,' says Jack Robinson.

Says the lady, says she, 'I have changed my state.'
'Why, you don't mean,' says Jack, 'that you've got a mate?
You know you promised—' Says she, 'I could not wait,
For no tidings could I gain of you, Jack Robinson;
And somebody, some day, come up to me and said
That somebody else, had somewhere read
In some newspaper, as how you were dead.'
'I've not been dead at all,' says Jack Robinson.

Then he turned his quid, and finished his glass,
Hitched up his trousers, 'Alas, alas,
That ever I should live to be made such an ass!
To be bilked by a woman!' says Jack Robinson.
'But to fret and to stew about it's all in vain,
I'll get a ship and go to Holland, France and Spain,
No matter where, to Portsmouth I'll never come again.'
And he was off before you could say Jack Robinson.

139. *Rude Boreas*

Come rude Boreas, blustering railer, list ye landsmen all to me,
Shipmates hear a brother sailor sing of the dangers of the sea.
From bounding billows, first in motion, when the distant
    whirlwinds rise,
To the tempest-troubled ocean, when the skies contend with skies.

Hark the bosun's hoarsely bawlin', by tops'l sheets an' halyards
    stand,
Down t'gans'ls quick be haulin', down yer stays'ls, hard, boys, hard!
See it freshens, set taut the braces, tops'ls sheets now let her go,
Luff, boys, luff, don't make wry faces, up yer tops'ls nimbly clew.

Now all ye on down beds a-sportin', fondly locked in Beauty's arms,
Fresh enjoyments, wanton courtin', safe from all but love's alarms;
Round us roars the angry tempest, see what fears our minds enthral,
Harder yet, it blows still harder, hark again the bosun's call.

The tops'l yard points to the wind, boys, see all clear to reef each
    course,
Let the foresheet go, don't mind, boys, though the weather should
    get worse;
For 'n' aft the sprits'l yard get, reef the mizen, see all clear,
Hands up each preventer-brace get, man the foreyard, cheer,
    boys, cheer!

All the while fierce thunder's roarin', peel on peel contendin'
    flash;
On our heads fierce rainfall pourin', in our eyes blue lightning
    flash;
All around is one wide water, all above us one black sky,
Different deaths at once surround us, hark! what means that dreadful
    cry?

The foremast's gone! cried every tongue out, o'er the lee twelve foot
    above deck,
A leak there is beneath the chesstrees sprung, pipe all hands to clear
    the wreck.
Come cut the lanyards all to pieces, come, me hearts, be stout an'
    bold,
Plumb the well, the leak increases, four foot water in the hold.

O'er the ship the wild waves beatin', we for wives and children moan,
Alas from here there's no retreatin', alas, to them there's no return;
Still the leak is gainin' on us, both chain-pumps are jammed below,
Heaven have mercy here upon us, for only that can save us now.

On the lee beam there is land, boys, let the guns overboard be
    thrown,
To the pump come every hand, boys, see our mizen mast is gone;
The leak we've found it can't pour faster, we've lightened her a foot
    or more,
Up an' rig a jury foremast, she's right, she's right, boys, we're off
    shore.

Now once more on shore we're thinkin', since kind heaven has saved
    our lives,
Come the cup now let's be drinkin' to our sweethearts an' our wives;
Fill it up, about ship wheel it, close to our lips a-brimmin' fine,
Where the tempest now, who feels it? None! the danger's drowned
    in wine!

140. *The Manchester Ship Canal*

Oh the SS *Irwell* left this port the stormy sea to cross,
They heaved the lead and went ahead on a voyage to Barton Moss.
No fairer ship e'er left the slip from this port to Natal,
Than the boats that plough the waters of the Manchester Canal.

The third day out or thereabout a great storm swept the main,
The captain called his officer, I just forget his name.
'You see that light there on the right?' 'Aye aye,' he did exclaim,
'Well, it's the Wilson Brewery lightship at the end of Ancoats Lane.'

The captain's brow was darkened for he saw a storm was brewing,
And the engineer reported that the horse it wanted shoeing.
'Is there a chart aboard this barque?' he asked of one or two,
The captain he was ashy pale and so were all the crew.

'By gum, we've lost our reckoning, whatever shall we do?
We must be near to Bailey Bridge on the banks of Pinmill Brew.'
Then all became confusion as the stormy winds did roar,
And the captain wished himself and crew were safe again on shore.

'Let go the anchor, boy,' he cried, 'for I am sorely puzzled,
The mate is drunk and in his bunk, see that the cook is muzzled.
We're short of grub in this 'ere tub and we are far from land,
There's not an oat on this 'ere boat and the engine's broken down.'

'Close reefs the sails,' the bosun cried, 'we're in a great dilemma,
Just row her to Pomona Bay, she cannot stand the weather.
She's sprung a leak, now all is lost, let each man do his best,
For soon she'll be a total wreck on the shoals of Throstle's Nest.'

But soon the storm abated, it was rather over-rated.
When captain, crew and officers were quickly congregated,
They searched the chart in every part to find their situation,
They were east-north-east of Bailey Bridge, just south of Salford
    Station.

141. *The Sound of the Drum*

In merry month of May,
When bees from flower to flower did hum,
Soldiers through the town marched gay,
And the villagers ran to the sound of the drum.

The cobbler he's thrown down his awl,
With last and apron he has done,
Left wax and thread for powder ball,
He's left it all to follow the drum.

The tailor he got off his board,
And said he'd wallop his foes, Good Lord,
When he's left his bodkin for a sword,
And gone with the rest to follow the drum.

Robin swore he'd leave the plough,
His team and furrow just begun,
With country life he'd had enow,
He'd leave it all and follow the drum.

Three old dames, the one was lame.
Another blind, a third nigh dumb,
They said it was a burning shame
That they couldn't go and follow the drum.

In the merry month of May,
When bees from flower to flower did hum,
Soldiers through the town marched gay,
And the villagers ran to the sound of the drum.

142. *Bonnets So Blue*

Down in green valleys a town in Yorkshire,
I lived at my ease and was free from all care.
I lived at my ease and I got a sweetheart now,
He's my bonny Scotch laddie and his bonnet so blue.

A regiment of soldiers, oh you soon shall hear,
From England to Ireland they did both steer.
There is one lad among them and I do love so true,
For very well he becomes his bonnet so blue.

'Twas early one morning she rose from her bed,
She called to her Sally, her young waiting-maid,
'Dress me as neat as your two hands can do,
For I am going to see the lad that wears the bonnet so blue.'

And when she came there they stood all on parade.
She stood with great pleasure to hear what was said.
His name was John Stuart and I know him true,
For dearly do I love his bonnet so blue.

My love he passed by me with a gun all in his hand,
And then I strove to speak to him, but still 'twas all in vain.
But then I strove to speak with him, from me he did flew
And my heart went along with his bonnet so blue.

She said, 'My dearest soldier, I will buy your discharge
And free you from the army and set you at large.
If thou couldst but love me my heart will go true,
For dearly do I love thy sweet bonnet so blue.'

He said, 'My honoured lady, if you'll buy my discharge
And free me from the army and set me at large,
And if I only love thee thy heart will prove true;
And what will my poor little Scotch lassie do?

'For I have a sweetheart in my own country,
I never will despise her for all her poverty,
For she is the truest maid and always did prove true
And never put a stain on my bonnet so blue.'

I'll send to old England, to Ireland also,
I'll have my love's likeness drawed out in full
And in my bedchamber oftentimes will view,
For dearly do I love his sweet bonnet so blue.

143. *The Trooper's Horse*

There was an old woman lived under the hill
 And it's green, oh green the leaves do grow
And she had good beer and ale for to sell
 And it's ha young man, why do you tell me so?

The woman's daughter and her name it was Nelly
And she took sick with a fever in her belly.

It was a bold trooper rode up to the inn,
He's perishing cold and wet to the skin.

He drank up his beer and called for another.
He kissed pretty Nelly, likewise her old mother.

The night coming on, the day being spent,
They both went to bed with the mother's consent.

The old woman put them in bed together
To see if the one couldn't cure the other.

'Oh what's this here so stiff and warm?'
'It's my fine nag and his name is Bald.'

'Oh what's this here hanging under his chin?'
'It's only his head, he'll do you no harm.

'But what's this here?' 'It's only my well
Where your fine nag can drink his fill.'

'But what if my nag should chance to fall in?'
'He must catch on the grass that grows round the brim.'

'But what if the grass should prove to be rotten?'
'He must bob up and down until he hits bottom.

'How can you tell when your nag's had his fill?'
'He'll hang down his head, turn away from the well.'

'How can you tell when your nag wants some more?'
'He'll raise up his head and come knock at the door.'

144. *The Royal Light Dragoon*

Come all you saucy landladies, what makes you look so gay?
Oh I do well assure you, the Light Horse comes in today,
Well mounted on their short-tail nags comes prancing into town
And the very first thing that they will do, they'll put your hayricks
    down.

The landlord gives them diet, the best he can afford,
Oh for to keep the Light Horse quiet and from drawing of the sword.
In bed they lies like gentlemen with arms all round the room
And 'tis death to those that do oppose the Royal Light Dragoon.

They gets up of a summer morn and goes to exercise
Whiles the pretty girls stand all round the boys with tears all in their
    eyes.
We get up of a summer's morn and do our work by noon
And spend a summer evening with the saucy Light Dragoon.

Now if we should kiss those pretty girls, and that perhaps we may,
They'll speak unto our officers, and they will send us away
Into some foreign country, where riots soon will be,
And 'tis death to those who do oppose the Royal Light Dragoon.

Now if we should marry those pretty girls and make them our lawful
    brides
They'd tire us of our comfort and weary us of our lives,
For we must rock the cradle, boys, from stable time till noon,
And 'tis death to those who do oppose the Royal Light Dragoon.

So now the rout has come, my boys, and now we must away
Into a place called Holland our orders to obey.
Here's a good success to the pretty girls and I wish them well for me.
They do like to spend a time in a soldier's company.

145. *A Bold Dragoon*

In the dragoon's ride from out the north
He came up to a lady,
And then she knew him by his horse
And she loved him very dearly.
    Oh dearly, oh dearly.

She took the horse by the bridle rein
To lead him to the stable.
She said, 'There's hay and corn for the horse
So let him eat whilst able.
    Oh able, oh able.'

She said, 'There's cake and wine for you,
There's corn and hay for horses,
There's bread and ale for the king's soldier,
Aye and there's pretty lasses.
    Oh lasses, oh lasses.'

She stepped upstairs, she made the bed,
She made it plump and easy,
And into bed she nimble jumped
And said 'Dragoon, I'm ready.
    Oh ready, oh ready.'

Oh he pulled off his armour bright,
He cast it on the table,
And into bed he nimbly jumps
To kiss whilst he was able.
    Oh able, oh able.

They spent the night till break of dawn,
They saw the full light grieving.
'O hark! I hear the trumpet sound.
Sweet maid, I must be leaving.
    Oh leaving, oh leaving.'

rout] muster

'I would the trumpet ne'er might call,
Oh cruel does it grieve me.
My heart, my very heart will break
Because, dragoon, you leave me.
  Oh leave me, oh leave me.

'Oh when shall we, love, meet again?
Oh when shall we be married?'
'When cockle shells turn silver bells,
Then you and I shall be married.
  Married, oh married.'

'Oh what have I for Saturday night
And what have I for Sunday,
And what have I for all the week,
And what have I for Monday?
  Monday, oh Monday.'

'Here's half a crown for Saturday night,
Sheep's head and lung for Sunday.
Here's bread and cheese for all the week,
And devil a cat for Monday.
  Oh Monday, oh Monday.'

146. *The Bold Dragoon*

'My father is a knight and a man of high renown.
If I should marry a soldier 'twould pull his honour down
For your birth and my birth it never 'twon't agree,
So take it as an answer, bold dragoon,' said she.

'Your answer, your answer I do not mean to take.
I'd rather lay my life down all for your sweet sake.'
And the hearing of these words made the lady's heart to bleed.
Oh and then she consented, and married was with speed.

After they had been married and returning home again
She saw her honoured father and seven armèd men.
'Oh now,' says the lady, 'we both shall be slain,
For yonder comes my father with seven armèd men.'

'There is no time to talk, love, there is no time to prattle.
If you will hold my horse, love, then I will fight the battle.'
He pulled out his sword and pistol, he made their bones to rattle,
While the lady held the horse and the dragoon fought the battle.

'Hold your hand, bold dragoon, hold your hand,' said he,
'And you shall have my daughter and ten thousand pounds in fee.'
'Fight on,' said the lady, 'your portion 'tis too small.
Hold your hand, dear dragoon, and you shall have it all.'

All you honourable ladies that have got gold in store,
You should never despise a soldier because he's sometimes poor,
And all you lads of honour a-lying on the ground
So send it to Victoria that wears the British crown.

147. *High Germany*

'O Polly, my dear Polly, the war has now begun
And I must march away by the beating of the drum.
Go dress yourself in your best and come along with me,
I'll take you to the war, my love, in the Isle of Germany.'

'O Billy, my dear Billy, listen to what I say.
My feet they are so very sore I cannot march away.
Besides, my dearest Billy, I am with child by thee;
I'm not fitting for the war, my love, in the Isle of Germany.'

'I'll buy you a horse, my love, my Polly, you shall ride
And all my delight shall be a-walking by your side.
We'll call to every ale-house that ever we pass by,
We'll sweetheart on the road, my love, get married by and by.'

Cruel, cruel was the war when first the rout began
And out of old England went many a smart young man.
They pressed my love away from me, likewise my brothers three,
They sent them to the war, my love, in the Isle of Germany.

The drum that my love's beating is covered in green,
The pretty lambs are sporting, 'tis pleasure to be seen.
And when my pretty babe is born, sits smiling on my knee,
I'll think upon my own true love in the Isle of Germany.

148. *Why, Soldiers, Why?*

How stands the glass around?
For shame, ye take no care, my boys!
How stands the glass around?
Let mirth and wine abound.
The trumpets sound,
The colours they are flying, boys,
To fight, kill or wound.
May we still be found
Content with our hard fare, my boys,
On the cold, cold ground.

Why, soldiers, why
Should we melancholy be, boys,
Whose business 'tis to die!
What, sighing? Fie!
Damn fear, drink on, be jolly boys,
'Tis he, you or I,
Cold, hot, wet or dry,
We're always bound to follow, boys,
And scorn to fly.

'Tis but in vain
(I mean not to upbraid you, boys),
'Tis but in vain
For soldiers to complain.
Should next campaign
Send us to Him who made us, boys,
We're free from pain.
But should we remain,
A bottle and kind landlady
Cures all again.

149. *Arthur McBride*

I once knew a fellow named Arthur McBride,
And he and I rambled down by the seaside,
A-looking for pleasure or what might betide,
And the weather was pleasant and charming.

So gaily and gallant we went on our tramp,
And we met Sergeant Harper and Corporal Cramp,
And the little wee fellow who roused up the camp
With his row-de-dow-dow in the morning.

'Good morning, young fellow,' the sergeant he cried.
'And the same to you, sergeant,' was all our reply.
There was nothing more spoken, we made to pass by,
And continue our walk in the morning.

'Well now, my fine fellows, if you will enlist,
A guinea in gold I will slap in your fist,
And a crown in the bargain to kick up the dust
And drink the Queen's health in the morning.'

'Oh no, mister sergeant, we aren't for sale,
We'll make no such bargain, and your bribe won't avail.
We're not tired of our country, and don't care to sail,
Though your offer is pleasant and charming.

'If we were such fools as to take your advance,
It's right bloody slender would be our poor chance,
For the Queen wouldn't scruple to send us to France
And get us all shot in the morning.'

'How now, you young blackguards, if you say one more word,
I swear by the errins, I'll draw out my sword
And run through your bodies as my strength may afford.
So now, you young buggers, take warning.'

Well we beat that bold drummer as flat as a shoe,
And we made a football of his row-de-dow-dow,
And as for the others we knocked out the two.
Oh, we were the boys in that morning.

We took the old weapons that hung by the side
And flung them as far as we could in the tide.
'May the devil go with you,' says Arthur McBride,
'For delaying our walk this fine morning.'

errins] ?corruption of heavens

150. *The Recruiting Sergeant*

Sergeant
Here, mower, take my shiners bright,
You'll prove a hero in the fight;
The very man, in strength and size,
To mow down all your enemies.

Mower
I thank you, sergeant, all the same,
But no, I hardly like the game.
For if I go to fight, you see,
The sword of war may mow me down.

151. *The Rambling Soldier*

I am a soldier blithe and gay
That has rambled for promotion.
I've laid the French and Spaniards low,
Some miles I've crossed the ocean.
I've travelled England and Ireland too,
I've travelled bonny Scotland through,
I've caused some pretty girls to rue
I am a roving rambling soldier.

When I was young and in my prime,
Twelve years I was recruiting.
Through England, Ireland, Scotland too,
Wherever it was suiting.
I led a gay and splendid life,
In every town a different wife,
And seldom was there any strife
With the rambling roving soldier.

In Woolwich town I courted Jane,
His sister and her mother.
I mean to say, when I was there
They were jealous of each other.

Our orders came, I had to start,
I left poor Jane with a broken heart,
Then I straight to Colchester did depart,
The gay and rambling soldier.

The King's permission granted me
To range the country over,
From Colchester to Liverpool,
From Plymouth down to Dover.
And in whatever town I went
To court all damsels I was bent,
And marry none was my intent
But live a rambling soldier.

With the blooming lasses in each town
No man was ever bolder.
I thought that I was doing right
As the King did want new soldiers.
I told them tales of fond delight,
I kept recruiting day and night,
And when I had made all things right
Off went the rambling soldier.

And now the wars are at an end
I am not ashamed to mention
The King has given me my discharge
And granted me a pension.
No doubt some lasses will me blame
But me they never once can shame,
And if you want to know my name
'Tis Bill the rambling soldier.

152. *The Girl I Left Behind Me*

I'm lonesome since I crossed the hill
And o'er the moor and valley,
Such heavy thoughts my heart do fill
Since parting with my Sally.
I seek no more the fine or gay,
For each does but remind me
How swift the hours did pass away
With the girl I left behind me.

Oh ne'er shall I forget the night,
The stars were bright above me,
And gently lent their silvery light
When first she vowed to love me.
But now I'm bound to Brighton camp,
Kind heaven, then, pray guide me,
And send me safely back again
To the girl I left behind me.

Her golden hair, in ringlets fair,
Her eyes like diamonds shining,
Her slender waist, with carriage chaste,
May leave the swan repining.
Ye gods above, oh hear my prayer
To my beauteous fair to bind me,
And send me safely back again
To the girl I left behind me.

153. *The Banks of the Nile*

'O hark, the drums do beat, my love, I can no longer stay.
The bugle calls are sounding and we must march away.
We're ordered out of Portsmouth and for many a weary mile,
To join the British army on the banks of the Nile.'

'O Willie, dearest William, don't leave me here to mourn,
Or I must curse and rue the day that ever I was born.
For parting from my love would be like parting from my life,
So stay at home, dear William, and I will be your wife.'

'O Nancy, dearest Nancy, sure that would never do,
The government has ordered and we are bound to go.
The government has ordered and the Queen she gives command
And I am bound away, my love, to serve in a foreign land.'

'Then I'll cut off my yellow hair and I'll go along with you,
I'll dress myself in uniform and I'll see Egypt too.
I'll march beneath your banner while fortune it do smile
And we'll comfort one another on the banks of the Nile.'

'Oh your waist is too slender, love, your fingers are too small,
And the sultry sun of Egypt your rosy cheeks would spoil.
Your delicate constitution will not stand the unwholesome soil
And the dry and sandy deserts on the banks of the Nile.'

'My curse attend that cruel war and the hour it began,
For it has robbed our country of many the gallant man.
They've robbed us of our sweethearts and protectors of the soil
And their blood does steep the grass that's deep upon the banks of
    the Nile.'

'O when the war is over, love, back home I will return
Unto my wife and family I've left behind to mourn,
And we'll take up the plough, my boys, and till the fertile soil,
No more we'll go a-roving on the banks of the Nile.'

154. *The Plains of Waterloo*

As I was a-walking one midsummer's morning
Down by the gay banks of a clear pleasant stream,
There I met a fair maid making sad lamentation,
So I drew myself in ambush to hear her sad refrain.
Through the woods she marched along, caused the valleys to ring-o,
And the fine feathered songsters around her they flew,
Saying, 'The war it is now over and peace it is returned again,
Yet my William's not returning from the plains of Waterloo.'

I stepped up to this fair maiden and said, 'My fond creature,
Oh dare I make inquiry as to what's your true love's name?
For it's I have been in battle where the cannons loud do rattle
And by your description I might have known the same.'
'Willie Smith's my true love's name, he's a hero of great fame,
And he's gone and he's left me in sorrow, it's true.
Now no-one shall me enjoy but my own darling boy
And yet he's not returning from the plains of Waterloo.'

'If Willie Smith's your true love's name then he's a hero of great
    fame,
He and I have fought in battle through many's the long campaign
Through Italy and Russia, through Germany and Prussia.
He was my loyal comrade through France and through Spain

Till at length by the French arms then we were surrounded
And like heroes of old then we did them subdue.
We fought for three days till at length we did defeat you,
That bold Napoleon Boney on the plains of Waterloo.

'And on the sixteenth day of June it ended the battle,
Leaving many's the bold hero in sorrow to mourn,
Where the war drums they do beat and the cannons loud do rattle,
It was by a French soldier your William was slain.
And as I passed by near where he lay a-bleeding,
I skirted the field for to bid him adieu.
With a kind, faltering voice these words he kept repeating,
"Fare you well, my lovely Annie, you are far from Waterloo."'

And when that this fair maid heard my sad acclamation,
Her two rosy cheeks they turned pale, cold and wan,
And lamenting this young man her sad lamentations.
But he cried, 'My lovely Annie, I am your very own.
And here is the ring that between us was broken,
In the depths of all days, love, to remind me of you.'
And she fell into his arms when she saw the token,
Saying, 'You're welcome, lovely William, from the plains of
    Waterloo.'

155. *The Recruited Collier*

Oh what's the matter with you, my lass,
And where's your dashing Jimmy?
The soldier boys have picked him up
And sent him far, far from me.
Last pay day he set off to town
And them red-coated fellows
Enticed him in and made him drunk,
And he'd better gone to the gallows.

The very sight of his cockade
It set us all a-crying,
And me I nearly fainted twice,
I thought that I was dying;
My father would have paid the smart,
And he run for the golden guinea,
But the sergeant swore he'd kissed the book,
So now they've got young Jimmy.

When Jimmy talks about the wars
It's worse than death to hear him,
I must go out and hide my tears
Because I cannot bear him.
A brigadier or a grenadier
He says they're sure to make him,
And aye he jibes and cracks his jokes
And begs me not forsake him.

As I walked o'er the stubble field,
Below it runs the seam,
I thought of Jimmy hewing there,
But it was all a dream.
He hewed the very coals we burn,
And when the fire I's lighting,
To think the lumps were in his hands
It sets my heart to beating.

So break my heart, and then it's o'er
So break my heart, my deary,
And I'll lie in the cold, cold ground,
For of single life I'm weary.

156. *The Orphan Boy*

The snow is fast descending
And loud the winds do roar,
A poor little boy quite friendless
Came up to a lady's door.
The lady sat at her window,
He raised his eyes with joy,
Saying, 'Lady gay, take pity I pray
On a poor little soldier's boy.

'My mother died when I was young
And my father he went to the wars,
But in battle brave he nobly fell
All covered with wounds and scars.
For many a mile on his knapsack
He has carried me with joy,
But now I am left, of pity bereft,
I'm a poor little soldier's boy.

'The snow is fast descending
And night is coming on.
Unless you are befriending
I shall perish before the morn.
Then how it will grieve your heart
And your peace of mind destroy
To find me dead at your door in the morn,
A poor little soldier's boy.'

The lady rushed from her window
And she opened her mansion's doors.
'Come in,' she cried, 'misfortune's child,
You never shall want any more.
For my only son in battle fell,
He was my only joy.
And whilst I live shelter I'll give
To a poor little soldier's boy.'

157. *The Old Battalion*

If you want to find the sergeant,
I know where he is, I know where he is;
If you want to find the sergeant,
I know where he is:
He's lying on the canteen floor.
I've seen him, I've seen him,
Lying on the canteen floor.
I've seen him,
Lying on the canteen floor.

If you want to find the quarter-bloke,
I know where he is, I know where he is;
If you want to find the quarter-bloke,
I know where he is:
He's miles and miles behind the line.
I've seen him, I've seen him,
Miles and miles behind the line.
I've seen him,
Miles and miles behind the line.

If you want to find the sergeant-major,
I know where he is, I know where he is;
If you want to find the sergeant-major,
I know where he is:
He's boozing up the privates' rum.
I've seen him, I've seen him,
Boozing up the privates' rum.
I've seen him,
Boozing up the privates' rum.

If you want to find the CO,
I know where he is, I know where he is;
If you want to find the CO,
I know where he is:
He's down in the deep dugouts.
I've seen him, I've seen him,
Down in the deep dugouts.
I've seen him,
Down in the deep dugouts.

If you want to find the old battalion,
I know where they are, I know where they are;
If you want to find the old battalion,
I know where they are:
They're hanging on the old barbed wire.
I've seen them, I've seen them,
Hanging on the old barbed wire.
I've seen them,
Hanging on the old barbed wire.

Crime and Punishment

158. *Little Sir Hugh*

It rains, it rains in merry Lincoln,
It rains both great and small,
When all the boys came out to play,
To play and toss the ball.

They play, they toss the ball so high,
They toss the ball so low,
They toss it over the Jews' garden
Where all the fine Jews go.

The first that came out was the Jew's daughter,
Was dressed all in green.
'Come in, come in, my little Sir Hugh,
To have your ball again.'

'I cannot come there, I will not come there,
Without my playmates all,
For I know full well from my mother dear
'Twill cause my blood to fall.'

The first she offered him was a fig,
The next a finer thing;
The third was a cherry as red as blood,
Which tolled the young thing in.

She sat him up in a gilty chair,
She gave him sugar sweet;
She laid him out on a dresser board
And stabbed him like a sheep.

One hour and the school was over,
His mother came out to call,
With a little rod under her apron
To beat her son withal.

'Go home, go home, my heavy mother,
Prepare a winding sheet,
And if my father should ask of me,
You tell I'm fast asleep.

'My head is heavy, I cannot get up,
The well is cold and deep;
Besides, a penknife sticks in my heart,
So out I cannot creep.'

159. *The Outlandish Knight*

An outlandish knight he came from the north land,
And he came a-wooing to me;
Now he told me he'd take me to the north land
And there he would marry me.

'Go fetch me some of your father's gold,
And some of your mother's fee,
Two of the best horses out of the stable,
Where there stand thirty and three.'

She fetched him some of her father's gold,
And some of her mother's fee,
Two of the best horses out of the stable,
Where there stood thirty and three.

She mounted on her milkwhite steed,
And he on the dapple grey.
They rode till they came unto the seaside,
Not long before it was day.

'Light off, light off your milkwhite steed,
Deliver it now unto me,
For six pretty maids I have drownded here,
The seventh one thou shalt be.

'Put off, put off your silken gown,
Deliver it now unto me,
I think it is looking too rich and too good
For to rot all in the salt sea.'

'Now if I have to pull off my fine silken gown,
And deliver it now unto thee,
I don't think it fitting a ruffian like you
A naked woman should see.'

Now he turned himself the other way,
A-watching those leaves growing green,
She caught him round his middle so small,
And she tumbled him in the stream.

Now he plunged high and he plunged low,
Until he came to the side.
'Take hold of my hand, thou pretty fair maid,
And I will make you my bride.'

'Lie there, lie there, you false-hearted man,
Lie there instead of me,
For it's six pretty maids you have drownded here,
And the seventh she has drownded thee.'

She mounted on her milkwhite steed,
She led the dappled grey,
She rode till she came to her own father's hall,
Not long before it was day.

Now the parrot was up in the window so high,
And he to the lady did say,
'I'm afraid that some ruffian has led you astray,
That you have been so long away.'

'Don't prittle, don't prattle, my pretty Polly,
Don't tell no tales of me,
And your cage will be made of the glittering gold,
And the doors of the best ivory.'

Now the king sat up in his chamber so high,
And he heard what that parrot did say.
'Whatever's the matter, my pretty Polly,
You are prattling so long before day?'

'It's no laughing matter,' the parrot did say,
'That so loudly I call unto thee,
For the cat he got up in the window so high,
I'm afraid he will have me.'

'Well done, well done, my pretty Polly,
You have tuned your note well for me.
Now your cage will be made of the glittering gold,
And the doors of the best ivory.'

160. *Geordie*

As I came over London Bridge
One misty morning early,
I overheard a fair pretty maid
Lamenting for her Geordie.

'Come bridle me my milkwhite horse,
Come bridle me my pony,
That I may ride to London's court
To plead for the life of Geordie.

And when she entered in the hall,
There was lords and ladies plenty.
Down on her bended knee she fall,
To plead for the life of Geordie.'

'Oh, Geordie stole no cow or calf,
Nor sheep he never stole any,
But he stole sixteen of the king's wild deer,
And sold them in Bohenny.

'Oh, two brave children I've had by him,
And the third lies in my bosom;
And if you would spare my Geordie's life,
I'd freely part from them every one.'

The judge looked over his left shoulder,
And said, 'I'm sorry for thee.
My pretty fair maid, you come too late,
For he's condemned already.

'Let Geordie hang in golden chains,
Such chains as never was any.
Because he came of the royal blood,
And courted a virtuous lady.'

'I wish I was in yonder grove,
Where times I have been many,
With my broad sword and pistol too,
I'd fight for the life of Geordie.'

161. *Young Edwin in the Lowlands Low*

Come all you wild young people and listen to my song,
Which I will unfold concerning gold, that guides so many wrong.
Young Emma was a servant maid and loved a sailor bold,
He ploughed the main, much gold to gain for his love, as we've been
 told.

He ploughed the main for seven years and then he returned home.
As soon as he set foot on shore, unto his love did go.
He went unto young Emma's house, his gold all for to show,
That he had gained upon the main, all in the Lowlands low.

'My father keeps a public house down by the side of the sea,
And you go there and stay the night, and there you wait for me.
I'll meet you in the morning, but don't let my parents know
Your name it is Young Edwin that ploughed the Lowlands low.'

Young Edwin he sat drinking till time to go to bed.
He little thought a sword that night would part his body and head,
And Edwin he got into bed and scarcely was asleep
When Emily's cruel parents soft into his room did creep.

They stabbed him, dragged him out of bed, and to the sea did go.
They sent his body floating down to the Lowlands low.
As Emily she lay sleeping, she had a dreadful dream:
She dreamed she saw Young Edwin's blood a-flowing like the
 stream.

'O father, where's the stranger come here last night to lay?'
'Oh, he is dead, no tales can tell,' her father he did say.
'Then father, cruel father, you'll die a public show,
For the murdering of Young Edwin that ploughed the Lowlands
 low.

'The fishes of the ocean swim o'er my lover's breast,
His body rolls in motion, I hope his soul's at rest.
The shells along the seashore that are rolling to and fro
Remind me of my Edwin that ploughed the Lowlands low.'

So many a day she passed away and tried to ease her mind,
And Emma, broken-hearted, was to Bedlam forced to go,
Crying, 'O my friends, my love is gone, and I am left behind.'
Her shrieks were for Young Edwin that ploughed the Lowlands
low.

162. *The Constant Farmer's Son*

It's of a merchant's daughter,
In London town did dwell,
She was modest, fair and handsome
And her parents loved her well.
She was admired by lords and squires,
It was their hopes in vain,
For there was one, 'twas a farmer's son
Poor Mary's heart could gain.

Long time young William courted her
And fixed the wedding day,
Their parents all consented
But her brothers both did say,
'There lives a lord shall pledge the word
And him she shall not shun,
For we will betray and then we'll slay
Her constant farmer's son.'

A fair was held not far from town,
Those brothers went straightway.
They asked young William's company
With them to pass the day.
But mark! returning home again
They swore his race was run,
Then with a stick the life did take
Of the constant farmer's son.

Those villains soon returned home.
'O sister,' they did say,
'Pray think no more of your false love
But let him go his way.
For it is the truth we tell in love
He's fallen with some other one,
Therefore we came to tell the same
Of your constant farmer's son.'

As on the pillow Mary laid
She dreamed a dreadful dream.
She dreamed she saw his body laying
Down by some crystal stream.
Young Mary rose, put on her clothes,
For to seek her love did run.
Then dead and cold she did behold
Her constant farmer's son.

Her dream she felt was realised,
As on his face she gazed;
She sat down by his body cold
With wonder sore amazed.
She gathered leaves all from the trees,
To keep him from the sun,
One night and day she passed away
With the constant farmer's son.

But hunger it came creeping on,
Poor girl, she shaked with woe.
For to find out his murderer
She straightway home did go,
Crying, 'Parents dear, you soon shall hear
What a dreadful deed is done.
In the yonder vale lying dead and pale
My constant farmer's son.'

Up came her oldest brother
And he said, 'It is not me.'
The same replied the younger one
And he swore most bitterly.
Young Mary said, 'Don't turn so red
Nor try the laws to shun;
You've a-done the deed and you shall bleed
For my constant farmer's son.'

These villains soon they owned their guilt
And for the same did die.
Young Mary fair in deep despair
And never ceased to cry.
Their parents they did fade away,
The glass of life was run.
Young Mary cried, in sorrow died
For the constant farmer's son.

163. *Mary in the Silvery Tide*

'Twas of a lovely creature who dwelled by the seaside,
For her lovely form and features she was the village pride;
There was a young sea captain who Mary's heart would gain,
But she was true to Henry, was on the raging main.

'Twas in young Henry's absence this noble man he came
A-courting pretty Mary, but she refused the same.
She said, 'I pray you begone, young man, your vows are all in vain,
Therefore begone, I love but one, he's on the raging main.'

With mad desperation this noble man he said,
'To prove the separation I'll take her life away;
I'll watch her late and early and then alone,' he cried,
'I'll send her body a-floating in the rippling tide.'

This noble man was walking out to take the air,
Down by the rolling ocean he met the lady fair.
He said, 'My pretty fair maid, you consent to be my bride,
Or you shall swim far from here in the rolling silvery tide.'

With trembling limbs cried Mary, 'My vows I never can break,
For Henry I dearly love and I'll die for his sweet sake.'
With his handkerchief he bound her hands and plunged her in the
    main
And shrinking her body went floating in the rolling silvery tide.

It happened Mary's true love soon after came from sea,
Expecting to be happy and fixed the wedding day.
'We fear your true love's murdered,' her aged parents cried,
'Or she caused her own destruction in the rolling silvery tide.'

As Henry on his pillow lay he could not take no rest,
For the thoughts of pretty Mary disturbed his wounded breast.
He dreamed that he was walking down by a river side,
He saw his true love weeping in the rolling silvery tide.

Young Henry rose at midnight, at midnight gloom went he
To search the sandbanks over down by the raging sea.
At daybreak in the morning poor Mary's corpse he spied
As to and fro she was floating in the rolling silvery tide.

He knew it was his Mary by the ring upon her hand.
He untied the silk handkerchief which put him to a stand,
For the name of her cruel murderer was full thereon he spied,
Which proved who ended Mary's days in the rolling silvery tide.

This noble man was taken, the gallows was his doom
For ending pretty Mary's days, she had scarce attained her bloom.
Young Henry brokenhearted he wandered till he died.
His last words were for Mary in the rolling silvery tide.

164. *Gilderoy*

Now Gilderoy was a bonny boy, and he would not the ribbons wear;
He pulled off his scarlet coat, he gartered below his knee.
He was beloved by the ladies so fair, he was such a rakish boy;
He was my sovereign, my heart's delight, my charming young
    Gilderoy.

Young Gilderoy and I were born all in one town together,
And at the age of sixteen years we courted one another.
Our dads and mothers both did agree and crowned with mirth and
    joy,
To think upon our wedding day, with me and my Gilderoy.

Now Gilderoy and I walked out all in the fields together,
He took me round the waist so small, and down we went together;
And after he done all a man could do he rose and kissed his joy,
He was my sovereign, my heart's delight, my charming young
    Gilderoy.

What a pity is it that a man should be hanged for stealing woman,
Where he neither robbed house nor land, he stole neither horse nor
    mare.
He was beloved by the old and young, he was such a rakish boy,
He was my sovereign, my heart's delight, my charming young
    Gilderoy.

Now Gilderoy for some time has been dead and a funeral we must
    have,
With a brace of pistols by his side to guard him to his grave;
For he was beloved by the old and young, he was such a rakish boy,
He was my sovereign, my heart's delight, my charming young
    Gilderoy.

165. *Lambkin*

Lambkin, the finest mason that e'er laid a stone,
He built a lord's mansion and for payment got none.
He built it without and he sealed it within,
And he made a false window for himself to get in.

His Lordship going to London once upon a time,
The Lambkin thought fit to commit his great crime.
'I fear the Lambkin,' the lady did say,
'I fear the Lambkin when your lordship's away.'

'I fear not the Lambkin, nor any of his kind,
When my gates are well barred and my windows pinned down.'
So in stepped the Lambkin in the middle of the night,
Without coal or candle to show him the light.

'Where is his lordship?' then said the Lambkin.
'He's in London buying pearls,' said the false nurse to him.
'Where's her ladyship?' said the Lambkin.
'She's in her chamber sleeping,' says the false nurse to him.

'How will I get at her?' says the Lambkin.
'Stab the baby in the cradle,' says the false nurse to him.
'It's a pity, it's a pity,' said the Lambkin.
'No pity, no pity,' says the false nurse to him.

CRIME AND PUNISHMENT

So the Lambkin he rocked and the false nurse she sung,
And with a small penknife he dabbed now and then.
So the Lambkin he rocked and the false nurse she sung,
And the tearing of the cradle made the blood cold to run.

'Please my child, nurse, please him with the keys.'
'He won't be pleased, madam, you may do as you please.'
'Please my child, nurse, please him with the bell.'
'He won't be pleased, madam, till you come down yoursel'.'

'How can I come down, as my candle is out,
And the room is so dark that I cannot move about?'
'You have three golden mantles as bright as the sun;
Throw one of them round you, it will show you light down.'

As soon as her ladyship entered the stairs,
So ready was Lambkin to catch her with his snares.
'Good morrow, good morrow,' says the Lambkin;
'Good morrow,' says the lady to him.

'Where is his lordship?' says the Lambkin.
'He's in London buying pearls for my lying-in.'
'You never will enjoy them,' says the Lambkin.
'The more is the pity,' says the lady to him.

'Spare my life, Lambkin, spare it but one day;
I will give you as much gold as you can carry away.'
'If you give me as much gold as I could heap in a sack,
I could not keep my penknife from your lily-white neck.'

'Spare my life, Lambkin, spare it but one hour;
I'll give you my daughter, Bessie, your bride for to be.'
'Bring down your daughter, Bessie, she's both neat and trim,
With a silver basin to hold your life-blood in.'

'Oh no, no; that, Lambkin, that would never do;
If you say that, then Bessie will never be for you.
Bessie, lovely Bessie, stay up in your room,
Watch for your father coming home, and that will be soon.'

Bessie sat watching that cold winter night,
With her father coming home with his men at daylight.
'Father, dear father, what kept you so long;
Your lady is murdered and your own darling son.

'There is blood in the kitchen, there is blood in the hall;
But the blood of my mamma is the worst blood of all.
For the Lambkin will be hung high up on a tree,
And the false nurse will be burned, such a villain is she.'

166. *The Cruel Mother*

There was a lady lived in York,
    All alone and a loney,
A farmer's son he courted her,
    All down by the greenwood sidey.

He courted her for seven long years,
At last she proved with child by him.

She pitched her knee against a tree,
And there she found great misery.

She pitched her back against a thorn,
And there she had her baby born.

She drew the fillet off her head,
She bound the baby's hands and legs.

She drew a knife both long and sharp,
She pierced the baby's innocent heart.

She wiped the knife upon the grass,
The more she wiped, the blood run fast.

She washed her hands all in the spring,
Thinking to turn a maid again.

As she was going to her father's hall,
She saw three babes a-playing at ball.

One dressed in silk, the other in satin,
The other star-naked as ever was born.

'O dear baby, if you was mine,
I'd dress you in silk and satin so fine.'

'O dear mother, I once was thine,
You never would dress me coarse or fine.

'The coldest earth it was my bed,
The green grass was my coverlet.

'O mother, mother, for your sin,
Heaven gate you shall not enter in.

'There is a fire beyond hell's gate,
And there you'll burn both early and late.'

167(a). *Henry My Son*

'Where have you been all day, Henry my son,
Where have you been all day, my beloved one?'
'In the fields, dear mother, in the fields, dear mother,
Make my bed for I'm afraid in my heart,
And I want to lie down.'

'Where did you see your father, Henry my son,
Where did you see your father, my beloved one?'
'In the fields, dear mother, in the fields, dear mother,
Make my bed for I'm afraid in my heart,
And I want to lie down.'

'What did your father give you, Henry my son,
What did your father give you, my beloved one?'
'Water, dear mother, water, dear mother,
Make my bed for I'm afraid in my heart,
And I want to lie down.'

'What shall I give your father, Henry my son,
What shall I give your father, my beloved one?'
'A rope to hang him, a rope to hang him,
Make my bed for I'm afraid in my heart,
And I want to lie down.'

'Where shall I make your bed, Henry my son,
Where shall I make your bed, my beloved one?'

'In the churchyard, dear mother, in the churchyard, dear mother,
Make my bed for I'm afraid in my heart,
And I want to lie down.'

'How shall I make your bed, Henry my son,
How shall I make your bed, my beloved one?'
'Long and narrow, long and narrow,
Make my bed for I'm afraid in my heart,
And I want to lie down—for ever.'

167(b). *Green and Yellow*

'Where have you been all day, Henry my son,
Where have you been all day, my pretty one?'
'In the woods, dear mother, in the woods, dear mother.
Oh mother, be quick, 'cause I want to be sick, and lay me down and
die.'

'What did you do in the woods today, Henry my son,
What did you do in the woods today, my saveloy?'
'Ate, dear mother, ate, dear mother.
Oh mother, be quick, 'cause I want to be sick, and lay me down and
die.'

'What did you eat in the woods today, Henry my son,
What did you eat in the woods today, my currant bun?'
'Eels, dear mother, eels, dear mother.
Oh mother, be quick, 'cause I want to be sick, and lay me down and
die.'

'What colour were them eels, Henry my boy,
What colour were them eels, my pride and joy?'
'Green and yeller, green and yeller.
Oh mother, be quick, 'cause I want to be sick, and lay me down and
die.'

'Them weren't eels, them was snakes, Henry my son,
Them weren't eels, them was snakes, my pretty one.'
'Ugh, dear mother, ugh, dear mother.
Oh mother, be quick, 'cause I want to be sick, and lay me down and
die.'

'What colour flowers d'you want on your grave, Henry my boy,
What colour flowers d'you want on your grave, my pride and joy?'
'Green and yeller, green and yeller.
Oh mother, be quick, 'cause I want to be sick, and lay me down and
   die.'

168. *The Swan Swims So Bonny*

A farmer there lived in the north country
   Hey ho my nanny O
And he had daughters, one, two, three
   Where the swan swims so bonny O.

These daughters they walked by the river's brim,
And the eldest pushed the youngest in.

'O sister, O sister, pray lend me your hand,
And I will give you house and land.'

'I'll neither give you hand nor glove,
Unless you give me your own true love.'

Sometimes she sank, sometimes she swam,
Until she came to the miller's dam.

The miller's daughter, dressed in red,
She went for some water to make her bread.

'O father, O daddy, here swims a swan,
And it's very like to a gentlewoman.'

They laid her on the bank to dry,
There came a harper passing by.

He made a harp of her breast-bone,
And the harp began to play alone.

He made harp-pins of her fingers so fair,
He made harp-strings of her golden hair.

He brought it to her father's hall,
There was the court assembled all.

He laid the harp upon a stone,
And straight it began to play alone.

'Oh yonder sits my father, the king,
And yonder sits my mother, the queen.

'Oh yonder sits my brother Hugh,
And by him William, sweet and true.

'And there does sit my false sister Anne,
Who drowned me for the sake of a man.'

169. *The Execution of Luke Hutton*

I am a poor prisoner condemned to die,
    Ah woe is me, woe is me, for my great folly!
Fast fettered in irons in place where I lie,
    Be warned, young wantons, hemp passeth green holly.
My parents were of good degree,
By whom I would not counselled be.
    Lord Jesu forgive me, with mercy relieve me,
    Receive, O sweet Saviour, my spirit unto thee.

My name is Hutton, yea Luke of bad life,
Which on the high way did rob man and wife,
Enticed by many a graceless mate
Whose counsel I repent too late.

Not twenty years old, alas, was I,
When I begun this felony.
With me went still twelve yeomen tall,
Which I did my twelve apostles call.

There was no squire nor baron bold,
That rode the way with silver or gold,
But I and my twelve apostles gay
Would lighten their load ere they went away.

This news procured my kinsfolk's grief,
They hearing I was a famous thief,
They wept, they wailed, they wrung their hands,
That thus I should hazard life and lands.

They made me a jailer a little before,
To keep in prison offenders store;
But such a jailer was never one,
I went and let them out every one.

I wist their sorrow sore grieved me,
Such proper men should hangèd be.
My office there I did defy,
And ran away for company.

Three years I lived upon the spoil,
Giving many an earl the foil,
Yet never did I kill man nor wife,
Though lewdly long I kept my life.

But all too bad my deeds hath been,
Offending my country and my good Queen;
All men in Yorkshire talk of me
A stronger thief there could not be.

Upon St Luke's day was I born,
Whom want of grace hath made a scorn;
In honour of my birthday then,
I robbed in a bravery nineteen men.

The country weary to bear this wrong
With hues and cries pursued me long;
Though long I scaped, yet low at last,
London, I was in Newgate cast.

There did I lie with a grievèd mind,
Although the keeper was gentle and kind;
Yet was he not so kind as I,
To let me be at liberty.

At last the sheriff of Yorkshire came,
And in a warrant he had my name.
Said he, 'At York thou must be tried,
With me therefore hence must thou ride.'

Like pangs of death his words did sound,
My hands and arms full fast he bound.
'Good sir,' quoth I, 'I had rather stay,
I have no heart to ride that way.'

When no entreaty might prevail,
I called for beer, for wine and ale,
And when my heart was in woeful ease,
I drunk to my friends with a smiling face.

With clubs and staves I was guarded then,
I never before had such waiting men;
If they had ridden before amain,
Beshrew me if I had called them again.

And when into York that I was come,
Each one on me did pass their doom,
And while you lie this sentence note,
Evil men can never have good report.

Before the judges when I was brought,
Be sure I had a careful thought;
Nine score indictments and seventeen
Against me there was read and seen.

And each of these was felony found,
Which did my heart with sorrow wound.
What should I herein no longer stay,
For this I was condemned that day.

My death each hour I do attend,
In prayer and tears my time I spend,
And all my living friends this day
I do entreat for me to pray.

I have deserved long since to die,
A viler sinner lived not than I;
Oh friends, I hoped my life to save,
But I am fittest for the grave.

Adieu my loving friends, each one,
    Ah woe is me, woe is me, for my great folly!
Think on my words when I am gone.
    Be warned, young wantons, hemp passeth green holly.
When on the ladder you shall me view,
Think I am nearer heaven than you.
    Lord Jesu, forgive me, with mercy relieve me,
    Receive, O sweet Saviour, my spirit unto thee.

170. *Dick Turpin's Ride*

'Dick Turpin, bold Dick hie away,' was the cry
Of my pals, who were startled, you guess.
The pistols were levelled, the bullets whizzed by,
As I jumped on the back of Black Bess.

Three officers, mounted, led forward the chase,
Resolved in the capture to share;
But I smiled on their efforts, though swift was their pace,
As I urged on my bonny black mare.

Hark away, hark away! Still onward we press,
And I saw by the glimmers of morn,
Full many a mile on the back of Black Bess
That night I was gallantly borne.

High over, my Bet! Thy fatigue thou must bear.
Well cleared! Never falter for breath.
Hark forward, brave girl, my bonny black mare!
We are speeding for life or for death.

When the spires of York Minster now burst on my view,
And the chimes they were ringing a knell—
Halt, halt! my brave mare, they no longer pursue.
As she halted, she staggered, she fell.

Her breathings are over, all hushed to her grave,
My poor Black Bess, once my pride.
But her heart she had burst, her rider to save—
For Dick Turpin she lived and she died.

171. *Jack Hall*

My name it is Jack Hall, chimney sweep, chimney sweep,
My name it is Jack Hall, chimney sweep.
My name it is Jack Hall, and I'll rob both great and small,
And my life shall pay for all when I die.

I've twenty pounds in store, that's no joke,
I've twenty pounds in store, and I'll rob for twenty more,
And my life shall pay for all when I die.

I've candles lily-white, that's no joke,
I've candles lily-white, oh I stole them in the night,
For to light me to the place where I lie.

Oh I climbed up the ladder, that's no joke,
Oh I climbed up the ladder, and the hangman spread the rope
And the devil of a word said I coming down.

172. *The Sheffield Apprentice*

When I was bound for London a lady met me there,
She offered me high wages to serve her for one year,
To go with her to Holland with her I did agree,
Making my way from London, and cursèd was the day.

I did not serve my mistress one year or two
Until my wealthy mistress proved very fond of me.
She said she'd gold, she'd silver, she'd horses, she had lands,
If I would only marry her to be at her command.

I said, 'My honoured mistress, I cannot wed you both,
For I've already promised and made a solemn oath
I'd court no-one but Sally, your handsome waiting-maid,
Excuse me, dear mistress, she has my heart betrayed.'

My mistress in a passion and from me she did flew.
She said she'd play a project that'd prove my overthrow.
She slipped a ring from her middle finger as I did pass her by,
She slipped it in my pocket and she sweared that I should die.
My mistress said I'd robbed her. I was straightway sent to gaol.

173. *The Rambling Boy*

I am a wild and wicked youth,
I love young women and that's the truth,
I love them dearly and I love them well,
I love them better than tongue can tell.

In my seventeen I took a wife,
I loved her dearly as my life,
And to maintain her both well and gay
Robbing went I on the highway.

So when my money was getting low
On the highway I was forced to go,
A-robbing lords and ladies bright
And brought the gold to my heart's delight.

I robbed Lord Sandford I do declare,
And Lady Marmion in New Year's Square.
I shut the shutters, bid them goodnight
And away I went to my heart's delight.

My old mammy and my daddy too,
Affection told me it will never do,
I will not listen to what they say
But still go on my own wicked way.

When I am dead and in my grave
A decent funeral pray let me have,
Six highwaymen for to carry me,
Give them bright swords for their liberty.

Six blooming girls for to bear my pall,
Give them white gloves and pink ribbons all,
And when I'm dead they'll tell the truth:
There go a wild and wicked youth.

174. *Limbo*

I am a poor lad and my fortune is bad,
And if ever I get rich 'tis a wonder.
I've spent all my money on girls and strong beer,
And what riches I had are all plundered.
Field after field to market I sent,
Till my land was all gone and my money all spent.
My heart was so hard that I never would repent,
And 'twas that that brought me to Limbo.

Once I could run whilst other did lie,
And strut like a crow in the gutter;
The people all said that saw me pass by,
'There goes Mr Fop in a flutter.'
To the top and top-gallant I hoisted my sails,
With a fine, fringy cravat and a wig with three tails;
And now I am ready to gnaw my own nails
And drink the cold water of Limbo.

I had an old uncle lived down in the west,
And he heard of my sad disaster.
Poor soul, after that he could never take no rest,
For his troubles came faster and faster.
He came to the gaol to view my sad case,
And as soon as I saw him I knew his old face;
I stood gazing on him like one in amaze:
I wished myself safe out of Limbo.

'Jack, if I should set you once more on your legs,
And put you in credit and fashion,
Oh will you leave off those old rakish ways,
And try for to govern your passion?'
'Yes, Uncle,' says I, 'if you will set me free,
I surely will always be ruled by thee;
And I'll labour my bones for the good of my soul
And I'll pay them for laying me in Limbo.'

He pulled out his purse with three thousand pounds,
And he counted it out in bright guineas;
And when I was free from the prison gates
I went to see Peggy and Jeannie.

Limbo] debtors' prison

In my old ragged clothes they knew nought of my gold,
They turned me all out in the wet and the cold.
You'd a-laughed for to hear how those hussies did scold,
How they jawed me for laying in Limbo.

I'd only been there a very short time
Before my pockets they then fell to picking.
I banged them as long as my cane I could hold,
Until they fell coughing and kicking.
The one bawled out 'Murder', the other did scold;
I banged them as long as my cane I could hold,
I banged their old bodies for the good of their souls,
And I paid them for laying me in Limbo.

175(a). *Van Dieman's Land*

Come all you wild and wicked youths
Wherever you may be,
I pray you give attention
And listen unto me.
The fate of our poor transports
You shall understand,
The hardships they undergo
Upon Van Dieman's Land.

> *Young men all now beware*
> *Lest you are drawn into a snare.*

I and five more went out one night
To Squire Dunhill's park
To see if we could get some game
But the night it proved too dark.
And to our sad misfortune
They hemmed us in with speed
And sent us off to Warwick gaol
Which caused our hearts to bleed.

And at the March assizes
At the bar we did appear;
Like Job we stood with patience
To hear our sentence there.

We being old offenders
It made our case more hard;
Our sentence was for fourteen years
And I got sent on board.

The ship that bore us from the land
Speedwell was by name;
For about six months and upwards
We ploughed the raging main;
No land or harbour could we see,
Believe it is no lie,
Beneath us one black water
Above us one blue sky.

I often looked behind me
To see my native shore,
That cottage of contentment
That I shall see no more.
Nor yet my aged father,
He tore his old grey hair,
Likewise my aged mother,
In her womb she did me bear.

On the fifteenth of September
Was when we made the land.
At four o'clock next morning
All chained hand to hand,
To see my fellow sufferers
I'm sure I can't tell how:
Some were chained to a harrow
And others to a plough.

No shoes nor stockings had they on,
No hats had they to wear;
Leather breeches and linen drawers,
Their head and feet were bare.
They drove about in two and two,
Like horses in a team,
The driver he stood over them
With his malacca cane.

As we marched into Sydney town
Without no more delay,
A gentleman he bought me
His bookkeeper to be.
I took the occupation,
My master loved me well;
My joys were out of measure,
I'm sure no tongue could tell.

He had a female servant,
Rosanna was by name,
For fourteen years a convict,
From Wolverhampton came.
We often told our tales of love
While we were blest at home,
But now the rattling of our chains
In a foreign land to roam.
Young men now all beware
Lest you are drawn into a snare.

175(b). *Van Dieman's Land*

Come all you gallant poachers that ramble void of care,
While walking out one moonlight night with gun and dog and snare,
With your hares and lofty pheasants that you have at your command,
Not thinking of the last career upon Van Dieman's Land.

It's poor Tom Brown from Nottingham, Jack Williams and poor Joe,
They were three daring poachers the country did well know;
At night they were trepanned by the keepers hid in sand:
Fourteen years transported, boys, upon Van Dieman's Land.

The very day we landed upon that fateful shore,
The planters they stood round us full twenty score or more;
They ranked us up like horses and sold us out of hand,
They roped us to the plough, brave boys, to plough Van Dieman's
    Land.

The cottage that we lived in was built of clods and clay,
And rotten straw for bed, and we dare not say nay;
Our cots were fenced with fire, to slumber when we can,
To drive away wolves and tigers come by Van Dieman's Land.

There was a poor girl from Birmingham, Susan Simmons was her
   name,
Fourteen years transported, you all have heard the same.
Our planter bought her freedom, he married her out of hand;
She gave to us good usage upon Van Dieman's Land.

It's oft-times when I slumber I have a pleasant dream:
With my pretty girl I have been roving down by a sparkling stream;
In England I've been roving with her at my command,
But I wake broken-hearted upon Van Dieman's land.

Come all you daring poachers, give hearing to my song:
It is a bit of good advice although it is not long.
Lay aside your dogs and snares, to you I must speak plain,
For if you knew our hardships you'd never poach again.

176. *The Murder of Maria Marten*

Come all you thoughtless young men, a warning take by me,
And think on my unhappy fate to be hanged upon a tree;
My name is William Corder, to you I do declare,
I courted Maria Marten, most beautiful and fair.

I promised I would marry her upon a certain day,
Instead of that, I was resolved to take her life away.
I went into her father's house, the eighteenth day of May,
Saying, 'My dear Maria, we will fix the wedding day.

'If you will meet me at the Red Barn, as sure as I have life,
I will take you to Ipswich town, and there make you my wife.'
I then went home and fetched my gun, my pickaxe and my spade,
I went into the Red Barn, and there I dug her grave.

With heart so light, she thought no harm, to meet him she did go,
He murdered her all in the barn, and laid her body low;
After the horrible deed was done, she lay weltering in her gore,
Her bleeding mangled body he buried beneath the Red Barn floor.

Now all things being silent, her spirit could not rest,
She appeared unto her mother, who suckled her at her breast;
For many a long month or more, her mind being sore oppressed,
Neither night nor day she could not take any rest.

Her mother's mind being so disturbed, she dreamèd three nights
   o'er,
Her daughter she lay murdered beneath the Red Barn floor;
She sent her father to the barn, when he the ground did thrust,
And there he found his daughter mingling with the dust.

My trial is hard, I could not stand, most woeful was the sight
When her jawbone was brought to prove, which piercèd my heart
   quite;
Her aged father standing by, likewise his loving wife,
And in her grief her hair she tore, she scarcely could keep life.

Adieu, adieu, my loving friends, my glass is almost run,
On Monday next will be my last, when I am to be hanged;
So you, young men, who do pass by, with pity look on me,
For murdering Maria Marten, I was hanged upon the tree.

177. *Constance Kent*

Oh give attention, you maidens dear,
My dying moments are drawing near,
When I am sentenced alas to die
Upon a gallows gloomy and high.

Oh what sight it will be to see
A maiden die on the fatal tree.

I am a maiden in youth and bloom,
I a wretched murderer to die am doomed,
And in the city of Salisbury,
My days must end on a dismal tree.

My little brother, a darling sweet,
That fatal morning did soundly sleep,
I was perplexed, I invented strife,
Fully determined to take his life.

To the dirty closet I did him take,
The deed I done caused my heart to ache;
Into the soil I did him thrust down,
Where asleep in death he was quickly found.

CRIME AND PUNISHMENT

My own dear father they did suspect
That he would suffer they did expect;
I was apprehended, but got clear,
Though I was the murderess of my brother dear.

Long, long I pined in deep distress,
At length the murder I did confess,
The vile Road murder, as you may see,
Committed was by no-one but me.

Farewell my father, my father dear,
I know for me you will shed a tear,
Yes, your wicked daughter in shame must die
For that cruel murder on a gallows high.

How many maidens will flock to see
A female die upon Salisbury's tree?
Constance Emily Kent is my dreadful name,
Who in youth and beauty dies a death of shame.

I must go to my silent grave;
Father, is there no-one your child to save?
Oh the awful moments are drawing near,
Father, forgive your daughter dear.

Oh God in heaven, look down on me,
As I stand on the dreadful tree,
Forgive the crime I, alas, have done,
Wash me with the blood of Thy blessed Son.

I must not live, I am bound to go,
I must be hurried to the shadows below.
My guilty heart long did quake with fear;
Why did I kill my little brother dear?

I see the hangman before me stand,
Ready to seize me by the law's command.
When my life is ended on the fatal tree,
Then will be cleared up all mystery.

178. *Mary Arnold the Female Monster*

Of all the tales was ever told,
I now will you impart,
That cannot fail to terror strike,
To every human heart.
The deeds of Mary Arnold,
Who does in jail deplore,
Oh such a dreadful tale as this
Was never told before.

> *This wretched woman's dreadful deed*
> *Does everyone affright.*
> *With black beetles in walnut shells*
> *She deprived her child of sight.*

Now think you, tender parents,
What must this monster feel,
The heart within her breast must ten
Times harder be than steel.
The dreadful crimes she did commit
Does all the world surprise:
Black beetles placed in walnut shells
Bound round her infant's eyes.

The beetles in a walnut shell
The monster she did place,
This dreadful deed, as you may read,
All history does disgrace.
The walnut shell and beetles
With a bandage she bound tight
Around her infant's tender eyes,
To take away its sight.

A lady saw this monster
In the street when passing by,
And she was struck with terror
For to hear the infant cry.
The infant's face she swore to see,
Which filled her with surprise,
To see the fatal bandage
Tied round the infant's eyes.

With speed she called an officer,
Oh shocking to relate,
Who beheld the deed, and took the wretch
Before the magistrate.
Who committed her for trial,
Which did the wretch displease,
And she's now transported ten long years
Across the briny seas.

Is there another in the world
Could plan such wicked deed?
No-one upon this earth before
Of such did ever see.
To take away her infant's sight,
'Tis horrible to tell,
Binding black beetles round its eyes
Placed in walnut shells.

179. McCaffery

When I was eighteen years of age
To join the army I did engage;
I left the factory with good intent
To join the Forty-second Regiment.

To Fulwood Barracks I then did go
To spend a short period in that depot,
But out of trouble I could not be
And Captain Hansen took a dislike to me.

While standing sentry-go one day
Some soldiers' children came out to play,
And from his quarters my captain came
And ordered me to take their parents' names.

My officer's orders I had to fulfill,
Although it went against my will;
I took one's name but not all three,
And with neglect of duty they charged me.

CRIME AND PUNISHMENT

In the barrack court-room I did appear
But Captain Hansen my sad story would not hear;
Ten days in barracks and ten days' pay
For doing my duty the opposite way.

For fourteen weeks and thirteen days
My sentence rose and filled my gaze;
To shoot my captain dead on sight
Was all that I resolved to do each night.

One day upon the barrack-square
I saw him walking with Colonel Blair;
I raised my rifle and fired to kill
And shot my poor colonel against my will.

I did the deed, I shed his blood,
At Liverpool Assizes my trial I stood.
The judge he said, 'McCaffery,
Prepare yourself now for the gallows tree.'

I had no father to take my part,
I had no mother to break her heart,
I had one friend and a girl was she
Would lay down her life for McCaffery.

So now I lie in Walton gaol,
My thoughts and feelings no tongue can tell,
My thoughts and feelings no tongue can say,
The Lord have mercy on McCaffery.

So come all you young officers, take warning by me,
Have nothing to do with the British Army,
For bloody lies and tyranny
Have made a murderer of McCaffery.

Christian and Other Festivals

180. *The Holy Well*

As it fell out on a holiday,
A high holiday so high,
Sweet Jesus he asked his own mother dear
Whether he should go and play.

'To play, to play, my own dear son,
It's time that you are gone,
And don't let me hear no complaints of you
At night when you do come home.

'You'll go back to the merry little town
As far as the holy well,
And there you'll see as fine children
That as every tongue can tell.'

'They say they were lords' and ladies' sons,
The meanest among them all,
While I was nothing but a mild Mary's child
Born down in an oxen stall.'

'If you were nothing but a mild Mary's child
Born down in an oxen stall,
You shall be the ruler, the King of Heaven,
And ruler amongst them all.'

Sweet Jesus he turned himself right round,
Never a laugh nor a smile,
But the tears they falled from sweet Jesus' eyes
Like the water from the sky.

'Oh no, dear mother, such a thing shall never be,
And that you know full well,
There is too many a poor sinful souls
Crying out for the help of me.

'Oh hell is dark and hell it is dim
And hell is full of woe,
God grant it to any poor sinful souls
That is passed from sweet Jesus Christ.'

181. *The Bitter Withy*

As it fell out upon one day,
The stars from heaven did fall
And our Saviour asked his dear mother
If he could play at ball.

'To play at ball, dear child,
It's time that you were gone,
And don't let me hear of your ill-doings
At night when you come home.'

'If I do play with these children
And they do play with me:
"We are lords' and ladies' children
And born in a bowery hall,
And you are but a mild Mary's son
And born in an oxen stall."

'If I am but a mild Mary's child
And born in an oxen stall,
I'll make you appear at the very latter end,
I'm ruler above you all.'

Our Saviour built a bridge with the rays of the sun,
And over it went he.
There was three jolly Jordans went for to follow
And drownded were all three.

Then it's up the lane call and it's down the lane call,
The mothers they did run,
Saying, 'Mary mild, correct your child,
For he has drownded all.'

Sweet Mary took a bunch of the green withy
And placed our Saviour across her knee,
And with a bunch of green withy
She gave him lashes three.

'Oh the withy, the withy, the bitter withy
That has causèd me to smart,
The withy shall be the very first tree
For to perish all at the heart.'

182. *God Made a Trance*

Oh God made a trance on Sunday
All with His holy hand,
He made the sun fair on the moon
Like water on a dry land.

There's six good days all in a week
All for labouring man,
The seventh day to serve the Lord,
Both Father and the Son.

It's when you go to church, dear man,
Down on your knees down fall
And a-praying to our living Lord
For the saving of your soul.

For the saving of your soul, dear man,
Christ died along the road.
We shall never do for our Saviour Christ
As he has done for we.

Three drops of our good Saviour's blood
Were shed on Calvary.
We shall never do by our Saviour Christ
As he has done by we.

Come teach your children well, dear man,
The whiles that you are here.
It will be better for your soul, dear man,
When you lies upon the bier.

183(a). *The Seven Virgins*

All under the leaves, the leaves of life,
I met with virgins seven,
And one of them was Mary mild,
Our Lord's mother from heaven.

'Oh what are you seeking, you seven fair maids,
All under the leaves of life?
Come tell, come tell me what seek you
All under the leaves of life?'

'We're seeking for no leaves, Thomas,
But for a friend of thine;
We're seeking for sweet Jesus Christ,
To be our guide and thine.'

'Go you down, go you down to yonder town,
And sit in the gallery;
And there you'll find sweet Jesus Christ,
Nailed to a big yew-tree.'

So down they went to yonder town
As fast as foot could fall,
And many a grievous bitter tear
From the virgins' eyes did fall.

'Oh peace, mother, oh peace, mother,
Your weeping doth me grieve;
Oh I must suffer this,' he said,
'For Adam and for Eve.'

'Oh how can I my weeping leave
Or my sorrows undergo,
Whilst I do see my own son die,
When sons I have no mo'?'

'Dear mother, dear mother, you must take John,
All for to be your son,
And he will comfort you sometimes,
Mother, as I have done.'

'Oh come, thou John Evangelist,
Thou'rt welcome unto me,
But more welcome my own dear son,
That I mused upon my knee.'

Then He laid His head on His right shoulder,
Seeing death it struck Him nigh:
'The Holy Ghost be with your soul—
I die, mother dear, I die.'

Oh the rose, the rose, the gentle rose,
And the fennel that grows so green!
God give us grace in every place
To pray for our king and queen.

Furthermore for our enemies all
Our prayers they should be strong.
Amen, Good Lord, your charity
Is the ending of my song.

183(b). *The Leaves of Life*

Oh it's all under the leaves and the leaves of life,
Where I saw maidens seven,
And it's one of those was Mary mild,
Was our King's mother from heaven.

Then I asked them what they were looking for,
All under the leaves of life.
'I am looking for sweet Jesus Christ,
To be our heavenly guide.'

'Go you down, go you down to yonder town,
As far as you can see,
And there you will find sweet Jesus Christ
With his body nailed to a tree.'

'Dear mother, dear mother, do not weep for me,
Your weeping does me harm,
But John may be a comfort to you
When I am dead and gone.'

There's a rose and a rose and a gentle rose,
The charm that grows so green.
God will give us grace in every mortal place
For to pray to our heavenly Queen.

184. *Dives and Lazarus*

As it fell out upon one day,
Rich Diverus he made a feast,
And he invited all his friends
And gentry of the best.

As it fell out upon one day,
Poor Lazarus, he was so poor,
He came and laid him down and down,
Even down at Diverus' door.

Then Lazarus laid him down and down,
Even at Diverus' gate.
'Some meat, some drink, brother Lazarus,
For Jesus Christ his sake.'

'Thou art none of mine, brother Lazarus,
That lies begging at my gate.
No meat, no drink, will I give thee,
For Jesus Christ his sake.'

Then Diverus sent out his hungry dogs
To bite him as he lay.
They hadn't the power to bite one bite
But licked his sores away.

Then Diverus sent out his merry men
To worry him away.
They had not the power to strike one stroke,
But threw their whips away.

As it fell out upon one day,
Poor Lazarus, he sickened and died.
There came two angels out of heaven,
His soul therein to guide.

'Rise up, rise up, brother Lazarus,
And come along with me,
For you've a place prepared in Heaven,
For to sit upon an angel's knee.'

As it fell out upon one day,
Rich Diverus, he sickened and died.
There came two serpents out of hell,
His soul therein to guide.

'Rise up, rise up, brother Diverus,
And come along with me.
There is a place prepared in hell,
For to sit upon a serpent's knee.'

185. *Jacob's Well*

At Jacob's well a stranger sought
His drooping frame to cheer,
Samaria's daughter little thought
That Jacob's God was near.

This had she known, her fainting mind
For richer draughts had sighed.
Nor had Messiah ever kind
Those richer draughts denied.

This ancient well, no glass so true
Britannia's image shows.
Now Jesus travels Britain through,
But who the stranger knows?

186. *Christchurch Bells*

Hark, the bonny Christchurch bells!
One, two, three, four, five, six;
They sound so sweet, so wondrous sweet,
They sound so merry, merry.

Hark, the first and second bell!
At every day goes four and ten,
Cries, 'Come, come come, come, come to prayer
Or the verger stoops before the dean.'

Ting a ling ling, goes the small bell of ten,
To call the bearers home;
There's never a man will lose his can
Till he hears the mighty Tom.

187. *The Man that Lives*

The man that lives must learn to die,
Christ will no longer stay.
Our time is short, death's near at hand
To take our lives away.

What are our lives that we must live
And what's our carcass then?
'Tis food for worms to feed upon,
Christ knows the time and when.

Our lives are like the grass, O Lord,
Like flowers in the field.
So welcome death, praise ye the Lord,
Willing I am to yield.

Now we must die and leave this world
Which we have lived in,
Nothing but our poor winding-sheet
To wrap our bodies in.

Happy the man that never swears
Against his living Lord,
And never took God's name in vain
At any trifling word.

When shall we see that happy heaven
That blessèd resting place
Where we like angels then shall feed
Upon God's royal grace.

The bitter plagues, the fiery hell
Where sinners they are slain,
His beast shall die, his sheep shall rot,
Cold clay shall be his grave.

Besides himself sickness shall have
No physic shall him cure,
We never shall live to see old age
Our lives shall not endure.

188. *Our Saviour's Love*

Here is a fountain of Christ's blood
Wide open set to drown our sins,
Where Christ stands with open arms
With mercy to invite you in.

For you will see his bleeding wounds
And hear him breathe forth dying groans.
He shed His rich redeeming blood
Only to do poor sinners good.

A crown of thorns, spit on with scorn,
His soul was pained and His flesh was torn,
With ragged nails through hands and feet
They nailed our rich Redeemer sweet.

When all His precious blood was spent,
The thunder roared, the rocks were rent.
The richness of His precious blood
Did open graves and raise the dead.

The sun and moon in mourning went,
The sea did roar and the temples rent.
The earth did quake and the clouds did tumble
Which made hell shake and devils tremble.

189. *The Dilly Song*

I'll sing you one O
  Green grow the rushes O
What is your one O?
  One is one and all alone
  And evermore shall be so.

[*rising one by one to*]

I'll sing you twelve O
  Green grow the rushes O
What is your twelve O?
Twelve for the twelve apostles,
Eleven for the eleven who went to heaven,
Ten for the ten commandments,
Nine for the nine bright shiners,
Eight for the eight bold rangers,
Seven for the seven stars in the sky,
Six for the six proud walkers,
Five for the symbol at your door,
Four for the Gospel makers,
Three for the rivals,
Two, two, the lily-white boys,
Clothèd all in green O,
One is one and all alone
And evermore shall be so.

190. *The New Dial*

In those twelve days let us be glad,
  For God of His power hath all things made.
What are they that are but one?
  What are they that are but one?
One God, one Baptism, and one Faith,
One Truth there is, the Scripture saith.

What are they that are but two?
Two Testaments, the old and new,
We do acknowledge to be true.

What are they that are but three?
Three Persons are in Trinity,
Which makes one God in unity.

What are they that are but four?
Four sweet Evangelists there are,
Christ's birth, life, death, which do declare.

What are they that are but five?
Five senses, like five kings, maintain
In every man a several reign.

What are they that are but six?
Six days to labour is not wrong,
For God himself did work so long.

What are they that are but seven?
Seven liberal arts hath God sent down,
With divine skill man's soul to crown.

What are they that are but eight?
Eight beatitudes are there given,
Use them right and go to heaven.

What are they that are but nine?
Nine Muses, like the heavens' nine spheres,
With sacred tunes entice our ears.

What are they that are but ten?
Ten statutes God to Moses gave,
Which, kept or broke, do spill or save.

What are they that are but eleven?
Eleven thousand virgins did partake,
And suffered death for Jesus' sake.

What are they that are but twelve?
Twelve are attending on God's Son;
Twelve make our Creed. The Dial's done.

191. *Down in the Forest*

Down in the forest there stands a hall
    The bells of Paradise, I heard them ring
Is covered all over with purple so tall
    And I love my Lord Jesus above anything.

In that high hall there stands a bed,
Is covered all over with scarlet and red.

All in that bed there lies a knight,
Whose wounds they do bleed with main and with might.

And under that bed there runs a flood,
The one half runs water, the other runs blood.

And at the foot's bed there lies a hound
A-licking the blood as it daily runs down.

All at the bed's head there flowers a thorn
Which never so blossomed since Jesus was born.

192. *The Truth from Above*

This is the truth sent from above,
The truth of God, the God of love,
Therefore don't turn me from your door,
But hearken all both rich and poor.

The first thing which I do relate
Is that God did man create;
The next thing which to you I'll tell—
Woman was made with man to dwell.

And we were heirs to endless woes,
Till God the Lord did interpose;
And so a promise soon did run
That he would redeem us by His Son.

And at that season of the year
Our blest Redeemer did appear;
He here did live, and here did preach,
And many thousands did He teach.

Thus he in love to us behaved,
To show us how we must be saved;
And if you want to know the way,
Be pleased to hear what He did say.

193. *The Moon Shines Bright*

The moon shines bright and the stars give a light
A little before it was day.
What our Lord God has suffered on the cross
For us whom He loved so dear.

The life of a man it is but a span,
It's like a morning flower;
We're here today, tomorrow we're gone,
We're dead all in one hour.

Oh teach them well your children, dear man,
While you have got them here.
It will be better for your soul, dear man,
When your corpse lays on the bier.

Today you may be living, dear man,
With a many thousand pound;
Tomorrow you may be dead, dear man,
And your corpse lay under the ground.

With the green turf at your head, dear man,
And another at your feet,
Your good deeds and your bad, dear man,
Will all together meet.

My song is done and I must be gone,
No longer can I stay here.
God bless you all, both great and small,
And send you a happy new year.

194. *The Carnal and the Crane*

As I passed by a riverside,
And there as I did rein,
In argument I chanced to hear
A carnal and a crane.

The carnal said unto the crane,
'If all the world should turn,
Before we had the Father,
But now we have the Son.

'From whence does the Son come?
From where and from what place?'
He said, 'In a manger,
Between an ox and ass.'

'Pray thee,' said the carnal,
'Tell me before thou go,
Was not the mother of Jesus
Conceived by the Holy Ghost?'

'She was the purest virgin,
And the cleanest from sin;
She was the handmaid of our Lord,
And mother of our King.'

'Where is the golden cradle
That Christ was rockèd in?
Where are the silken sheets
That Jesus was wrapped in?'

'A manger was the cradle
That Christ was rockèd in
The provender the asses left
So sweetly he slept on.'

carnal] crow

195. *The Cherry-tree Carol*

Joseph was an old man,
And an old man was he,
And he married Mary,
The Queen of Galilee.

When Joseph was married
And Mary home had brought,
Mary proved with child,
And Joseph knew it not.

Joseph and Mary walked
Through a garden gay,
Where the cherries they grew
Upon every tree.

Oh then bespoke Mary,
With words both meek and mild,
'Oh gather me cherries, Joseph,
They run so in my mind.'

And then replied Joseph
With words so unkind,
'Let him gather thee cherries
That got thee with child.'

Oh then bespoke our Saviour
All in his mother's womb,
'Bow down, good cherry-tree,
To my mother's hand.'

The uppermost sprig
Bowed down to Mary's knee:
'Thus you may see, Joseph,
These cherries are for me.'

'Oh eat your cherries, Mary,
Oh eat your cherries now;
Oh eat your cherries, Mary,
That grow upon the bough.'

As Joseph was a-walking,
He heard an angel sing:
'This night shall be born
Our heavenly King.

'He neither shall be born
In housen or in hall,
Nor in the place of paradise,
But in an ox's stall.

'He neither shall be clothèd
In purple nor in pall,
But all in fair linen,
As were babies all.

'He neither shall be rockèd
In silver nor in gold,
But in a wooden cradle
That rocks upon the mould.

'He neither shall be christened
In white wine nor red,
But with fair spring water
With which we were christened.'

Then Mary took her young son
And set him on her knee:
'I pray thee now, dear child,
Tell how this world shall be.'

'Oh I shall be as dead, mother,
As the stones in the wall;
Oh the stones in the street, mother,
Shall mourn for me all.

'And on a Wednesday
My vow I will make,
And upon Good Friday
My death I will take.

'Upon Easter-day, mother,
My rising shall be;
Oh the sun and the moon
Shall uprise with me.

'The people shall rejoice,
And the birds they shall sing,
To see the uprising
Of the heavenly King.'

196. *The Virgin Unspotted*

The virgin unspotted the prophets foretold
To bring forth our Saviour which now you behold,
To be our Redeemer from death, hell and sin
Which Adam's transgression involved us in.

Then let us be merry, cast sorrow away,
Our Saviour Christ Jesus is born on this day.

Then presently after the shepherds did spy
Vast numbers of angels for to stand in the sky.
How happy they conversed, most sweetly they sang,
Glory and praise to her heavenly Son.

Through Bethlehem's city in Judah it was
Where Joseph and Mary together did pass,
And then to be taxèd which then they came,
Since Caesar Augustus commanded the same.

Mary's full time is come as you find,
She brought forth her first-born to save all mankind.
The inn being so full for this heavenly guest,
No place could be found for to lay him at rest.

The manger being his cradle where oxen did feed
Was the great God of mercy which proved our redeem.

197. *The Holly and the Ivy*

The holly and the ivy
Are plants that are well known
Of all the trees that grow in the woods
The holly bears the crown.

The rising of the sun
And the running of the deer,
The playing of the merry organ,
Sweet singing in the choir.

Its head it points to heaven
And shows its berries red
In token of the drops of blood
Which on Calvary were shed.

And in the holly prickles
You can plainly see
The crown of thorns our Saviour wore
When going up to Calvary.

And although up in heaven
His love can still be seen
In the holly colour,
The everlasting green.

198. *Christmas Now is Drawing Near*

Now Christmas Day is drawing near at hand,
Pray serve the Lord and be at His command.
Oh for our portion God he will provide
And give a blessing to our souls beside.

Can you remember that man he was made of clay?
All in this world we have not got long to stay.
This wicked world will never give content
With all the blessings which our Lord God sent.

Down in the garden where flowers grow by ranks
Down on your knees and 'turn the Lord God thanks;
Down on your knees, and pray both night and day
And leave off sin and leave off pride, I say.

So proud and lofty do some people go,
They've dressed themselves like puppets in a show;
They'll paste, they'll paint and dress with the idol stuff
As though God had not made them fine enough.

Come, come, Lord God, pray take me for your own,
Come, Jesus Christ, receive me to Thy throne.
Come, Holy Ghost, and cede it for us all
And crown my soul with the higher Trinity.

199. *On Christmas Day*

On Christmas Day it happened so,
Down in those meadows for to plough,
As he was ploughing all on so fast,
Up came sweet Jesus himself at last.

'O man, O man, why dost thou plough
So hard upon Our Lord's birthday?'
The farmer answered him with great speed,
'For to plough this day I have got need.'

Now his arms did quaver through and through,
His arms did quaver, he could not plough,
For the ground did open and lose him in,
Before he could repent of sin.

His wife and children's out of place,
His beasts and cattle they're almost lost,
His beasts and cattle they die away,
For ploughing on old Christmas Day.
His beasts and cattle they die away,
For ploughing on Our Lord's birthday.

200. *Softly the Night*

Softly the night is sleeping on Bethlehem's peaceful hill,
Silent the shepherds watching their gentle flocks are still.
But hark the wondrous music falls from the opening sky,
Valley and cliff re-echo glory to God on high.
Glory to God it rings again,
Peace on the earth, goodwill to men.

Come with the gladsome shepherds quick hastening from the fold,
Come with the wise men bringing incense and myrrh and gold,
Come to him poor and lowly all round the cradle throng,
Come with our hearts of sunshine and sing the angels' song.
Glory to God tell out again,
Peace on the earth, goodwill to men.

Wave ye the wreath unfading, the fir tree and the pine,
Green from the snows of winter to deck the holy shrine;
Bring ye the happy children for this is Christmas morn,
Jesus the sinless infant, Jesus the Lord is born.
Glory to God, to God again,
Peace on the earth, goodwill to men.

201. *New Year's Carol*

Awake, awake, ye drowsy souls,
And hear what I shall tell.
Remember Christ the Lamb of God
Redeemed our souls from hell.
He's crowned with thorns, spit on with scorn,
The Jews have hid themselves.
So God send you all in a joyful New Year.

They bound Christ's body to a tree
And wounded him full sore;
From every wound the blood ran down
Till Christ could bleed no more.
His dying wounds they rent and tore
All covered with pearly gore.

Then Jesus He called to Thomas
And bid him come and see,
And thrust thy fingers in My wounds
Which are in My body,
And be not faithless but believe,
And happy you shall be.

Then Jesus called His disciples
And tried them over death.

He said, 'All power shall be given to you
In heaven and on earth
Go forth and teach all nations
Despising you of your rest.

'Go seek every wandering sheep
As far as earth remains
Till I Myself have paid your debts
And turned you back again.
Come all you heavy laden
I'll ease you of your pain.'

202. *May Song*

A branch of may, it does look gay,
As before your door it stands;
It is but a sprout, but it's well spread about,
By the work of our poor hands.

I have a bag upon my arm,
It is drawn with a silken string;
It only wants a few more pence
To line it well within.

Arise, arise, my pretty fair maids,
And take our may bush in,
For if it is gone before morning comes
You'll say we have never been.

Come give us a jug of your sweet cream,
Or a jug of your brown beer,
And if we live to tarry the town,
We'll call another year.

203. *May Carol*

Awake, awake, good people all,
Awake and you shall hear
That Christ has died for our sins
For He loved us so dear.

243

So dearly, so dearly has Christ loved us
And for our sins was slain;
Christ bids us leave off our wickedness
And turn to the Lord again.

The early cock so early crows,
That is passing the night away,
For the trumpet shall sound and the dead shall be raised,
Lord, at the great judgment day.

A branch of may I have brought to you,
And at your door it stands;
It is but a sprout, but it's well budded out
By the work of our Lord's hands.

Now my song, that is done, and I must be gone,
No longer can I stay;
So God bless you all, both great and small,
And I wish you a joyful May.

204. *Thames Head Wassailers' Song*

Wassail, wassail, all over the town,
Our toast is white and our ale is brown,
Our bowl it is made of a maplin tree,
And so is good beer of the best barley.

Here's to the ox and to his long horn;
May God send our master a crop of good corn.
A crop of good corn, and another of hay,
To pass the cold wintry nights away.

Here's to the ox and to his right ear;
May God send our master a happy New Year.
A happy New Year, as we all may see,
With our wassailing bowl we will drink unto thee.

Here's to old Jerry and to her right eye;
May God send our mistress a good Christmas pie.
A good Christmas pie, as we all may see,
And a wassailing bowl we will drink unto thee.

Here's to old Boxer and to his long tail;
I hope that our master'll have ne'er a horse fail.
Ne'er a horse fail, as we all may see,
And a wassailing bowl we will drink unto thee.

Come pretty maidens—I suppose there are some!
Never let us poor young men stand on the cold stone;
The stones they are cold and our shoes they are thin,
The fairest maid in the house let us come in.
Let us come in and see how you do.

Here's to the maid and the rosemary tree,
The ribbons are wanted, and that you can see;
The ribbons are wanted, and that you can see,
With our wassailing bowl we will drink unto thee.

Now, bottler, come fill us a bowl of the best,
And we hope that thy soul in heaven may rest.
But if you do bring us a bowl of the small,
Then down shall go bottler, bowl and all,
Bowl and all, bowl and all,
Then down shall go bottler, bowl and all.

Now, master and mistress, if you are within,
Send down some of your merry, merry men,
That we may eat and drink before the clock strikes ten,
Our jolly wassail,
When joy comes to our jolly wassail.

205. *Gloucestershire Wassail*

Wassail, wassail, all over the town!
Our toast it is white and our ale it is brown.
Our bowl it is made of the white maple tree;
With the wassailing bowl we'll drink to thee.

So here is to Cherry and to his right cheek;
Pray God send our master a piece of good beef,
And a piece of good beef that may we all see;
With the wassailing bowl we'll drink to thee.

And here is to Dobbin and to his right eye;
Pray God send our master a good Christmas pie,
And a good Christmas pie that may we all see;
With our wassailing bowl we'll drink to thee.

So here is to Broad May and to her broad horn;
May God send our master a good crop of corn,
And a good crop of corn that may we all see;
With our wassailing bowl we'll drink to thee.

And here is to Filpail and to her left ear;
Pray God send our master a happy New Year,
And a happy New Year as e'er he did see;
With our wassailing bowl we'll drink to thee.

And here is to Colly and to her long tail;
Pray God send our master that never may fail
A bowl of strong beer; I pray you draw near
And our jolly wassail it's then you shall hear.

Come, butler, come fill us a bowl of the best,
Then we hope that your soul in heaven may rest;
But if you do draw us a bowl of the small,
Then down shall go butler, bowl and all.

Then here's to the maid in the lily-white smock,
Who tripped to the door and slipped back the lock,
Who tripped to the door and pulled back the pin,
For to let these jolly wassailers in.

206. *Somerset Wassail*

Wassail and wassail, all over the town,
The cup it is white and the ale it is brown;
The cup it is made of the good ashen tree,
And so is the malt of the best barley.

For it's your wassail, and it's our wassail,
And it's joy be to you, and a jolly wassail.

O master and missus, are you all within?
Pray open the door and let us come in;
O master and missus a-sitting by the fire,
Pray think upon poor travellers, a-travelling in the mire.

Oh where is the maid, with the silver-headed pin,
To open the door and let us come in;
O master and missus, it is our desire,
A good loaf and cheese, and a toast by the fire.

There was an old man and he had an old cow,
And how for to keep her he didn't know how;
He built up a barn for to keep his cow warm,
And a drop or two of cider will do us no harm.

No harm, boys, harm; no harm, boys, harm;
And a drop or two of cider will do us no harm.

The girt dog of Langport he burnt his long tail,
And this is the night we go singing wassail;
O master and missus, now we must be gone;
God bless all in this house till we do come again.

207. *Apple Wassail*

Here stands a good old apple tree,
Stand fast root, stand fast bough,
Every little twig bears an apple big,
Every little bough bears an apple now.
   Hatful, capful, pocketful, lapful,
   Holla, boys, holla, hip hip hurrah!

208. *Bee Wassail*

Bees, bees of paradise,
Do the work of Jesus Christ,
Do the work that no man can.

God made bees,
Bees make honey,
God made men,
Men make money,
God made men
To harrow and to plough,
And God made the little boy
To holla off the crow.
   Holla, boys, holla, hip hip hurrah!

209. *Souling Song*

God bless the master of this house
And the good missus too,
And all the little children
That about the table go.

Go bless your man and maiden,
Your cattle and your store,
And all that is within your gates
I wish you ten times more.

Your pockets lined with silver,
Your barrels full of beer,
Your pantry full of pork pies,
I wish I had some here.

Your streets are very dirty,
The night is very cold,
And this night to come a-souling
We do make bold.

The roads are very dirty,
My shoes are very thin,
I've got a little pocket
To put a penny in.

Go down into your cellar
And see what you can find;
The barrel is not empty,
I hope you will prove kind.

I hope you will prove kind
With your apples and strong beer,
And we'll come no more a-souling
Till this time next year.

The Country Year

210. *The Cuckoo*

The cuckoo is a merry bird,
He sings as he flies,
He brings us glad tidings
And tells us no lies.

He sucks the birds' eggs
To make his voice clear,
And the more he cries 'Cuckoo'
The summer draws near.

The cuckoo is a lazy bird,
She never builds a nest,
She makes herself busy
By singing to the rest.

She never hatches her own young,
And that we all know,
But leaves it for some other bird
While she cries 'Cuckoo.'

And when her time is come
Her voice we no longer hear,
And where she goes we do not know
Until another year.

The cuckoo comes in April,
She sings a song in May,
In June she beats upon the drum,
And then she'll fly away.

beats upon the drum] When the cuckoo omits the last syllable of its call, singing 'Cuck-cuck', it is said to 'beat the drum'. It is believed to be a sign of impending departure.

211. *John Barleycorn*

There were three men came out of the west,
Their fortune for to try,
And these three men made a solemn vow,
John Barleycorn should die.
They ploughed, they sowed, they harrowed him in,
Throwed clods upon his head,
And these three men made a solemn vow,
John Barleycorn was dead.

Then they let him lie for a very long time
Till the rain from heaven did fall,
Then little Sir John sprung up his head,
And soon amazed them all.
They let him stand till midsummer
Till he looked both pale and wan,
And little Sir John he growed a long beard
And so became a man.

They hired men with the scythes so sharp
To cut him off at the knee,
They rolled him and tied him by the waist
And served him most barbarously.
They hired men with the sharp pitchforks
Who pricked him to the heart,
And the loader he served him worse than that,
For he bound him to the cart.

They wheeled him round and round the field
Till they came unto a barn,
And there they made a solemn mow
Of poor John Barleycorn.
They hired men with the crabtree sticks
To cut him skin from bone,
And the miller he served him worse than that,
For he ground him between two stones.

Here's little Sir John in a nut-brown bowl,
Here's brandy in a glass;
And little Sir John in the nut-brown bowl
Proved the stronger man at last.

And the huntsman he can't hunt the fox,
Nor so loudly blow his horn,
And the tinker he can't mend kettles or pots
Without a little of Barleycorn.

212. *What's the Life of a Man?*

As I was walking one morn at my ease,
A-viewing the leaves as they fell from the trees,
Their rolling full motion appeared fine and gay,
Like the leaf they must wither and soon fade away.

What's the life of a man any more than a leaf,
For the man has a season and why should he grieve?
Below in the wide world he appears fine and gay,
Like the leaf he must wither and soon fade away.

If you seen the green leaves a short time ago,
A rolling full motion appearing to grow;
But the frost came upon them and withered them all;
Like the leaf he must wither and down he must fall.

If you look in the churchyard many names there you'll see,
They went from this world like a leaf from a tree.
Afflicted and wounded at last they must fall;
Like the green life it did wither and down it did fall.

213. *A Sweet Country Life*

A sweet country life is most pleasant and charming,
All for to walk abroad on a fine summer's morning,
Bright Phoebus did a-shine and the hills was adorning
As Molly she sat milking on a fair summer's morning.

No fiddle, no flute, no hautboy nor spinet
Is not to be compared to the lark or the linnet.
Down as I did lie all among the green rushes
'Twas there I did hear the charms of the blackbirds and thrushes.

214. *The North Country Maid*

A north country maid up to London had strayed
Although with her nature it did not agree.
She sobbed and she sighed and she bitterly cried,
How I wish once again in the north I could be,
Where the oak and the ash and the bonny rowan tree
Are all growing green in my north country.

As sadly I roam, I remember my home
Where lads and young lasses are making the hay,
Where the birds sweetly sing and the merry bells ring
And the maidens and meadows are pleasant and gay,
Where the oak and the ash and the bonny rowan tree
Are all growing green in my north country.

No doubt should I please I could marry with ease,
Where maidens are fair many lovers will come,
But he whom I wed must be north country bred
And carry me back to my north country home,
Where the oak and the ash and the bonny rowan tree
Are all growing green in my north country.

215. *Lace Tell*

Nineteen long lines hanging over my door
The faster I work it will shorten my score
But when I do play it will stand at my stay
So my little finger must twink it away
For after tomorrow comes my wedding day
My shoes are to borrow, my husband to seek
For I cannot get married till after next week
And after next week it will be all my care
To pink and to curl and to do up my hair
Six pretty maidens so neat and so clean
Shall dance at my wedding next Monday morning
Down in the kitchen the cook she will run
And tell Mr Bellman to ring the ting tang

I'll tell father when father comes home
What a day's work my mother has done
She's earned a penny, she's spent a crown
She's burnt a great hole in her holiday gown
She's earned a penny, she's spent a groat
She's burnt a great hole in her holiday coat
Father came home in an angry fit
And swore a pottle loaf should last us a week
He cut himself up into wee little bits
I all the time wonder at his naughty tricks
Father whipped mother and mother whipped me
So there was such a racket you seldom do see
Then mother she sent me a long way from home
She sent me to go by the beats of the drum
The beats of the drum and sweet music did play
For that was my grandmother's grand wedding day
The miller was driving his waggon along
The trees were in blossom, the nuts were so brown
They hang so ripe they won't come down
You buy plums, I'll buy flour
We'll have a pudding in half an hour.

216. 'A-begging buttermilk I will go'

A-begging buttermilk I will go,
I know I shan't be a beggar long,
For there's an old woman at yonder farm
Will give me plenty if I ask for some.

I'll sell it all for one pennee,
Fol the lol the laddle dee,
And with that penny I will buy eggs,
And I shall have seven for my pennee.

I'll set my seven eggs under a hen,
If cocks then they should chance to be,
I'll make seven young gamesters out of them,
And there will be seven half-crowns for me.

There will be seven half-crowns for me,
Fol the lol the laddle dee,
And with that money I will buy land,
All with my single, one pennee.

As this young boy was going along
Under a stony wall,
He hitched his foot against a stone,
And down came buttermilk, pitcher and all.

Then this poor boy got up again,
His lands and livings then were stretched,
And his mother made him this reply,
'Thou'st reckoned thy chickens before they were hatched.'

217. *The Nobleman and Thresherman*

A nobleman lived in a valley of late,
Who met a poor thresherman whose family was great.
'I say thou'st got seven children, I find it to be true.
How dost thou maintain them as well as thou do?'

'Sometimes I do reap and sometimes I do mow,
Sometimes out a-hedging and ditching I do go.
There's nothing comes amiss from the harrow to the plough
That I have got to get my bread by the sweatings of my brow.

'Although the times are bad and we are very poor
We can scarcely keep the raging wolf from the door.
My wife she is willing to join in my yoke
And live like turtle doves and never do provoke.'

'Now since thou hast spoken so well of thy wife,
I'll provide for thee all the days of my life.
Here's fifty acres of good land I'll freely give to thee,
To maintain thy wife and thy loving family.'

218. *Good Company*

When I sit by myself at the close of the day,
And watch the blue twilight turn amber and grey,
With fancies as twinkling and vague as the stars,
And as distant as they from this life's petty jars—
I know not, I think not where fortune may be,
But I feel I am in very good company.

When I sit with a friend at the glow of the hearth,
And fight some great battle of wisdom or mirth,
And strike from our armour the sparkle of wit,
That follows the shafts of our thoughts when they hit—
I know not, I think not where fortune may be,
But I feel I am in very good company.

When I sit with my darling who loves me so well,
And read in her eyes what no language can tell,
Or trace on her lips, free as cherubs' from guile,
The meanings and mysteries hid in a smile—
I know not, I think not where fortune may be,
But I feel I am in very good company.

219. *How Happy the Man*

How happy the man that is free from all care,
That loves to make merry o'er a pot of strong beer;
With his pipe and his friend passing hours away,
Singing song after song till he hail the new day.

How happy this isle, that is doubly blest
With meat that's delightful, and drink of the best!
We live free from control, and are blest with great store,
For we have what we want. What can mortals have more?

Our soldiers are bold, they fear not the foe;
Our sailors are valiant, which our enemies know;
They are feared in each clime, they're the dread of each shore
When the trumpet shall sound and the loud cannons roar.

But since we enjoy such blessings divine,
We'll throw off all discord, and to mirth we'll incline;
We'll drink and we'll sing, passing hours away,
And sing song after song till we hail the new day.

220. *The Beggar*

I've sixpence in my pocket and I've worked hard for it,
Kind landlord, here it is.
Never a Jew nor a Turk shall make me work
While begging is as good as it is.

> *Let the back and sides go bare, my boys,*
> *Let the hands and feet go cold.*
> *We'll give to the belly, boys, beer enough*
> *Whether it be new or old.*

I went up to some nobleman's gate
Begging for bread and beer;
Some were lame and some were blind
And some they could not hear.

221. *Now We've Met*

Now we've met let's merry, merry be,
In spite of all our foes,
And he that will not merry be
We'll pull him by the nose.

> *Let him be merry, merry there,*
> *Whilst we are merry, merry here,*
> *For who can go where we shall go*
> *To be merry another year.*

He that will not merry, merry be,
With a generous bowl and toast,
May he in Bridewell be shut up,
Fast bound unto a post.

He that will not merry, merry be
In the company of jolly boys,
May he be plagued with a scolding wife
To confound him with her noise.

He that will not merry, merry be,
And take his glass in course,
May he be obliged to drink small beer,
Never a penny in his purse.

He that will not merry, merry be
With his sweetheart by his side,
May he be laid in the cold churchyard,
With a headstone for his bride.

222. *The Dunmow Flitch of Bacon*

Come all you married couples gay,
Get up before the break of day,
To Dunmow then pray haste away,
To gain the flitch of bacon.
There is such pleasure, mirth and glee,
The married folks will have a spree,
They'll try for love and victory
And the Dunmow flitch of bacon.

> *So lads and lasses haste away,*
> *And do not make the least delay,*
> *And to Dunmow town pray haste away,*
> *And carry off the bacon.*

There's special trains for distant parts,
Young and old, with joyful hearts,
In coaches, gigs and donkey carts,
Have come to the flitch of bacon.

Sound the trumpets, beat the drums,
See how the lads and lasses run,
To Burton's meadow they have come
To view the flitch of bacon.

THE COUNTRY YEAR

A man and wife must married be
Just a twelvemonth and a day,
And never have a quarrel they say
To get the flitch of bacon.
And when they gain the prize, we hear,
They'll carry them round the town on a chair,
And give them many a lusty cheer,
And show the flitch of bacon.

There's a grand procession through the town,
And Mr Smith, he has come down,
We'll drink his health in glasses round—
Success to the flitch of bacon.
Young men and maids like summer bees,
We'll roam beneath the shady trees.
Come marry me quick now, if you please,
And next year we'll get the bacon.

Some will laugh, and some will shout,
Some on the grass will roll about,
While smart young men, without a doubt,
Will dance with the pretty ladies.
Bands of music sweetly play,
Smart young men and maidens gay,
To Burton's meadow they will stray
To talk of the flitch of bacon.

The velocipedes will races run,
The fight with clowns will cause some fun,
And maypole dancing will be done,
To please the folks of Dunmow.
There's Punch and Judy, all so gay,
The clowns they will at cricket play,
To the circus the folks will haste away,
To see Bluebeard at Dunmow!

Now when the sport it is all done,
And the flitch of bacon carried home,
Some scores will to the pop-shop run,
With bolsters, quilts and blankets;
Coats and waistcoats, gowns and shawls,
Shirts, chignons and parasols,
Will have to go to the golden balls
To pay for the spree at Dunmow.

So now to finish up my lay,
Take my advice, young ladies gay,
Get married now without delay,
And try for the flitch of bacon,
For the Essex ladies they are so sly,
And you had better mind your eye,
Or next year you may have a girl or a boy
Marked with a flitch of bacon!

223. *Ground for the Floor*

I lived in a wood for a number of years
With my dog and my gun for to drive away all fears;
I've a neat little cottage and the roof it is secure,
And if you look underneath you'll find ground for the floor.

Ground for the floor, ground for the floor,
I've a neat little cottage and it's ground for the floor.

My cottage is surrounded with brambles and thorn,
And so sweet are the notes of the birds in the morn;
It's a neat little cottage, and the roof it is secure,
And if you look underneath you'll find ground for the floor.

As for grate I have none, for my fire's on the ground,
As for chairs I have none, for to sit myself down;
I've a three-legged stool, that's my chiefest of store,
And a neat little cottage that's ground for the floor.

My bed is made of straw, my poor limbs to repose,
I've nothing to cover me, or to keep me from the cold,
But I've a guinea in my pocket, and many others in store,
And a neat little cottage that's ground for the floor.

God bless my old father, he's dead and he's gone,
I hope he's safe in heaven, and never to return;
He's left me all his riches that he heaped in store,
And a neat little cottage that's ground for the floor.

224. *Country Statutes*

Come all you lads of high renown and listen to my story,
For now the time is coming on that is all to your glory;
For Jumping Joan is coming here the statutes to admire,
To see the lads and lasses standing waiting to be hired.

> *So to the hirings we have come, all for to look for places,*
> *If with the master we agree and he will give good wages.*

The master that a servant wants will now stand in a wonder;
You all must ask ten pounds a year and none of you go under.
It's you that must do all the work, and what they do require,
So now stand up for wages, lads, before that you do hire.

There's rolling Gin the hemp will spin and Sal will mind the dairy,
And John will kiss his mistress when the master he is weary.
There's Tom and Joe will reap and mow; they'll thrash and ne'er be
    tired;
They'll load the cart and do their part, so they're the lads to hire.

There's carter John with whip so long rises early in the morn;
He's always ready at his work before daylight can dawn.
Hey up, gee wo, the plough must go, till he is very weary,
But a jug of ale both stout and stale it soon will make him merry.

There's Poll so red will make the bread, likewise good cheese and
    butter,
And Bet so thick will spread the rick, she's never in a flutter.
She'll feed the sows and milk the cows and do what she is able;
Although she's mean she's neat and clean, when waiting at the table.

There's black-eyed Fan with the frying pan will cook your eggs and
    bacon,
With beef and mutton, roast and boiled, if I am not mistaken.
She'll make the puddings fat and good, all ready for your dinner,
But if you grumble when she's done she'll cure you with the skimmer.

The farmer's wife so full of pride must have a lady's maid,
All for to dress and curl her hair and powder it beside;
But the girl of heart to dress so smart, they call her charming Nancy,
She can wink and blink in such a style, she's all the young men's
    fancy.

And when the mop it is all o'er, you that are young and hearty
Must take your girl all in your hand and join a drinking party;
But when you are returning home, enjoying sweet embraces,
With love and honour spend the night at statutes, fairs and races.

225. *Country Hirings*

Come all you blooming country lads and listen unto me,
And if I do but tell the truth I know you will agree.
It's of the jolly farmers who servants want to have,
For to maintain them in their pride and to be to them a slave.

    Servant men, stand up for your wages
    When to the hirings you do go,
    For you must work all sorts of weather,
    Both cold and wet and snow.

While the farmer and his wife in bed so snug and warm can lie,
But you must face the weather both cold, wet or dry;
For the rates they are so heavy and the taxes they are high,
So we must pull the wages down, the farmers they do cry.

The farmers twenty years ago their rates and taxes pay,
But now they are so full of pride and increase every day,
Which makes the landlords raise the rent and the farmers for to scold
On the poor young servant lads and rob them of their gold.

The farmers and the servants together used to dine,
But now they're in the parlour with their pudding, beer and wine.
The master and the mistress, their sons and daughters all alone,
They will eat the meat and you may pick the bones.

The farmers' daughters they used to dress so neat and clean and
    brown,
And now with bustles, frills, and furbelows and flounces to their
    gowns,
They go dressed like dandy Bess, more fitted for the stage,
Which cause the farmers' rent to rise and put them in a rage.

The description of your living I am sure it is the worse,
For the pottage it is thin and the bread is very coarse,
While the masters they do live as you shall understand
On butter and good cheese and the fat from the land.

A roasted goose for dinner, likewise a leg of lamb,
With soups and potatoes and everything that's grand,
While servants in the kitchen they do both sport and play,
Speaking about the fun they'll get on the hiring day.

But I could tell you of a better plan without any fears or doubts,
If you would only kiss the mistress when the master he is out,
You may kiss her, you may squeeze her, you may roll her round about
And then she would find you better grub without any fear or doubt.

> *So good lads, stand out for your wages*
> *When to the hirings you do go,*
> *For you will have to stand all sorts of weather*
> *Both cold, wet and snow.*

226. *The Farmer's Boy*

The sun went down behind yon hill,
Across yon dreary moor,
Weary and lame a poor boy came
Up to a farmer's door.
'Can you tell me if any there is
That will give me employ,
For to plough and sow,
To reap and mow,
And to be a farmer's boy,
To be a farmer's boy.

'For my father's dead, and mother's left
With her five children small;
And what is worse for mother still,
I'm the eldest of them all.
Though little I be, I fear no work
If you will me employ,
For to plough and sow,
To reap and mow,
And to be a farmer's boy,
To be a farmer's boy.

'And if that you won't me employ,
One favour I have to ask:
Will you shelter me till break of day
From this cold winter's blast?
At break of day I'll trudge away
Elsewhere to seek employ,
For to plough and sow,
To reap and mow,
And be a farmer's boy,
To be a farmer's boy.'

The farmer said, 'Pray, take the lad,
No further let him seek.'
'Oh yes, dear father,' the daughter cried,
While the tears ran down her cheek;
'For those that will work it's hard to want
And wander for employ,
To plough and sow,
To reap and mow,
And to be a farmer's boy,
To be a farmer's boy.'

In course of time he grew a man,
And the good old farmer died;
He left the lad the farm he had,
And his daughter for his bride.
So the boy that was now farmer is;
He sits and thinks with joy
Of the lucky, lucky day he came that way
To be a farmer's boy,
To be a farmer's boy.

227. *A Lincolnshire Shepherd*

Yan, tan, tethera, tethera, pethera, pimp
Yon owd yowe's far-welted, and this yowe's got a limp.
Sethera, methera, hovera, and cover-a up to dik,
Aye, we can deal wi' them all, and where's me crook and stick.

I count 'em up to figgits, and figgits have a notch—
There's more to being a shepherd than being on watch;
There's swedes to chop and lambing time and snow upon the rick,
Sethera, methera, hovera, and cover-a up to dik.

From Caistor down to Spilsby, from Sleaford up to Brigg,
There's Lincoln sheep all on the chalk, all hung wi' wool and big.
And I, here in Langton wi' this same old flock,
Just as me grandad did afore they meddled wi' the clock.

We've bred our tups and gimmers for wool and length and girth,
And sheep have lambed, have gone away all o'er all the earth.
They're bred in foreign flocks to give the wool its length and crimp,
Yan, tan, tethera, pethera, pimp.

They're like a lot of bairns, they are, like children of me own,
They fondle round about owd Shep afore they're strong and grown;
But they gets independent-like, before you know, they've gone.
But yet again, next lambing time, we'll 'a' more to carry on.

Yan, tan, tethera, pethera, pimp,
Fifteen notches up to now and one yowe with a limp.
You reckons I should go away, you know I'll never go,
For lambing time's on top of us, and it'll surely snow.

Well, one day I'll leave me yowes, I'll leave me yowes for good,
And then you'll know what breeding is in flocks and human blood;
For our Tom's come out o' t'army, his face as red as brick,
Sethera, methera, hovera, and cover-a up to dik.

Yan, tan, etc] see Notes and References   yowe] ewe
far-welted] on its back   tups and gimmers] young male and female sheep

Now lambing time comes reg'lar-like, just as it's always been,
And shepherds have to winter 'em and tent 'em till they're weaned.
My fambly had it 'fore I came, they'll have it when I sleep,
So we can count our lambing times as I am counting sheep.

228. *Sheep Shearing*

How delightful to see
In those evenings of spring
When the sheep are a-going to the fold,
The master do sing
As he goes on his way
And the dog goes before them when told.

The sixth month of the year
In the month called June,
When the weather's too hot to be borne,
The master doth say
As he goes on his way,
Tomorrow my sheep shall be shorn.

Now as for those sheep,
They're delightful to see,
They're a blessing to man on his farm;
It's the best of all food,
For their flesh it is good,
And the wool it will clothe us up warm.

Now the sheep they're all shorn
And the wool carried home.
Here's a health to our master and flock,
And if we should stay
Till we all goes away,
I'm afraid 'twill be past twelve o'clock.

tent] tend

229. *All Jolly Fellows that Follow the Plough*

'Twas early one morning by the break of the day,
The cocks were a-crowing, the farmer did say,
'Now arise, my good fellows, now arise with good will,
Your horses are empty, their bellies to fill.'

So we jumped out of bed and put on our clothes,
And away to the stable so nimble we goes,
A-rubbing and a-scrubbing; I declare and I'll vow
We're all jolly fellows that follow the plough.

When six o'clock came we to breakfast did go
With a good bread and cheese and a burst of stingo,
Besides fill our pockets; I declare and I'll vow
We're all jolly fellows that follow the plough.

So we harness our horses and to plough we did go
With our hands in our pockets like a gentleman go.
When four o'clock came, our master came round,
Saying, 'What have you been doing this long summer's day?
You've not ploughed an acre, I'll declare and I'll vow,
You're all idle fellows that follow the plough.'

The boy turned round and made his reply:
'O master, O master, what have you been saying?
What have you been saying? It is a big lie,
For we ploughed more than an acre, I'll declare and I'll vow,
We're all jolly fellows that follow the plough.'

The master turned round with a smile and a joke:
''Tis half-past four o'clock, boys, 'tis time to unyoke.
Unharness your horses and rub them down well,
And I'll give you a jug of the best of brown ale.'

230. *Once I Was a Shepherd Boy*

Oh once I was a shepherd boy,
Kept sheep on Compton Down,
'Twas about two miles from Illesley,
It was called a market town.

> *With my fol de rol, a the riddle oddy O*
> *With my fol de rol i day.*

And in the morn when we do rise,
When daylight do appear,
Our breakfast we do get,
To our fold we all do steer.

And when we gets to our sheepfold,
We merrily pitched him round
And all the rest part of the day
We sailed the downs all round.

When we gets up on the down,
Gazing ourselves all round,
We see the storm is rising
And coming on all round.

And now the storm is coming on,
The rain fast down do fall,
Neither limb nor tree to shelter me,
I must stand and take it all.

And there we stood in our wet clothes,
A-shining and shaking with cold.
We dare not go to shift ourselves
Till we drive our sheep to fold.

And when the storm is over
And that you may plainly see,
I'll never keep sheep on the down any more,
For there's neither a limb nor a tree.

231. *The Jolly Waggoner*

When first I went a waggoner,
A waggoner I'd go,
I bear my aged parents' hearts
With sorrow, grief and woe.
And many are the hardships
That we have been through.

  And sing wo, my lads, sing wo,
  Drive on the waggons O,
  There's none can lead the life
  Like the jolly waggoner do.

Now summer it is come
What pleasures we shall see;
The small birds are singing
On every green tree,
The blackbirds and thrushes
Are whistling in the grove.

It's a cold stormy night,
We got wet through our clothes;
We'll bear it with contentment
Until we reach the inn,
And then we will get drinking
With the landlord and his friends.

Now Michaelmas is coming,
What pleasure we shall find;
We'll make the gold to fly, my boys,
Like chaff before the wind.
And many a lad will take his lass
And sit her on his knee.

232. *The Husbandman and Serving-man*

'Well met, well met, my friend, all on the highway riding
So simply all alone.
I pray come tell to me what may your calling be,
Are you some serving-man?'
'Oh no, my brother dear, what makes you to inquire
Of any such thing at my hand?
Indeed I'll not refrain but I will tell you plain,
I am a downright husbandman.'

'If a husbandman you be, pray come along with me
And instantly out of hand.
All in a little space I will help you to some place
Where you shall be a serving-man.'
'As for thy diligence I return thee many thanks.
I require no such thing at your hand.
But something to me show where oft-time I may know
The pleasures of a serving-man.'

'Why, at court we must be dressed in our livery the best,
Fine and gay with our hats in our hands;
Our shirts are white as milk, our stockings made of silk,
There's clothing for a serving-man.'
'As for thy rich attire it's not fitting for to wear
Nor to ramble the bushes among.
Give me a good greatcoat and in my purse a groat.
There's clothing for a husbandman.'

'A servant man do eat the best of dainty meat,
Such as peacock, capons, goose and swan;
Where lords and ladies dine they drink sugar in their wine,
That's living for a serving-man.'
'As for thy goose and capon, give me good beans and bacon,
Some butter and some cheese now and then;
To have good brawn and sauce all in a farmer's house,
That's living for the husbandman.'

'Is it not a fine thing to ride out with the king,
A duke, lord, or any such a one,
To hear the horns to blow, see the hounds all in a row?
There's pleasure for the servant man.'

'My pleasure's more than that, to my oxen fat,
My corn for to flourish in my land.
My ploughing and my sowing, my reaping and my mowing,
That's pleasure for the husbandman.'

'Well sir, I must confess your calling is the best,
So I'll give you the upper hand.
Neither lord nor duke nor king nor any such a one
Can do without the husbandman.'
'So both now and for ever I'll do my best endeavour
To support the servant man.
For evermore I'll pray by night and day,
May heaven bless the husbandman.'

233. *The Carter*

I once was a bold fellow and went with a team,
And all my delight was in keeping them clean.
With brushes and curries I'd show their bright colour,
And the name that they gave me was a hearty good fellow.

As every evening I go to my bed,
The thought of my horses comes into my head;
I rise the next morning to give them some meat,
As soon as I can get the shoes on my feet.

The first was a white horse, as white as the milk,
The next was a grey horse, as soft as the silk;
The next was a black horse, as sleek as a mole,
The next was a brown horse, like diamonds did show.

As I go a-driving all on the highway,
When light goes my load, then I feed them with hay,
And give them some water when we comes to a pond,
And after they've drunk, boys, go steady along.

My feet they grow weary walking by their side;
I said to my mate, 'I will get up for a ride.'
And as I was riding, I made a new song,
And as I did sing it you must learn it along.

234. *The Miller and His Sons*

It's of a crafty miller and he
Had able sons one, two and three.
He called them all to make his will
To see which one should take the mill.

With me wack fol the riddle ol
The riddle ol the dee

The miller called for his eldest son,
Said he, 'My days are almost done,
And if the will to you I make
What toll dost thou intend to take?'

'Father,' he said, 'my name is Jack,
From every bushel I'll take a peck,
And every bushel that I grind
The profits they'll be large I'll find.'

'Thou art a fool,' the old man said,
'Thou hast not learned well thy trade;
To take such toll no man would live,
To thee the mill I ne'er will give.'

The miller called for his second son,
Said he, 'My days are almost done,
And if the will to you I make
What toll dost thou intend to take?'

'Father,' he said, 'my name is Ralph,
From every bushel I'll take a half
And every bushel that I grind
The profits they'll be large I'll find.'

'Thou art a fool,' the old man said,
'Thou hast not learned well thy trade;
To take such toll no man would live,
To thee the mill I ne'er will give.'

The miller called for his youngest son,
Said he, 'My days are almost done,
And if the will to you I make
What toll dost thou intend to take?'

'Father,' he said, 'I am your boy,
To take the toll will be my joy.
Before I shall good living lack,
I'll take it all, forswear the sack.'

'Thou art my boy,' the old man said,
'And thou hast learned well thy trade.
I give the mill to thee,' he cried,
Then he turned on his side and died.

235. *Poor Old Horse*

Once I was a young horse all in my youthful prime,
My mane hung o'er my shoulders and my coat he did so shine;
But now I'm getting old, my features do decay,
My master he looks down on me and his words I heard him say:

Poor old horse, poor old horse,
Poor old horse, let him die.

My master used to ride me at every chase all round,
My legs they were so nimble I could trip over the ground,
But now I'm getting old and scarcely able to crawl,
My master he looks down on me, saying I am no use at all.

Once all in the stable I used good corn and hay
That grows in yonder fields and likewise meadows so gay.
But now I'm getting old I scarcely get hay at all,
For I'm obliged to nibble the short grass that grows against the wall.

Once all in the stable I was kept so fine and warm
To keep my tender limbs from all aching pain and harm,
But now I'm getting old to the fields I'm obliged to go,
Let it hail, rain or sunshine, or the winds blow high or low.

My hide unto the huntsman so freely will I give,
My body to the hounds, for I'd rather die than live,
Then lay my legs so low that have run so many a mile,
Over the hedges, over ditches, over turnpike gates and stiles.

Poor old horse, poor old horse,
Poor old horse, let him die.

236. *Bold Reynard the Fox*

A great many gentlemen take great delight
In hunting bold Reynard the fox.
At Ashbittle copse I did lay,
An extraordinary rate I did live
In picking the bones of the fat geese and ducks
Till the farmers they all did me hate.

Oh for the lord's hounds did descend,
The huntsman swore I should die.
I left little brother behind,
They love little lambs better than I.

Oh through the lord's park they did run me,
The gamekeeper shot at my thigh.
I beg your pardon, huntsman and hounds,
From this bloody wound I must die.

I made away back to my home,
The place that I always did use,
And when I got back to my home
The holes were all stopped up close.

I been run by day many times,
Dogs that could run like a cow,
But never in all my whole time
I've not stopped a breath before now.

All through the wild woods they did run me,
Those bloodthirsty dogs did me follow,
And made my old coat stand on end
When I heard the loud huntsman to holloa.

All down stony land they did run me,
Those bloodthirsty dogs did me follow,
They tore my old coat all in pieces
Which made the loud huntsman to holloa.

So now the old Reynard he's dead,
We'll go to the Dolphin and dine,
We'll dip his forefoot in a bumper
And drink my lord's health in good wine.

237. *We'll All Go A-Hunting Today*

What a fine hunting day, it's as balmy as May,
When the hounds to our village did come.
Every friend will be there and all trouble and care
Will be left far behind them at home.
See servants on steeds on their way
And sportsmen in scarlet display.
Let us join the glad throng that goes laughing along,
And we'll all go a-hunting today.

So we'll all go a-hunting today,
All nature looks smiling and gay.
Let us join the glad throng that goes laughing along,
And we'll all go a-hunting today.

Farmer Hodge to his dame says 'I'm sixty and lame,
Times are hard, yet my rent I must pay;
But I don't care a jot if I raise it or not,
For I must go a-hunting today.
There's a fox in the spinney, they say,
We'll find him and have him away;
I'll be the first in the rush and I'll ride for his brush,
For I must go a-hunting today.'

As the judge sits in court he gets wind of the sport
And he calls for the court to adjourn,
As no witness had come and there's none left at home—
They have gone with the hounds and the horn.

Says he, 'Heavy fines you must pay
If you will not your summons obey;
But it's very fine sport so we'll wind up the court,
And we'll all go a-hunting today.'

And the village bells chime, there's a wedding at nine,
When the parson unites the fond pair.
When he heard the sweet sound of the horn and the hound,
And he knew it was time to be there,
Says he, 'For your welfare I pray,
I regret I no longer can stay;
You've been safely made one, we must quickly be gone,
For we must go a-hunting today.'

None were left in the lurch for all friends were at church
With beadle and clerk, aye and all;
All determined to go and to shout 'Tallyho',
And the ringers all joined in the rear.
With bride and bridegroom in array
They one to the other did say,
'Let us join the glad throng that goes laughing along,
And we'll all go a-hunting today.'

There's the doctor in boots to a breakfast that suits
Of home-brewed ale and good beef.
To his patients in pain says, 'I've come once again
To consult you in hope of relief.'
To the poor his advice he gave way,
And the rich he prescribed them to pay,
But to each one he said, 'You will quickly be dead
If you don't go a-hunting today.'

And there's only one cure for a malady, sure,
Which reaches the heart to adjure.
It's the sound of a horn on a fine hunting morn,
And where is the heart wishing more?
For it turneth the grave into gay,
Makes pain into pleasure give way,
Makes the old become young and the weak become strong,
If they'll all go a-hunting today.

238. *The Nottinghamshire Poacher*

In Thorney Moor Woods in Nottinghamshire,
   Fal the dal airol ay ti loddidy
Three keepers' houses stood at three square,
   Fal the dal airol ay
Three keepers' houses stood at three square,
About a mile from each of them were,
With orders it was to look after the deer,
   Ri fal the dal airol ay day.

So me and my mates went out that night,
With my two dogs close at my heels,
So me and my mates went out that night,
With my two dogs close at my heels,
To catch a fat buck in Nottingham fields.

The very first night we had bad luck:
Jack, my very best dog, got struck.
He came to me both bloody and lame
And sorry I was to see him the same;
He was not able to follow the game.

So I'll take my pikestaff in my hand,
I'll scour the woods till I find that man;
I'll take my pikestaff in my hand,
I'll scour the woods till I find that man,
Then I'll tan his hide right well if I can.

The very first thing that we found
Was a big fat buck nearly dead on the ground;
The very first thing that we found
Was a big fat buck nearly dead on the ground.
I know my dogs gid him his death wound.

I pulled out my knife and I cut the buck's throat,
I pulled out my knife and I cut the buck's throat,
And you'd have laughed to have seen Limping Jack
Go hopping along with the buck on his back;
He carried him like some Yorkshireman's pack.

We found a butcher to skin the game,
Likewise another to sell the same.
The very first joint we offered for sale
Was to an old woman who brewed bad ale,
That caused we poor lads in jail.

Assizes are opened and we are all here,
Assizes all over we're all clear.
The judges felt a sorrowful scorn
That such an old woman should be foresworn
And all into pieces she ought to be torn.

239. *The Three Tall Men*

Come friends and listen to my song,
You shall not find it dull.
It is the strange and merry lay
About the Bloxwich bull.

It was the wake of seventy-nine,
The village green was full;
They said no town afar or near
Could boast so fine a bull.

The dogs were brought, the stakes were driven,
And then there came a lull
While three tall men went o'er the green
To fetch the famous bull.

Now when they reached the stable door,
Long faces did they pull,
For lo! some knave had been afore
And taken away the bull.

The folk they raved, the folk they swore,
They said it was a gull;
They said they'd bait the three tall men
Unless they found the bull.

The three tall men were sore afraid,
They with grief were full.
'Give us an hour's space,' they said,
'And we will find the bull.'

They searched from noon till twilight grey
And then to evening dull,
But nevermore the people spied
The tall men or the bull.

240. *The Cock of the Game*

Here's to the blood, in his mettle and pride,
To the hunter who takes every fence in his stride,
And here's to the hounds and a straight running fox,
And I'll drain off my glass to the fighting game-cocks.

> *Let us drink all night till the dawn of the day,*
> *Then you back the crow wing and I'll back the grey.*
> *Such courage and beauty none other can claim,*
> *For the pride of my heart is a cock of the game.*

Long years ago on the old village green
At Easter and Whitsun great battles were seen,
When the cocks in their fury made feathers to fly,
Clipped out, and well heeled with a gleam in their eye.

Now the Lord has created the game cock to fight,
But the Law has decreed that this cannot be right,
So we're out on the moors where no-one can see
Till the Lord and Law decide to agree.

From the woods of Low Furness to the wild Broughton Moor,
By Brayton and Wigton you'll find them for sure,
May the day never dawn when I no longer hear
The crow of the game cock so loud and so clear.

Choose for a wife like the bonny game hen,
If she comes of good family, a breed that you ken,
A right bonny lassie with fire in her eyes,
Small in the belly and strong in the thighs.

Fight for your rights like the game-cock of old,
The rights that belong you to have and to hold,
Though fortune provides neither riches nor fame,
May she leave you a son like the cock of the game.

There are plenty among us all sport would deny,
When our country's in peril they alter their cry,
For then they've no wish for our spirits to tame,
For they're looking for lads like the cock of the game.

241. *Master McGrath*

Eighteen sixty-nine being the date and the year,
Those Waterloo sportsmen and more did appear
To gain the great prizes and bear them away,
They were counting on Ireland and Master McGrath.

On the twelfth of November, that day of renown,
McGrath and his keeper they left Lurgan town;
A gale in the channel, it soon drove them on,
On the thirteenth they landed on England's fair shore.

Oh, and when they arrived there in big London town,
Those great English sportsmen all gathered round;
And one of those gentlemen standing nearby
Said, 'Is that the great dog you call Master McGrath?'

And one of those gentlemen standing around
Said, 'I don't give a damn for your Irish greyhound.'
And another he sneered with a scornful 'Ha ha,
We'll soon humble the pride of your Master McGrath.'

Lord Lurgan stood up and he said 'Gentlemen,
Is there any amongst you with money to spend?
For your grand English nobles don't give a straw,
It's five thousand to one upon Master McGrath.'

Oh, McGrath he looked up and he waggled his tail,
Informing his lordship, 'I know what you mean.
Don't fear, noble brown lord, don't fear him awa,
We'll soon tarnish their laurels,' said Master McGrath.

Oh, the Rose stood uncovered, that great English pride,
Her master and keeper were close by her side.
They led them away and the crowd cried hoorah,
For the pride of old England and Master McGrath.

Oh, the Rose and the Master they both ran along.
'Oh I wonder,' said Rose, 'What brought you from your home?
You should have stayed there in your Irish domain,
Not come to gain laurels on Albion's plain.'

'Well I know,' said the Master, 'we're wild at the bogs,
But by God in Ireland we're good men and dogs.
Lead on, bold Britannia, give no more of your jaw,
Stuff that up your nostrils,' said Master McGrath.

Well, the hare she led on just as fast as the wind,
He was sometimes before her, and sometimes behind.
He jumped on her back and held up his old paw.
'Long live the Republic,' said Master McGrath.

242. *The Bullard's Song*

Come all you bonny boys
Who love to bait the bonny bull,
Who take delight in noise,
And you shall have your bellyful.
On Stamford's town bull-running day,
We'll show you such right gallant play;
You never saw the like, you'll say,
As you shall see at Stamford.

Earl Warren was the man
That first began this gallant sport;
In the castle he did stand
And saw the bonny bulls that fought.
The butchers with their bulldogs came,
These sturdy, stubborn bulls to tame,
But more with madness did inflame;
Enraged, they ran through Stamford.

bullard] bull-runner

Delighted with the sport,
The meadows there he freely gave;
Where these bonny bulls had fought,
The butchers now do hold and have;
By charter they are strictly bound
That every year a bull be found:
Come, dight your face, you dirty clown,
And stump away to Stamford.

Come, take him by the tail, boys,
Bridge, bridge him if you can;
Prog him with a stick, boys,
Never let him quiet stand.
Through every street and lane in town
We'll chevy-chase him up and down:
You sturdy bungstraws ten miles around
Come stump away to Stamford.

243. *When This Old Hat Was New*

I am a poor old man, come listen to my song.
Provisions now are twice as dear as when that I was young;
When this old hat was new and stood above my brow,
Oh what a happy youth was I when this old hat was new.

But four score years ago, the truth I do declare,
When men they took each other's word, they thought it very fair;
No oaths they did require, men's words they were so true,
'Twas thus in all my youthful days when this old hat was new.

And when the harvest came and we went off to shear,
How often we were merry made with brandy, ale and beer;
When corn it was brought home and put upon the mow,
The workers' paunches were well filled when this old hat was new.

At the board's head stood the farmer, the table for to grace,
And greeted all as they came in, each took his proper place;
His wife stood at the table to give each man his due,
And oh, what plenty did abound when this old hat was new.

dight] clean   prog] poke   bungstraws] threshers

But how the times are changed, the poor are quite done o'er,
They give to them their wages like beggars at the door;
In the house we must not go, although we are but few,
It was not so when Bess did reign and this old hat was new.

The commons are taken in and cottages pulled down,
Moll has got no wool to spin her linsey-wolsey gown;
'Tis cold and clothing's thin and blankets are but few,
But we were clothed both back and side when this old hat was new.

When Romans ruled this land, the commons they did give
Unto the poor in charity to help them for to live;
The poor are quite done o'er, we know it to be true,
It was not so when Bess did reign and this old hat was new.

244. *The New-Fashioned Farmer*

Good people all, I pray attend
And listen to my story,
How the farmers used to live
In our native country.
When masters lived as masters ought
And happy in their station,
Until at length their stinking pride
Has ruined half the nation.

Fol de lol lo, fol de lol lol lido

A good old-fashioned long grey coat
The farmers used to wear, sir,
And on old Dobbin they would ride
To market or to fair, sir.
But now fine geldings they must mount,
To join all in the chase, sir,
Dressed up like any lord or squire,
Before their landlord's face, sir.

In former times, both plain and neat,
They'd go to church on Sunday,
And then to harrow, plough or sow
They'd go upon a Monday;

But now, instead of the plough-tail,
O'er hedges they are jumping,
And instead of sowing of their corn,
Their delight is in fox-hunting.

The good old dames, God bless their names,
Were seldom in a passion,
But strove to keep a right good house,
And never thought on fashion;
With fine brown beer their hearts to cheer,
But now they must drink swipes, sir.
It's enough to make a strong man weak,
And give him the dry gripes, sir.

The farmer's daughters used to work
All at the spinning wheel, sir,
But now such furniture as that
Is thought quite ungenteel, sir.
Their fingers they're afraid to spoil
With any kind of sport, sir;
Sooner than handle a mop or broom,
They'd handle a pianoforte, sir.

Their dress was always plain and warm,
When in their holyday clothes, sir;
Besides, they had such handsome cheeks,
As red as any rose, sir.
But now they're frilled and furbelowed,
Just like a dancing monkey,
Their bonnets and their great black veils
Would almost fright a donkey.

When wheat it was a guinea a strike,
The farmers bore the sway, sir,
Now with their landlords they will ride
Upon each hunting day, sir.
Besides, their daughters they must join
The ladies at the ball, sir,
The landlord says, we'll double the rents,
And then their pride must fall, sir.

swipes] small beer
strike] local measure of corn, ranging from a half bushel to four

I hope no-one will think amiss,
At what has here been penned, sir,
But let's hope that these hard times
May speedily amend, sir.
It's all through such confounded pride
Has brought them to reflection,
It makes poor servants' wages low,
And keeps them in subjection.

245. *The Cottager's Complaint*

How sweetly did the moments glide,
How happy were the days,
When no sad fear my breast annoy'd
Or e'er disturbed my ease;
Hard fate! that I should be compelled
My fond abode to lose,
Where threescore years in peace I've dwell'd
And with my life to close.

> *Oh the time! the happy, happy time*
> *Which in my cot I've spent;*
> *I wish the churchyard was his doom*
> *Who murders my content.*

My ewes are few, my stock is small,
Yet from my little store
I find enough for Nature's call,
Nor would I ask for more.
That word, Enclosure!, to my heart
Such evil doth bespeak,
I fear I with my All must part
And fresh employment seek.

What little of the spacious plain
Should power to me consign,
For want of means I can't obtain,
Would not long time be mine.
The stout may combat fortune's frowns,
Nor dread the rich and great;
The young may fly to market towns,
But where can I retreat?

What kind of feelings must that man
Within his mind possess,
Who from an avaricious plan
His neighbours would distress?
Then soon, in pity to my case,
To Reason's ear incline;
For on his heart it stamps disgrace
Who formed the base design.

246. *My Master and I*

Says the master to me, 'Is it true, I am told
Your name on the books of the Union enrolled;
I can never allow that a workman of mine
With wicked disturbers of peace should combine.'

Says I to the master, 'It's perfectly true
That I am in the Union, and I'll stick to it too,
And if between Union and you I must choose,
I have plenty to win and little to lose.

'For twenty years mostly my bread has been dry,
And to butter it now I shall certainly try;
And though I respect you, remember I'm free,
No master in England shall trample on me.'

Says the master to me, 'A word or two more.
We never have quarrelled on matters before.
If you stick to the Union, ere long I'll be bound,
You will come and ask me for more wages all round.

'Now I cannot afford more than two bob a day
When I look at the taxes and rent that I pay,
And the crops are so injured by game as you see,
If it is hard for you it's hard also for me.'

Says I to the master, 'I do not see how
Any need has arisen for quarrelling now,
And though likely enough we shall ask for more wage
I can promise you we shall not get first in a rage.'

247. *Pity Poor Labourers*

You sons of England, now listen to my rhymes,
And I'll sing you a short sketch of the times,
Concerning poor labourers we all must allow
Who work all day at the tail of the plough.

Oh pity poor labourers, oh pity them all,
For five or six shillings they work the whole week.

There's many poor labourers to work they will go
Either hedging or ditching, to plough or to sow;
And many poor fellows are used like a Turk,
They do not get paid fair for half a day's work.

And many poor labourers, I'm sorry to say,
Are breaking of stones for eighteen pence a day.
Bread and water's the fare of the poor lab'ring man,
While the rich they can live on the fat of the land.

Some pity the farmers, but I tell you now,
Pity poor labourers that follow the plough.
Oh pity poor children half-starving and then
Divide every great farm up into ten.

There's many young fellows you'll see every day
For snaring a hare they are banished away
To Van Dieman's Land or to some foreign shore,
And their wives and their children are left to deplore.

There's many a farmer that's making a fuss,
While the poor and the starving can scarce get a crust.
Do away with their hounds and their hunters so gay
And give the poor labourers a little fair play.

Fair play is a stranger these many years past,
And pity's bunged up in an old oaken cask;
But the time's fast approaching, it's very near come,
When we'll have the farmers all under our thumbs.

248. *The Labouring Man*

You Englishmen of each degree,
One moment listen unto me;
To please you all I do intend,
So listen to these lines I've penned.
From day to day you all may see
The poor are frowned upon by degrees
By them, you know, who never can
Do without the labouring man.

> *Old England's often led the van*
> *But not without the labouring man.*

In former days you must all know,
The poor man cheerful used to go,
Quite neat and clean, upon my life,
With his children and his darling wife;
And for his wages, it is said,
A fair day's wages he was paid;
But now to live he hardly can—
May God protect the labouring man.

There is one thing we must confess,
If England finds they're in a mess
And has to face the daring foe,
Unto the labouring man they go
To fight their battles, understand,
Either on sea or on the land;
Deny the truth we never can,
They call upon the labouring man.

Some for soldiers they will go,
And jolly sailors too, we know,
To guard old England day and night,
And for their country boldly fight;
But when they do return again
They are looked upon with great disdain;
Now in distress throughout the land
You may behold the labouring man.

When Bonaparte and Nelson too,
And Wellington at Waterloo,
Were fighting both by land and sea,
The poor man gained these victories.
Their hearts are cast in honour's mould,
The sailors and the soldiers bold;
And every battle, understand,
Was conquered by the labouring man.

The labouring man will plough the deep,
Till the ground and sow the wheat,
Fight the battles when afar,
Fear no danger or a scar;
But still they're looked upon like thieves
By them they keep at home at ease,
And every day throughout the land
They try to starve the labouring man.

Now if the wars should rise again
And England be in want of men,
They'll have to search the country round
For the lads that plough the ground.
Then to some foreign land they'll go,
To fight and drub the daring foe;
Do what they will, do what they can,
They can't do without the labouring man.

249. *The Painful Plough*

Come all you jolly ploughmen
With courage stout and bold,
They'll labour all the winter
Through stormy winds and cold
To clothe your fields with plenty,
Your farmyards to renew,
To crown them with contentment
Remains the painful plough.

Adam was a ploughman
When ploughing first began,
The next that did succeed him
Was Cain his eldest son.

THE COUNTRY YEAR

Some of their generation
Their calling doth pursue,
That bread may not be wanted
Remains the painful plough.

'O ploughman,' says the gardener,
'Don't count your trade with ours.
There's walking in the garden
To view those early flowers,
There's all those curious borders
And pleasant walks to view,
There's no such peace and contentment
Promoted by the plough.'

'O gardener,' says the ploughman,
'Our calling don't despise.
Every man for his living
Doth in his trade relies.
Were it not for the ploughman
Both rich and poor must rue,
For we're all depending
Upon the painful plough.

'Behold the wealthy merchants
That trades upon the seas,
That brings the golden treasures
To those that live at ease,
That brings the fruit and spices
And silks too also,
They are brought from the Indies
By virtue of the plough.

'And the men that do bring them,
We've only to be true,
They could not sail the ocean
Without the painful plough.
For they must have bread, biscuits,
Flour, pudding, beef and peas
To feed the jolly sailors
As they sail upon the seas.'

I hope no-one's offended
With me for singing this,
For I never was intended
For anything amiss.
If you consider it rightly
You'll find what I say is true:
Not a man that you can mention
Can live without the plough.

250. *An Old Man's Advice*

My grandfather worked when he was very young,
And his parents felt grieved that he should;
To be forced in the fields to scare away the crows,
To earn himself a bit of food.
The days they were long and his wages were but small,
And to do his best he always tried;
But times are better for us all
Since the old man died.

> *For the Union is started, unite, unite,*
> *Cheer up, faint-hearted, unite, unite;*
> *The work's begun, never to stop again*
> *Since the old man died.*

My grandfather said in the noontide of life,
Poverty was a grief and a curse;
For it brought to his home sorrow, discord and strife,
And kept him poor, with empty purse.
So he took a bold stand, he joined the Union band,
To help his fellow men he tried;
A Union man he vowed he'd stand
Till the day he died.

My grandfather's dead; as we gathered round his bed,
These last words to us he did say:
'Don't let your Union drop nor the agitation stop,
Or else you will soon rue the day.
Get united to a man for it's your only plan,
Make the Union your care and your pride.
Help on reform in every way you can.'
Then the old man died.

251. *Adieu to Old England*

Oh once I could ride in my coach
And horses to draw me along,
But now I am poor and far in distress,
I have nothing to call it my own.

> *Adieu to old England, adieu,*
> *Adieu to some hundreds of pounds.*
> *If the world had been ended when I was young,*
> *My sorrows I never should have known.*

Oh once I could eat of the best,
The bestest of bread so brown,
But now I am glad for the hard mouldy crust
And I have got it to eat.

Oh once I could lay on a bed
And a bed that was made of fine down,
But now I am glad of a lock of clean straw
To lay this poor body down on.

Oh once I could drink the best beer
And the beer that was made of fine brown,
But now I am glad of a drop of cold water
That runs from town to town.

252. *The English Labourer*

Come lads and listen to my song, a song of honest toil;
'Tis of the English labourer, the tiller of the soil;
I'll tell you how he used to fare, and all the ills he bore,
Till he stood up in his manhood, resolved to bear no more.

> *This fine old English labourer,*
> *One of the present time.*

He used to take whatever wage the farmer used to pay,
And work as hard as any horse for eighteen pence a day;
And if he grumbled at the nine and dared to ask for ten,
The angry farmer cursed and swore, and sacked him there and then.

He used to tramp off to his work while townsfolk were abed,
With nothing in his belly but a slice or two of bread;
He dined upon potatoes, and never dreamed of meat,
Except a lump of bacon fat sometimes by way of treat.

He used to find it hard enough to give his children food,
But sent them to the village school as often as he could;
But though he knew that school was good, they must have bread and
   clothes,
So he had to send them to the fields to scare away the crows.

He used to walk along the fields and see his landlord's game
Devour his master's growing crops, and think it was a shame;
But if the keeper found him with a rabbit or a wire,
He got it hot when brought before the parson and the squire.

But now he's wide awake and doing all he can,
At last for honest labour's rights he's fighting like a man;
Since squires and landlords will not help, to help himself he'll try,
And if he doesn't get fair wage he'll know the reason why.

They used to treat him as they liked in the evil days of old;
They thought there was no power on earth to beat the power of gold;
They used to threaten what they'd do if ever work was slack,
But now he laughs their threats to scorn with the Union at his back.

253. *The Owslebury Lads*

The thirtieth of November last, eighteen hundred and thirty,
The Owslebury lads they did prepare all for the machinery.
And when they did get there, my eye, how they let fly,
The machinery flew to pieces in the twinkling of an eye.

The mob, such a mob you had never seen before,
And if you live for a hundred years, you never will no more.

THE COUNTRY YEAR

Oh then to Winchester we were sent, our trial for to take,
And if we do have nothing, said our counsel, we shall keep.
When the judges did begin, I'm sorry for to say,
So many there was transported for life and some was case to die.

Sometimes our parents they come in for to see us all,
Sometimes they bring some baccy or a loaf that is so small.
They thought there was no power on earth to beat the power of gold;
They used to threaten what they'd do if ever work was slack,

At six o'clock in the morning our turnkey he comes in,
With a bunch of keys all in his hands tied up all in a ring.
And we can't get any further than back and forward in the yard;
A pound and a half of bread a day, and don't you think it hard?

At six o'clock in the evening the turnkey he comes round,
The locks and bolts they rattle like the sounding of a drum.
And we are all locked up all in the cells so high
And there we stay still morning whether we lives or die.

And now it's to conclude and finish my new song.
I hope you gentlemen round me will think that I'm not wrong,
For all the poor in Hampshire for rising of their wages,
I hope that none of our enemies will know for the want of places.

The Rise of Industry

254. The Poor Man Pays for All

As I lay musing all alone
Upon my resting bed,
Full many a cogitation
Did come into my head;
And waking from my sleep I
My dream to mind did call:
Methought how I saw before mine eyes
How poor men pay for all.

Methought I saw how wealthy men
Did grind the poor men's faces,
And greedily did prey on them,
Not pitying their cases.
They make them toil and labour sore
For wages too too small;
The rich men in the taverns roar,
But poor men pay for all.

Methought I saw a usurer old
Walk in his fox-furred gown,
Whose wealth and eminence controlled
The most men in the town.
His wealth he by extortion got,
And rose by others' fall;
He had what his hands earned not,
But poor men pay for all.

Methought I saw a courtier proud
Go swaggering along,
That unto any scarce allowed
The office of his tongue.
Methought, wert not for bribery,
His peacock plumes would fall;
He ruffles out in bravery,
But poor men pay for all.

Methought I was i' th'country,
Where poor men take great pains,
And labour hard continually,
Only for rich men's gains.
Like th'Israelites in Egypt,
The poor are kept in thrall;
The taskmasters are playing kept
But poor men pay for all.

Methought I saw poor tradesmen
I' th'city and elsewhere,
Whom rich men keep as beadsmen
In bondage, care and fear.
They'll have them work for what they list,
The weakest go to the wall:
The rich men eat and drink the best,
But poor men pay for all.

Methough I saw two lawyers base
One to another say,
'We have had in hand this poor man's case
A twelvemonth and a day;
And yet we'll not contented be
To let the matter fall;
Bear thou with me, and I'll bear with thee,
While poor men pay for all.'

Methought I saw a red-nose host,
As fat as he could wallow,
Whose carcase, if it should be roast,
Would drop seven stone of tallow.
He grows rich out of measure
With filling measure small;
He lives in mirth and pleasure
But poor men pay for all.

And so likewise the brewer stout,
The chandler and the baker,
The malt-man also, without doubt,
And the tobacco-taker.

playing kept] i.e. not working   beadsmen] suppliants

Though they be proud and stately grown,
And bear themselves so tall,
Yet to the world it is well known
That poor men pay for all.

Even as the mighty fishes still
Do feed upon the less,
So rich men, might they have their will,
Would on the poor men cess.
It is a proverb old and true,
That weakest go to th'wall:
Rich men can drink till th'sky look blue,
But poor men pay for all.

But now, as I before did say,
This is but a dream indeed;
Though all dreams prove not true, some may
Hap right as I do read.
And if that any come to pass,
I doubt this my dream shall,
For still 'tis found too true a case,
That poor men pay for all.

255. *Poverty Knock*

Poverty, poverty knock!
Me loom is a sayin' all day.
Poverty, poverty knock!
Gaffer's too skinny to pay.
Poverty, poverty knock!
Keepin' one eye on the clock.
Ah knows ah can guttle
When ah hear me shuttle
Go poverty, poverty knock!

Up every mornin' at five,
Ah wonder that we keep alive.
Tired an' yawnin' on the cold mornin',
It's back to the dreary old drive.

cess] levy   **255** guttle] eat

THE RISE OF INDUSTRY

Oh dear, we're goin' to be late,
Gaffer is stood at the gate.
We're out o' pocket, our wages they're docket,
We'll 'a' to buy grub on the slate.

An' when our wages they'll bring,
We're often short of a string.
While we are fratchin' wi' gaffer for snatchin',
We know to his brass he will cling.

We've got to wet our own yarn
By dippin' it into the tarn.
It's wet an' soggy and makes us feel groggy,
An' there's mice in that dirty old barn.

Oh dear, me poor 'ead it sings,
Ah should have woven three strings,
But threads are breakin' and my back is achin',
Oh dear, ah wish ah had wings.

Sometimes a shuttle flies out,
Gives some poor woman a clout.
There she lies bleedin', but nobody's heedin'.
Who's goin' t'carry her out?

Tuner should tackle me loom,
'E'd rather sit on his bum.
'E's far too busy a-courtin' our Lizzie,
An' ah cannat get 'im to come.

Lizzie is so easy led,
Ah think that 'e teks her to bed.
She allus was skinny, now look at her pinny,
It's just about time she was wed.

Poverty, poverty knock!
Me loom is a-sayin' all day.
Poverty, poverty knock!
Gaffer's too skinny to pay.
Poverty, poverty knock!
Keepin' one eye on the clock.

string] cloth-length   fratchin'] arguing   Tuner] maintenance man

Ah know ah can guttle
When ah hear me shuttle
Go poverty, poverty knock!

256. *The Poor Cotton Weaver*

I'm a poor cotton weaver as many one knows.
I've nowt to eat i' th'house an' I've wore out my cloas.
You'd hardly give sixpence for all I have on,
My clugs they are brossen an' stockins I've none.
You'd think it wur hard to be sent into th'world
To clem an' do th'best ot you con.

Our church parson kept tellin' us long,
We should have better times if we'd but hold our tongues.
I've houden my tongue till I can hardly draw breath,
I think i' my heart he means to clem me to death.
I know he lives weel by backbitin' the de'il,
But he never picked o'er in his life.

We tarried six weeks an' thought every day were t'last.
We tarried and shifted till now we're quite fast.
We lived on nettles while nettles were good,
And Waterloo porridge were best of us food.
I'm tellin' you true, I can find folk enew,
That er livin' no better than me.

Old Bill o' Dan's sent bailiffs one day,
For a shop score I owed him that I couldn't pay,
But he were too late, for old Bill o' Bent
Had sent horse and cart and taen goods for rent.
We had nowt but a stoo', that wur a seat for two,
An' on it cowered Margit an' me.

The bailiffs looked round as sly as a mouse,
When they saw aw things wur taen out o' t'house.
Says one to the other, 'All's gone, thou may see.'
Aw sed, 'Lads, never fret, you're welcome to me.'
They made no more ado, but nipped up t'owd stoo',
An' we both went wack upo' t'flags.

clugs] clogs   brossen] bursting   clem] starve   pick o'er] weave
Waterloo porridge] thin gruel

I get howd o' Margit, for hoo're stricken sick,
Hoo sed hoo ne'er had such a bang sin hoo wur wick.
The bailiffs scoured off wi' owd stoo' on their backs,
They would not have cared had they brokken our necks.
They're mad at owd Bent cos he's taen goods for rent,
And wur ready to flay us alive.

I sed to our Margit as we lay upo' t'floor,
'We shall never be lower in this world, I am sure.
But if we alter, I'm sure we mun mend,
For I think i' my heart we both at far end.
For meat we have none, nor looms to weave on,
Egad, they're as weel lost as found.'

Then I geet up my piece, an' I took it 'em back,
I scarcely dare speak, mester lookit so black.
He said, 'You wur o'erpaid last time you coom.'
I said, 'If I wur, 'twas for weavin' bout loom.
In the mind as I'm in, I'll ne'er pick o'er again,
For I've woven mysel to t'fur end.'

Then aw coom out o' t'warehouse, an' left him to chew that,
When aw thought again, aw wur vext till aw sweat.
To think we mun work to keep him an' aw t'set,
All the days o' my life, an' die in their debt.
But I'll give o'er this trade and work wi' a spade,
Or go an' break stones upo' t'road.

Our Margit declares if hoo'd cloas to put on,
Hoo'd go up to Lundun an' see t'young Queen,
An' if things didn't alter when hoo had been,
Hoo swears hoo would fight, blood up to t'een.
Hoo's nought agen t'Queen, but hoo likes a fair thing,
An' hoo says hoo can tell when hoo's hurt.

257. *The Carpet-Weavers' Lament*

Good people give attention and listen unto me,
While I relate a story of our sad destiny;
Out of one pound that we do get, a fourth they want to take,
And at our present prices, we scarce get bread to eat.

hoo] she   wick] alive   bout] without

For now our masters have agreed our trade to overthrow,
Our wives and children as you see are filled with grief and woe;
But we will never yield to them nor their cruel laws,
But on the truth we will rely and still maintain our cause.

Were you to go round the town, their country seats to see,
You would then be convinced what they had gained by we;
To see their livery servants, their carriages also,
You would then be quite satisfied whether we are right or no.

The manufacturers of this town, their fortunes they have made,
And in the space of twenty years all by the carpet trade;
To see how they do ride about their pleasures for to take,
Leaving their poor journeymen with scarce a meal to eat.

Now to conclude and make an end, the truth I'll tell to you,
Out of the town of Kidderminster the carpet trade will go;
For if they so press their journeymen, a living we can't get,
So it's better for to leave the town than go to gaol for debt.

258. *The Weaver and the Factory Maid*

I am a hand weaver to my trade,
I fell in love with a factory maid;
And if I could but her favour win,
I'd stand beside her and weave by steam.

My father to me scornful said,
'How could you fancy a factory maid,
When you could have girls fine and gay,
And dressed like to the Queen of May?'

'As for your fine girls, I do not care;
And could I but enjoy my dear,
I'd stand in the factory all the day,
And she and I'd keep our shuttles in play.'

I went to my love's bedroom door,
Where oftentimes I had been before;
But I could not speak nor yet get in
To the pleasant bed my love laid in.

'How can you say it's a pleasant bed,
When nowt lies there but a factory maid?'
'A factory lass although she be
Blest is the man that enjoys she.'

Oh, pleasant thoughts come to my mind
As I turned down her sheet so fine,
And I seen her two breasts standing so,
Like two white hills all covered with snow.

Where are the girls? I'll tell you plain,
The girls have gone to weave by steam;
And if you'd find 'em you must rise at dawn
And trudge to the mill in the early morn.

259. *The Jute Mill Song*

Oh dear me, the mill's ga'in' fast,
The poor wee shifters canna get their rest;
Shiftin' bobbins coarse and fine,
They fairly make you work for your ten and nine.

Oh dear me, I wish the day was done,
Runnin' up and down the pass is no fun—
Shiftin', piecin', spinnin' warp, weft and twine,
To feed and cleed your bairn aff'n ten and nine.

Oh dear me, the world's ill divided,
Them that work the hardest are the least provided.
But I must bide contented, dark days or fine;
There's no' much pleasure livin' aff'n ten and nine.

cleed] clothe

260. *Funny Rigs of Good and Tender-Hearted Masters*

Come townsmen all and women too,
There is no end of fun
When masters will as masters may
The rig of fancy run.
Of old and steady workmen late
Our masters sadly tired,
Searched England through and through
And then some new ones briskly hired.

Lean-fleshed and lousy, scant of clothes,
Almost as when first born,
Cooked meat they never could have seen
Nor smelt John Barleycorn.
We wondered much, we asked how long
Unhandcuffed they had been,
And others asked if ever they
A carpet loom had seen.

No, they replied,
But masters want experiments to make.
They told us that their pleasure
Was apprentices to take.
Well, said our friends, that's brave,
Pray do your best and learn,
But mind when first you candles snuff
You don't your fingers burn.

Well, quickly unto looms they got,
To work they tried their best;
The masters and the foremen too
Thought they could do the rest.
The lishes, treddles, sword and all
Danced to such a crazy tune
That each loom thought its master
Turned into a crazy loon.

The shuttle vowed whene'er he stirred
He always went astray,
And then he swore that he'd not been
Once right throughout the day.
The draw boys too, God bless the lads
And keep them all from evil,
Wished that strange medley anywhere,
Perhaps unto the devil.

To good workmen they'd long been used,
Able, long-tried and sure,
But such tenpenny fools as these
They never could endure.
They knew by English feeling taught
When law the tyrant plays,
And vowed that rather than submit
They'd suffer all their days.

But masters I'd almost forgot,
And ragamuffins too,
How they went on when I know myself
I'll surely tell to you.
Meantime, could anything cause mirth
Among such great disasters,
It would be such funny rigs
Of good and tender-hearted masters.

261. *General Ludd's Triumph*

No more chant your old rhymes about bold Robin Hood,
His feats I do little admire.
I'll sing the achievements of General Ludd,
Now the hero of Nottinghamshire.
Brave Ludd was to measures of violence unused
Till his sufferings became so severe,
That at last to defend his own interests he roused,
And for the great fight did prepare.

The guilty may fear but no vengeance he aims
At the honest man's life or estate;
His wrath is entirely confined to wide frames
And to those that old prices abate.

Those engines of mischief were sentenced to die
By unanimous vote of the trade,
And Ludd who can all opposition defy
Was the grand executioner made.

And when in the work he destruction employs
Himself to no method confines;
By fire and by water he gets them destroyed,
For the elements aid his designs.
Whether guarded by soldiers along the highway,
Or closely secured in a room,
He shivers them up by night and by day
And nothing can soften their doom.

He may censure great Ludd's disrespect for the laws
Who ne'er for a moment reflects
That foul imposition alone was the cause
Which produced these unhappy effects.
Let the haughty the humble no longer oppress,
Then shall Ludd sheathe his conquering sword;
His grievances instantly meet with redress,
Then peace shall be quickly restored.

Let the wise and the great lend their aid and advice
Nor e'er their assistance withdraw,
Till full-fashioned work at the old-fashioned price
Is established by custom and law.
Then the trade when this arduous contest is o'er
Shall raise in full splendour its head;
And colting and cutting and squaring no more
Shall deprive honest workmen of bread.

262. *The Cropper Lads*

Come, cropper lads of great renown,
Who love to drink good ale that's brown
And strike each haughty tyrant down,
With hatchet, pike and gun.

colting, cutting squaring] see Notes and References

Oh the cropper lads for me,
And gallant lads they be,
With lusty strokes the shear frames broke,
The cropper lads for me.

What though the specials still advance,
And soldiers round in nightly prance;
The cropper lads still lead the dance
With hatchet, pike and gun.

And night by night when all is still,
And the moon is hid behind the hill,
We forward march to do our will
With hatchet, pike and gun.

Great Enoch still shall lead the van;
Stop him who dare, stop him who can.
Press forward every gallant man
With hatchet, pike and gun.

263. *July Wakes*

Looms are swept an' brass is drawn,
An' me an' Jack'll be up in t'morn,
We're off to beg or sell or pawn
For July Wakes.

We've sweat for one an' fifty week
An' human bones like looms'll creak;
We're gonna lay on Pendle cheek
An' stretch our limbs.

We'll roam in t'woods an' stretch in t'hay,
We'll watch great clouds spring up at play,
An' if they brast we'll torn that way
And taste clean rain.

Great Enoch] a big hammer used to smash machinery, named after the firm of
Enoch and James Taylor.
263 brast] burst   torn] turn

We'll foller t'river up t'sky,
We'll watch wick fishes skimmin' by
An' drink at brooks when throats is dry;
We'll stand up men.

Days'll flee till Jack downcast
'Il harken t' minutes racing past,
An' t'buzzers moan through t'linnet's blast;
To 'ell wi't' looms.

Monday'll see us stood in t'shed,
Shuttles spewin' out their thread,
Weavin' fifty-one weeks of bread
An' one of life.

264. *Brave Collier Lads*

As I walked forth one summer's morn, all in the month of June,
The flowers they were springing, and the birds were in full tune,
I overheard a lovely maid, and this was all her theme:
'Success attend the collier lads, for they are lads of fame.'

I stepped up to her, and bending on my knee,
I asked her pardon for making with her so free.
'My pardon it is granted, young collier,' she replies,
'Pray do you belong to the brave Union boys?'

'You may see I'm a collier as black as a sloe,
And all the night long I am working down below.'
'Oh I do love a collier as I do love my life,
My father was a pitman all the days of his life.

'Come now, my young collier, and rest here awhile,
And when I have done milking, I'll give you a smile.'
He kissed her sweet lips while milking her cow,
And the lambs were sporting all in the morning dew.

wick] live

309

Come all you noble gentlemen, wherever you may be,
Do not pull down their wages, nor break their unity.
You see they hold like brothers, like sailors on the sea,
They do their best endeavours for the wives and family.

Then she clapped her arms around him like Venus round the vine.
'You are my jolly collier lad, you've won this heart of mine.
And if that you do win the day, as you have won my heart,
I'll crown you with honour, and for ever take your part.'

The colliers are the best of boys, their work lies underground,
And when they to the alehouse go they value not a crown.
They spend their money freely and pay before they go;
They work underground while the stormy winds do blow.

So come all you pretty maidens wherever you may be,
A collier lad do not despise in any degree.
For if that you do use them well they'll do the same to thee,
There is none in this world like a pitboy for me.

265. *The Collier Lad's Lament*

In taking of my lonely walk on a cold and wintry day,
As through the colliers' country I wended my way,
I overheard a collier lad, most bitterly he cried,
'Oh how I rue the day that my own poor father died.

'When my father he was living, no tommy shops were there;
He did receive good wages and all things went on fair;
And when on Saturday he came home, he to my mother said,
"Come, let us go up into the town to buy our children bread."

'To the tommy shop now they're forced to go for all that they do eat,
They're forced to take their wages out in bread and cheese and meat;
And when on Saturday they go to get their wages paid,
The master says, "Do not forget the tommy shop today."

'Five and sixpence for a good day's work, it was a collier's due,
But now he thinks himself well off if he gets more than two;
And if he grumbles at the price, the master thus will say,
"To the workhouse with your children, and there get better pay."

tommy shop] see Notes and References

'Myself and my poor brother, in the morning we do go
To work upon the coalpit bank all in the frost and snow;
The little that we both do earn is needless for to tell,
It'll scarcely serve the one of us, the masters pay so well.

'But when I do grow up a man, if they don't give better pay,
I'll go and be a soldier for thirteen pence a day
Before I'll work in those dark pits, with others for to share
The benefit of what I earn in tommy shops and beer.

'If the Queen and all her ministers, they all were for to come
To live as these poor colliers do and work down underground,
And undergo the hardships and dangers of the fire,
I think they'd make the masters pay them better for their hire.

'If Johnny Russell he was here and worked upon the bank,
And Albert he was doggy, for he's of higher rank,
I think one week would settle them and cause them thus to say,
"Let these poor colliers have their rights, and give them better pay." '

266. *'Call the horse, marrow'*

Call the horse, marrow,
For I can call nane.
The heart of my belly
Is hard as a stane.
As hard as a stane
And as round as a cup.
Call the horse, marrow,
Till my hewer comes up.

Me and my marrow
And Christy Crawhall
Will play any three in the pit
At the football.
At the football
And at the coal-tram,
We'll play any three in the pit
For twelve-pence a gam.

Johnny Russell] Lord Russell was Prime Minister from 1846 to 1852
doggy] foreman in charge of underground workings

Hewing and putting
And keeping in the sticks,
I never so laboured
Since I took the picks.
I'm going to my hewer's house
On the Fell Side.
He hews his coals thick
And drives his bords wide.

The rope and the roll
And the long ower-tree,
The devil's flown o'er the heap
With them all three.
The roll hangs across the shaft;
De'il but it fall
And stick in the thill,
Twenty-four horned owls
Run away with the mill.

I'm going to my hewer
Wherever he may be.
He's hipt of a buddock
And blind of an e'e.
He's blind of an e'e
And lame of a leg.
My uncle Jack Fenwick
He kissed my aunt Peg.

267. *Fourpence a Day*

The ore is waiting in the tubs, the snow's upon the fells;
Canny folk are sleeping yet, but lead is reet to sell.
Come, my little washer lad, come let's away,
We're bound down to slavery for fourpence a day.

bord] excavation usually driven at right angles to the cleavage of the coal
roll] engine-drum   ower-tree] engine-beam   thill] floor of a coalmine

It's early in the morning we rise at five o'clock,
And the little slaves come to the door to knock, knock, knock.
Come, my little washer lad, come let's away,
It's very hard to work for fourpence a day.

My father was a miner and lived down in the town,
'Twas hard work and poverty that always kept him down.
He aimed for me to go to school but brass he couldn't pay,
So I had to go to the washing rake for fourpence a day.

My mother rises out of bed with tears on her cheeks,
Puts my wallet on my shoulders which has to serve a week.
It often fills her great big heart when she unto me does say,
'I never thought thou would have worked for fourpence a day.'

Fourpence a day, my lad, and very hard to work,
And never a pleasant look from a gruffy-looking Turk.
His conscience may it fail and his heart may it give way,
Then he'll raise us our wages to ninepence a day.

268. *The Oakey Street Evictions*

It wes in November an' aw nivor will forget,
The polises an' the candymen at Oakey's hooses met.
Johnny the bellman he was there, squintin' roond aboot,
An' he placed three men at ivory door te torn the pitmen oot.

> Oh, what wid aw dee, if aw'd the poower mesel?
> Aw'd hang the twenty candymen an' Johnny that carries the bell.

There they went fre hoose te hoose te pit things on the road,
But mind, they didn't hort thorsels wi' liftin' heavy loads.
Some wid carry the poker oot, the fender or the rake;
If they lifted two at once it was a great mistake.

Some o' these dandy candymen was dressed up like a clown.
Some had hats wivoot a flipe, an' some wivoot a crown.
Some had ne laps upon their coats, but there wes one chap warse—
Ivory time he had te stoop, it was a laughable farce.

candyman] rag-and-bone man   bellman] bailiff

There wes one chap had ne sleeves nor buttons upon his coat.
Another had a bairn's hippin lapped aroond his throat.
One chap wore a pair o' breeks that belang tiv a boy;
One leg wes a sort o' tweed, the tuthor was cordyroy.

Next there comes the maisters, aw think they should think shyem,
Deprivin' wives an' families of a comfortable hyem.
But then they shift fre where they live, aw hope they'll gan te hell,
Alang wi' the twenty candymen an' Johnny that carries the bell.

269. *The Blantyre Explosion*

By Clyde's bonny banks where I sadly did wander,
Among the pit-heaps as evening drew nigh,
I spied a fair maiden all dressed in deep mourning,
A-weeping and wailing with many a sigh.

I stepped up beside her and thus I addressed her,
'Pray tell me, fair maiden, of your trouble and pain.'
Sobbing and sighing, at last she did answer,
'Johnny Murphy, kind sir, was my true lover's name.

'Twenty-one years of age, full of youth and good-looking,
To work down the mines from High Blantyre he came.
The wedding was fixed, all the guests was invited.
That calm summer evening young Johnny was slain.

'The explosion was heard, all the women and children
With pale anxious faces they haste to the mine.
When the truth was made known, the hills rang with their moaning.
Three hundred and ten young miners were slain.

'Now husbands and wives and sweethearts and brothers,
That Blantyre explosion they'll never forget.
And all you young miners that hear my sad story,
Shed a tear for the victims who're laid to their rest.

hippin] nappy

314

270. *The Trimdon Grange Explosion*

Let's not think of tomorrow
Lest we disappointed be;
Our joys may turn to sorrow
As we all may daily see.
Today we're strong and healthy,
But how soon there comes a change,
As we may see from the explosion
That has been at Trimdon Grange.

Men and boys left home that morning
For to earn their daily bread,
Little thought before the evening
They'd be numbered with the dead.
Let us think of Mrs Burnett,
Once had sons and now has none—
With the Trimdon Grange explosion,
Joseph, George and James are gone.

February left behind it
What will never be forgot;
Weeping widows, helpless children
May be found in many a cot.
Little children kind and loving
From their homes each day would run,
For to meet their father's coming
As each hard day's work was done.

Now they ask if father's left them,
And the mother hangs her head,
With a weeping widow's feelings
Tells the child its father's dead.
Homes that once were blessed with comfort
Guided by a father's care,
Now are solemn, sad and gloomy,
Since the father is not there.

God protect the lonely widow,
Help to raise each drooping head;
Be a father to the orphans,
Never let them cry for bread.

Death will pay us all a visit;
They have only gone before.
We may meet the Trimdon victims
Where explosions are no more.

271. *The Gresford Disaster*

You've heard of the Gresford disaster,
And the terrible price that was paid.
Two hundred and forty-two colliers were lost,
And three men of a rescue brigade.

It occurred in the month of September,
At three in the morning, that pit
Was racked by a violent explosion
In the Dennis where gas lay so thick.

The gas in the Dennis deep section
Was packed there like snow in a drift,
And many a man had to leave the coal-face
Before he had worked out his shift.

A fortnight before the explosion,
To the shotfirer, Tomlinson cried,
'If you fire that shot we'll all be blown to hell!'
And no-one can say that he lied.

The fireman's reports they are missing,
The records of forty-two days:
The colliery manager had them destroyed
To cover his criminal ways.

Down there in the dark they are lying,
They died for nine shillings a day.
They have worked out their shift and now they just lie
In the darkness till Judgment Day.

The Lord Mayor of London's collecting
To help both our children and wives.
The owners have sent some white lilies
To pay for the poor colliers' lives.

Farewell, our dear wives and our children,
Farewell, our old comrades as well.
Don't send your sons down the dark dreary pit,
They'll be damned like the sinners in hell.

272. *The Old Miner*

Oh who'll replace this old miner,
And who will take my place below,
And who will follow the trepanner,
O dear God, when I go?

Oh who will wield my heavy pick
That I did wield for forty years,
And who will hew the black, black coal,
Who, dear God, when I go?

Oh who will ride the miners' train
That takes him to the dark coal face?
Who'll take my place upon that train,
Who, dear God, when I go?

Oh who will load this great iron tub,
Oh who will strain his bending back,
And who will work, sweat and ache like hell,
Who, dear God, when I go?

Oh who will cry when the roof caves in,
When friends are dying all round,
And who will sing the miners' hymn,
Who, dear God, when I go?

For forty years I've loved the mine,
For forty years I've worked down there.
Now who'll replace this old coal miner
When I've paid God my fare?

273. *The Strike*

Come, me canny Tynesiders, an' lissen
Tiv a song that aw's sartin ye'll like,
An' aw'll whisper a word kind an' cheerin'
Te the many poor fellows on strike.
Let 'em keep up their hearts as they hev deun,
Thor's a day for the true an' the brave,
An' the time wad come yet when the maisters
'Il find oot a mechanic's no slave.

Is Nine Oors an unreasonable movement?
Is't not plenty te labour for men?
Let them that condemned hev a try on't
An' see if they'll not alter the plan.
An' if lang oors industry increases,
Hev they found oot wi' the oors that they've tried?
Their capital grows through wor labour,
Wey, it's mair to their shyem, that they'll find.

But cheer up, there's good friends that support us,
Ay, an' England depends on us a';
An' we'll prove that we're true to the movement,
An' vict'ry shall let the world knaw
That Tynesiders'll nivor be conquered
By maisters that care nought for them.
An' if maisters is meant te be maisters,
Let 'em find there's men meant te be men!

274. *The Colliers' March*

The summer was over, the season unkind,
In harvest a snow how uncommon to find;
The times were oppressive, and well it be known
That hunger will strongest of fences break down.

'Twas then from their cells the black gentry stepped out
With bludgeons, determined to stir up a rout;
The prince of the party, who revelled from home,
Was a terrible fellow, and called Irish Tom.

He brandished his bludgeon with dexterous skill
And close to his elbow was placed Barley Will.
Instantly followed a numerous train,
Cheerful as bold Robin Hood's merry men.

Sworn to remedy a capital fault
And bring down the exorbitant price of the malt,
From Dudley to Walsall they trip it along
And Hampton was truly alarmed at the throng.

Women and children, wherever they go,
Shouting out, 'Oh the brave Dudley boys, O';
Nailers and spinners the cavalcade join,
The markets to lower their flattering design.

Six days out of seven poor nailing boys get
Little else at their meals but potatoes to eat;
For bread hard they labour, good things never carve,
And swore 'twere as well to be hanged as to starve.

Such are the feelings in every land,
Nothing Necessity's call can withstand;
And riots are certain to sadden the year
When sixpenny loaves but three-pounders appear.

275. *The Collier's Rant*

As me and me marrer was gannin' te work,
We met wi' the devil, it was in the dark,
Aa up wi' me pick, it was in the neet,
Aa knocked off his horns, likewise his club feet.

Oh follow the horses, Johnny me laddie,
Follow the horses, Johnny lad O,
Follow the horses, Johnny me laddie,
Oh follow them through, me Johnny lad O.

O marrer, O marrer, oh what do you think?
Aa've broken me bottle and spilt all the drink.
Aa've lost all me tools amang the big stanes,
Draw me to the shaft, it's time te gan hyem.

Hampton] Wolverhampton

As me and me marrer was loadin' a tram,
The light it went oot an' me marrer went wrang.
Ye would ha' laughed at such a fine game,
Old Nick got me marrer an' aa got the tram.

Now here is me horses and here is me tram,
Two horns full o' grease wull make her to gan;
There is me marrer all stretched oot on the ground,
You can tear up his shirt for his minin's all done.

276. *A Miner's Life*

A miner's life is like a sailor's,
'Board a ship to cross the waves;
Every day his life's in danger,
Still he ventures, being brave.
Watch the rocks, they're falling daily,
Careless miners always fail.
Keep your hands upon your wages
And your eyes upon the scale.

> *Union miners, stand together,*
> *Do not heed the owners' tale.*
> *Keep your hands upon your wages*
> *And your eyes upon the scale.*

You've been docked and docked again, boys,
You've been loading two to one.
What have you to show for working
Since this mining has begun?
Worn-out boots and worn-out miners,
Lungs of stone and children pale.
Keep your hands upon your wages
And your eyes upon the scale.

In conclusion, bear in mem'ry,
Keep the password in your mind;
God provides for every worker
When in union they combine.

Stand like men and linked together,
Victory for you will prevail.
Keep your hands upon your wages
And your eyes upon the scale.

277. *Jowl, Jowl and Listen*

Jowl, jowl and listen, lad,
And hear that coal face workin'.
There's many a marrer missin', lad,
Becaas he wadn't listen, lad.

Me feyther aalwes used te say,
Pit wark's mair than hewin',
Ye've got te coax the coal alang
And not be rivin' and tewin'.

Noo the depitty craals frae flat te flat,
While the putter rams the tyum 'uns,
But the man at the face hes te knaa his place
Like a mother knaas hor young 'uns.

278. *The Blackleg Miner*

Oh early in the evenin', just after dark,
The blackleg miners creep te wark,
Wi' their moleskin trousers an' dorty shirt,
There go the blackleg miners!

They take their picks an' doon they go
Te dig the coal that lies below,
An' there's not a woman in this toon'raw
Will look at a blackleg miner.

277 jowl] knock   rivin' and tewin'] pushing and pulling
depitty] charge-hand   putter] pusher   tyum 'uns] empty tubs

Oh Delaval is a terrible place,
They rub wet clay in a blackleg's face,
An' roond the pitheaps they run a foot-race
Wi' the dorty blackleg miners.

Now don't go near the Seghill mine;
Across the way they stretch a line
Te catch the throat an' break the spine
O' the dorty blackleg miners.

They'll take your tools an' duds as well,
An' hoy them doon the pit o' hell.
It's doon ye go, an' fare thee well,
Ye dorty blackleg miners.

So join the Union while ye may,
Don't wait till yer dyin' day,
For that may not be far away,
Ye dorty blackleg miners!

279. *Striking Times*

Cheer up, cheer up, you sons of toil, and listen to my song,
While I try to amuse you—it will not take me long.
The working men of England at length begin to see,
They've made a bold strike for their rights in 1853.

    And it's high time that working men should have it their own way,
    And for a fair day's labour receive a fair day's pay.

This is the time for striking, at least it strikes me so,
Monopoly has had some knocks, but this must be the blow;
The working men by thousands complain their lot is hard,
May order mark their conduct and success be their reward.

Some of our London printers this glorious work begun,
And surely they've done something, for they've upset the *Sun.*
Employers must be made to see they can't do what they like;
It is the masters' greediness that causes men to strike.

The labouring men of London on both sides of the Thames,
They made a strike last Monday, which adds much to their names.
Their masters did not relish it, but made them understand,
Before the next day's sun had set they gave them their demand.

The unflinching men of Stockport, Kidderminster in their train,
Three hundred honest weavers struck, their ends all for to gain.
Though masters find they lose a deal the tide must soon be turning;
They find the men won't quietly be robbed of half their earning.

Our London weavers mean to show their masters and the trade
That they will either cease to work or else be better paid.
In Spitalfields the weavers worked with joy in former ages,
But they're tired out of asking for a better scale of wages.

The monied men have had their way, large fortunes they have made,
For things could not be otherwise, with labour badly paid;
They roll along in splendour and with a saucy tone,
As Cobbett says, they eat the meat, the workman gnaws the bone.

At Liverpool the postmen struck and sent word to their betters,
Begging them to recollect that they were men of letters;
They asked for three bob more a week and got it in a crack,
And though each man has got his bag they have not got the sack.

The coopers and the dockyard men are all a-going to strike,
And soon there'll be the devil to pay without a little mike.
The farming men of Suffolk have lately called a go,
And swear they'll have their wages rose before they reap or sow.

280. *The Manchester Ship Canal*

I sing a theme deserving praise,
A theme of great renown, sir;
The Ship Canal in Manchester,
That rich and trading town, sir.
I mean to say, it once was rich
E'er these bad times came on, sir;
But good times will come back, you know,
When these bad times are gone, sir.

mike] leisure

In eighteen twenty-five,
When we were speculating all, sir,
We wise folks clubbed together
And we made this Ship Canal, sir.
I should have said we meant to do,
For we'd the scheme laid down, sir,
That would have made this Manchester
A first-rate seaport town, sir.

Near Oxford Road the dry dock is,
To cork and to careen, sir;
Our chief West India Dock
Is where the pond was at Ardwick Green, sir.
That is to say they might have been there,
Had these plans been done, sir,
And vessels might have anchored there
Of full five hundred ton, sir.

Instead of lazy Old Quay flats
That crawl three miles an hour, sir,
We'd fine three-masted steam ships,
Some of ninety horses' power, sir.
That is, had it been made we should;
And Lord! how fine 'twould be, sir,
When all beyond St Peter's Church
Was open to the sea, sir.

At Stretford, Prestwich, Eccles too,
No weaver could you see, sir,
His shuttle for a handspike changed,
Away to sea he went, sir.
I'm wrong, I mean he would have done so
Had it but been made, sir,
For who would starve at weaving
Who could find a better trade, sir?

Alas, then, for poor Cannon Street,
The hookers-in, poor odd fish!
Instead of catching customers,
Must take to catching cod fish.
That is, supposing it was made,
May it ne'er be, I wish, sir,
These cotton boats for customers
Would never do for fish, sir.

Alas, too, for poor Liverpool,
She'd surely go to pot, sir;
For want of trade her folks would starve,
Her custom house would rot, sir.
I'm wrong, they'd not exactly starve
Or want, for it is true, sir,
They might come down to Manchester,
We'd find them work to do, sir.

Success then unto Manchester,
And joking all aside, sir,
Her trade will flourish as before
And be her country's pride, sir.
That is to say if speculation
Can but be kept down, sir,
And sure we've had enough of that,
At least within this town, sir.

281. *The New Navigation*

This day for our new navigation,
We banish all care and vexation,
The sight of the barges each honest heart glads,
And the merriest of mortals are Birmingham lads.
Birmingham lads, jovial blades,
And the merriest of mortals are Birmingham lads.

With rapture each heart must be glowing,
Stamps, presses and lathes shall be going;
The lads to the wharf with their lasses repair
And smile at the streamers that play in the air.
Play in the air, free and fair,
And smile at the streamers that play in the air.

Let Stratford boast out of all measure
The fruits of her mulberry treasure;
Such treasure for once may cause jubilee joys
But riches spring daily from Birmingham toys.
Birmingham toys all men praise,
But riches spring daily from Birmingham toys.

mulberry treasure ... jubilee joys] see Notes and References

The Thames, Severn, Trent and the Avon
Our countrymen frequently rave on;
But none of their neighbours are happy as they
Who peaceably dwell on the banks of the Rea.
Banks of the Rea, ever gay,
Who peaceably dwell on the banks of the Rea.

Not Europe can match us for traffic,
America, Asia and Afric;
Of what we invent each partakes of a share,
For the best of wrought metals is Birmingham ware.
Birmingham ware, none so rare,
For the best of wrought metals is Birmingham ware.

Since by the canal navigation
Of coals we've the best in the nation,
Around the gay circle your bumpers then put,
For the cut of all cuts is a Birmingham cut.
Birmingham cut, fairly wrought,
For the cut of all cuts is a Birmingham cut.

282. *The Oxford and Hampton Railway*

Oh come and listen to my song,
And I will not detain you long,
About the folks they all did throng
Along the Oxford Railway.

Ri fan, ti fan, mirth and fun,
Don't you wonder how it's done?
Carriages without horses run
On the Oxford and Hampton Railway.

And to go along the line
Mother, father, son and daughter,
Going along at one o'clock
By fire, steam and water.

Rea] a small stream in Birmingham   cut] canal

THE RISE OF INDUSTRY

And from the villages and the towns
Ladies and gents all gathered round,
And music in the air did sound
Along the Oxford Railway.

There's butchers, bakers, nailers too,
And lots of gents all dressed in blue,
And they've all come to take a view
At the Oxford and Hampton Railway.

Now there's a girl in Worcester Town,
I think her name is Nancy,
She said a ride along the line
Would really please her fancy.

She'll go by steam, she'll come by steam,
By steam she'll unbehurried,
And if she do a husband find
By steam they will be married.

Now an old girl looking up the line
Said, 'I don't give a farthing,
For they've pulled down me cottage fine
And taken away me garden,

'Where I for many years did dwell
Growing cabbages and potatoes,
But worse than that my daughter now
Run off with a navigator.'

When line is finished at both ends
Then you can send your cocks and hens,
And go and visit all your friends
Along the Oxford Railway.

You can send your butter and cheese
At any time whenever you please.
You can send your hen and eggs
And them can ride as has no legs
On the Oxford and Hampton Railway.

283. *The Dalesman's Litany*

It's hard when folks can't find th'work
Weer they've been bred and born;
When I were young I allus thowt
I'd bide midst royits and corn.
But I've been forced to work in t'towns,
So here's my litany:
From Hull and Halifax and Hell,
Good Lord, deliver me.

When I were courting Mary Jane,
T'old squire he says, one day,
'I've got na bield for wedded folk,
Choose will ta wed or stay.'
I could na give up t'lass I loved,
So to t'town we 'ad to flee:
From Hull and Halifax and Hell,
Good Lord, deliver me.

I've worked i' Leeds an' 'Uddersfield
And addled honest brass.
At Bradford, Keighley, Rotherham,
I've kept my bairns an' t'lass.
I've travelled all three Ridings round
And once I went to sea:
From forges, mills an' sailin' boats,
Good Lord, deliver me.

I've walked at neet through Sheffield loyns—
'Twere same as being i' hell—
Where furnaces thrust out tongues of fire
And reared like t'wind on t' fell.
I've sammed up coils i' Barnsley pits
Wi' muck up to my knee:
From Sheffield, Barnsley, Rotherham,
Good Lord, deliver me.

royits] roots   bield] room   addled] learned   loyns] lanes
sammed up coils] picked up coal

I've seen fog creep across Leeds brig
As thick as Bastille soup.
I've lived weer folks were stowed away
Like rabbits in a coop.
I've seen snow float down Bradford Beck
As black as ebony:
From Hunslet, Holbeck, Wibsey Slack,
Good Lord, deliver me.

Well now when all us childer's fligged,
To t'country we've come back.
There's fourty mile a heathery moor
'Twixt us an' t'coilpits' slack.
And as I sit by t'fire at neet,
Well, I laugh an' shout wi' glee:
From Hull and Halifax and Hell,
Good Lord, deliver me.

284. *The Dandy Horse*

Queer sights we every day do find,
As the world we pass along,
The ladies' hoops and crinolines
And then their large chignons;
To come out in the French fashion,
Of course we must indeed,
And have a dandy horse—
The famed Velocipede.

> *The dandy horse, Velocipede,*
> *Like lightning flies, I vow, sir,*
> *It licks the railroad in its speed*
> *By fifty miles an hour, sir.*

The lasses of the period
Will cut along so fine,
With their hair just like a donkey's tail,
A-hanging down behind;

brig] bridge   Bastille] workhouse   fligged] departed

Upon a dandy horse will go,
And behind them footman John,
Whose duty will be to cry gee-wo!
And hold on their chignon.

The Velocipedes are all the go
In country and in town,
The patent dandy hobby-horse
It everywhere goes down.
A wheel before and one behind,
Its back is long and narrow,
It's a cross between the treading mill
And a razor-grinder's barrow.

All the world will mount Velocipedes,
Oh, won't there be a show
Of swells out of Belgravia,
In famous Rotten Row;
Tattersall's they will forsake,
To go there they have no need,
They will patronise the wheelwright's now
For a famed Velocipede.

All kinds of Velocipedes
Will shortly be in use,
The snob will have one like a last,
The tailor like a goose!
Bill Gladstone he will have one
To ride, so help-me-bob,
The head will be the Irish church,
The tail Ben Dizzy's nob.

Old Sal Brown to her husband said,
'There is no use of talking,
I must have a dandy hobby-horse,
For I am tired of rocking;
Your leather breeches I will spout,
And send you bare on Monday
If I don't have a Velocipede
To ride to church on Sundays.'

snob] cobbler   spout] pawn

What will the poor horse-dealers do,
I am sure I cannot tell,
Since the dandy horses have come up
Their horses they can't sell;
Oh, won't the cats and dogs be glad,
Their grub they will get cheap,
Or else it will be all bought up
To sell for paupers' beef.

The Velocipedes are rode by swells,
Tinkers too and tailors,
They will be mounted, too, by the police,
The soldiers and the sailors.
An old lady who lives in ——,
At least the story goes, sir,
Is a-going to race the omnibus
All down the —— road, sir.

The railways they will be done brown,
The steamboats too, beside,
For folks when they go out of town,
The Velocipedes will ride;
But I'd have you look out for squalls,
Or else you may depend,
You will go down, dandy horse and all,
And bruise your latter end.

285. My Grandfather's Days

Give attention to my ditty and I'll not keep you long;
I'll endeavour for to please you if you'll listen to my song.
I'll tell you an ancient story, the doings and the ways,
The manners and the customs of my grandfather's days.

Of many years that's gone and past, which hundreds do say hard,
When Adam was a little boy and worked in Chatham Yard,
We had no Waterloo soldiers dressed out in scarlet clothes;
The people were not frightened by one man's big, long nose.

THE RISE OF INDUSTRY

We had not got Lord Brougham to pass the Poor Law Bill;
We had not got policemen to keep the people still;
We had not got a treadmill to dance upon and grin;
Old women in the morning didn't drink a pint of gin.

If a young man went a-courting a damsel meek and mild,
And if she from misfortune should hap to have a child,
By going to a magistrate, a recompense to seek,
They'd make the man to marry her, or pay a crown a week.

But now by the new Poor Law he nothing has to pay,
Nor would he, even if he got twenty children every day.
We had not got a German queen to govern by her laws;
O'Connell had not come to town to fight for Ireland's cause.

A tradesman was not known to sigh, had no reason to complain;
Colonel Evans wasn't here to drag young Englishmen to Spain.
There then was none of Fieschi's gang to wheel about and prance;
They hadn't got the musket made to shoot the King of France.

In my grandfather's day, now very well you know,
They never learned to wheel about, nor learned to jump Jim Crow.
They walked, or rode on horseback, or travelled with a team;
They never thought of railroads or travelling by steam.

They travelled on the roads by day or in the morning, soon;
Green did not go to Holland in a dashing great balloon.
With silks and satins, women didn't decorate their backs;
The sleeves upon their gowns weren't like great 'tato sacks.

In my grandfather's days, the coats were made of cloth,
But now they're india rubber and styled a Mackintosh.
As through the streets they go along, the boys cry out quite pert,
'Oh crikey, there's a swellish cove, but what a dirty shirt.'

In my grandfather's days, if a journey you would take,
Then coaches ran so easy, no fear your bones they'd break;
Now we've omnibuses, patent cars and bedsteads upon springs,
Where children you may get by steam, such pretty little things.

Colonel Evans, Fieschi] see Notes and References

286. *Humphrey Hardfeature's Descriptions of Cast-Iron Inventions*

Since cast-iron has got all the rage,
And scarce anything's now made without it,
As I live in this cast-iron age,
I mean to say something about it.
There's cast-iron coffins and carts,
There's cast-iron bridges and boats,
Corn-factors with cast-iron hearts,
That I'd hang up in cast-iron coats.

Iron bedsteads have long been in use;
With cast-iron they now pave our streets;
Each tailor has a cast-iron goose,
And we soon shall have cast-iron sheets.
Tommy Whalebone has grown quite a blade,
So dextrous and clever his hand is,
Swears he now shall have excellent trade
Making cast-iron stays for the dandies.

We have cast-iron gates and lamp-posts,
We have cast-iron mortars and mills, too;
And our enemies know to their cost
We have plenty of cast-iron pills, too.
We have cast-iron fenders and grates,
We have cast-iron pokers and tongs, sir;
And we soon shall have cast-iron plates,
And cast-iron small-clothes ere long, sir.

So great is the fashion of late,
We have cast-iron hammers and axes;
And, if we may judge by their weight,
We have plenty of cast-iron taxes.
Cast-iron banknotes we can't use,
But should we e'er prove such ninnies,
A good Henry Hase to refuse,
They must issue out cast-iron guineas.

goose] pressing iron   Henry Hase] Chief Cashier of the Bank of England
1807–29; thus a banknote.

Now my cast-iron song's at an end;
I hope you'll not take it amiss, sir.
May your plaudits my efforts attend;
My heart it will burst if you hiss, sir.
I pray, my kind friends, don't say nay,
For, if I'm not out in my latitude,
Your goodness I'll never repay
With such feeling as cast-iron gratitude.

287. *A New Hunting Song*

All you that are low-spirited, I think it won't be wrong
To sing to you a verse or two of my new hunting song;
For hunting is in season, the sport has just begun,
And heroes they will have their fun with their fine dog and gun.

> *A-hunting we will go, my boys, a-hunting we will go,*
> *We'll lay out schemes and try all means to keep the poor man low.*

It's one of our brave huntsmen, my song I will commence,
Brave Bonaparte I will begin, he was a man of sense;
From Corsica he did set off to hunt upon a chance,
He hunted until he became the Emperor of France.

And Nelson for his hunting he got the nation's praise,
He was the greatest huntsman that hunted on the seas;
He and his warlike terror, a-hunting bore away,
A musket ball proved his downfall in Trafalgar Bay.

Now Wellington at Waterloo, he had the best of luck,
He hunted from a lieutenant till he became a duke;
But men that did fight well for him, and did him honour gain,
He tried the very best he could to get their pensions ta'en.

O'Connor round the country, a-hunting he did go,
With meetings called in every town to tell the truth, you know;
The tyrants tried to keep him down but that was all in vain,
The people swear they'll back him up and have their rights again.

O'Connor] Feargus O'Connor (1794–1855) Chartist leader and MP

Prince Albert to this country came a-hunting for a wife,
He got one that he said he loved far dearer than his life;
Oh yes, he got the blooming Queen to dandle on his knee,
With thirty thousand pounds a year paid from this country.

They're hunting up the beggars through the country every day,
And hawkers if they do not all a heavy licence pay;
They won't allow the poor to beg, it's against the law to steal,
For the beggars there's the Bastille and the others go to jail.

Now to conclude my hunting song, I hope you will agree,
The poor men they are starving while the rich will have their spree;
And to complain it is a crime, so poor you must remain,
The parson says, 'Contented be, and you will heaven gain.'

288. *London Adulterations*

Here tradesmen, 'tis plain, at no roguery stop,
They adulterate everything they've in their shop;
You must buy what they sell, and they'll sell what they please,
And they would, if they could, sell the moon for green cheese.

    Sing tantararara, rogues all, rogues all,
    Sing tantararara, rogues all.

Now it is well know imitation's the rage:
Everything's imitated in this rare old age;
There's tea, coffee, beer, butter, gin, milk, in brief,
No doubt they'll soon imitate mutton and beef.

The grocer sells ash leaves and sloe leaves for tea,
Tinged with Dutch pink and verdigris, just like bohea;
What sloe poison means Slomon now has found out;
We shall all to a T be poisoned, no doubt.

Some grocers for pepper sell trash called PD;
Burnt horse beans for coffee—how can such things be?
I really do think those who make such a slip
And treat us like horses, deserve a horse-whip.

Bastille] workhouse
288 Dutch pink] a colouring agent   bohea] tea   Slomon] probably one of
    the doctors who investigated adulterizations   PD] pepper dust

THE RISE OF INDUSTRY

The milkman, although he is honest, he vows,
Milks his pump night and morn quite as oft as his cows;
Claps plenty of chalk in your score—what a bilk—
And, egad, claps you plenty of chalk in your milk.

The baker will swear all his bread's made of flour,
But just mention alum, you'll make him turn sour;
His ground bones and pebbles turn men skin and bone:
We ask him for bread and he gives us a stone.

The butcher puffs up tough mutton like lamb,
And oft for South Down sells an old mountain ram;
Bleeds poor worn-out cows to pass off for white veal,
And richly deserves to die by his own steel.

A slippery rogue is the cheesemonger, zounds,
Who with kitchen stuff oft his butter compounds;
His fresh eggs are laid o'er the water, we know,
For which, faith, he over the water should go.

The brewer's a chemist, and that is quite clear,
We soon find no hops have hopped into his beer;
'Stead of malt he from drugs brews his porter and swipes—
No wonder so oft we all get the gripes.

The tobacconist smokes us with short-cut of weeds,
And finds his returns of such trash still succeeds;
With snuff of ground glass and of dust we are gulled:
For serving our nose so, his nose should be pulled.

The wine merchant, that we abroad may not roam,
With sloe juice and brandy makes port up at home;
Distillers their gin have with vitriol filled;
'Tis clear they're in roguery double-distilled.

Thus we rogues have in grain and in tea too, that's clear;
Don't think I suppose we have any rogues here.
The company present's excepted, you know,
Here's wishing all rogues their deserts they must have.

swipes] weak beer

289. *How Five and Twenty Shillings Were Expended in a Week*

It's of a tradesman and his wife,
I heard the other day,
Who did kick up a glorious row,
They live across the way.
The husband proved himself a fool,
When his money was all spent,
He called upon his wife, my life,
To know which way it went.

> *So she reckoned up and showed him,*
> *And she showed him all complete,*
> *How five and twenty shillings was*
> *Expended in a week.*

He said my wages are all gone,
And it does me perplex.
Indeed, said she, then list to me,
My bonny cock of wax.
Continually you make a noise,
And fill the house with strife,
I will tell you where your money goes,
I will upon my life.

There is two and threepence house rent,
Now attend to me, she said;
There is four shillings goes for meat,
And three and ninepence bread;
To wash your nasty dirty shirt
There is sixpence-halfpenny soap,
There's one and eightpence coals, old boy,
And tenpence wood and coke.

There's fourpence for milk and cream,
And one and twopence malt,
Three halfpence goes for vinegar
And twopence halfpenny salt;

A penny goes for mustard,
Three halfpence goes for thread,
And you gave me threepence the other night
For half a baked sheep's head.

A red herring every morning
Is fivepence farthing a week;
Sometimes you send me out for fish,
You say you can't eat meat.
Last Monday night home you got drunk,
There was ninepence went for capers,
You had a penny box of congreves,
And a halfpenny baked potato.

There's a penny goes for pepper too,
As you must understand;
Twopence halfpenny soda, starch and blue,
And a farthing's worth of sand.
Fourpence halfpenny goes for candles,
Three-farthings goes for matches,
And a penn'orth of pieces of cordury,
You had to mend your breeches.

A shilling potatoes, herbs and greens,
Tenpence butter now you see,
Sixpence coffee, eightpence sugar,
And one and fourpence tea.
There is twopence goes for this thing,
A penny for that and t'other;
Last night you broke a chamber pot,
And I had to buy another.

There's eightpence for tobacco,
And seven-farthings swipes,
There is threepence halfpenny snuff,
And twopence halfpenny tripes;
A penny you owed for strings
Over at the cobbler's shop,
And you know last Sunday morning
You had a bottle of ginger pop.

capers] scented tea   congreves] matches

There's twopence goes for blacking,
And eightpence halfpenny cheese,
A three-farthing rushlight every night,
To watch the bugs and fleas.
And while every night to a public house
You go to drink and sing,
I go to the wine vaults over the way
To have a drop of gin.

So reckon up again, old boy,
And you will find complete,
How five and twenty shillings were
Expended in one week.

290. *An Appeal by Unemployed Ex-Service Men*

Some thousands in England are starving,
And all through no fault of their own,
The troubles of poverty sharing,
And only to them is it known.
It's hard when the cupboard is empty,
And through the streets the poor men must roam,
And all the week through with nothing to do,
Yet with poor hungry children at home.

Then pity the ex-service workmen
Who starve all the week through,
They don't want to shirk any kind of hard work,
But, alas, they can't get it to do.

A man who is fond of his children
To keep them alive does his best
So to him it must be bewildering,
Yet brings sorrow to both parents' breast
To see his dear little ones starving,
In the midst of deep poverty hurled,
For no-one can tell what they must feel
So friendless and alone in the world.

339

The workman must live by his labour,
And that he needs have day by day,
And altho' he may have feeling neighbours
They have nothing they can give away.
For no-one knows where the shoe pinches,
But those who the pain have to bear,
With no work to do, all the week through,
And just *nothing* but sorrow and care.

There are many in towns and in cities
Who are walking the streets all foot-sore,
They surely deserve all your pity,
As dejected they pass by your door.
At factories and workshops they're calling
But they're told the same words every day:
There's no orders in hand, all over the land,
So no wages the masters can pay.

It used to be called happy England,
But where is its happiness now?
When people are slaving in thousands
At the factory, the loom and the plough.
In this country there's millions of money,
But those who have got it take care
Their sovereigns they nurse and they keep a full purse,
So the poor man can't get a share.

Then do what you can to assist them,
For they're all flesh and blood like yourselves.
Their poverty sadly oppresses them
With no food at all on the shelves.
The help that your fellow-man's needing
Should be given the country all through,
So help the poor man the best way you can,
Who *would* work if he had it to do.

Tradition in the Making

HARVEY ANDREWS

291. *Unaccompanied*

The hooter wakes me up to face the day again,
I wish that it would bloody go away again.
Monday's bad and Tuesday's worse,
Wednesday, Thursday, just a curse;
But Friday's payday, fill the purse
And pray again.

My wife she's growing round the waist, we're wild again;
The priest gives thanks that we've been blessed with child again.
After five I said no more,
I'd never touch her, that I swore;
But the priest said that's what loving's for—
Beguiled again.

They moved us to this bloody block of flats again;
Before we'd been there long we had the rats again.
The kids play on a piece of scrub,
We haven't even got a tub
But the priest he's formed a social club—
Rush mats again.

They built a special factory for work again,
Said it's a great job for you if you don't shirk again.
I stand around and tighten screws
And dream about a glass of booze.
Whichever way you turn you lose—
A berk again.

The car's packed up, I can't afford repairs again,
But the company's paid dividends on shares again.

The bloody telly's on the blink
And something's blocked the kitchen sink,
But the boss's mistress earned her mink—
Upstairs again.

The Thirties are a memory for Dad again,
He tells me it can never be that bad again.
But from Jarrow and from Clyde they'll come
With silent hearts and muffled drum:
We want the cake and not the crumb—
We're mad again.

PETER BELLAMY

292. *Sweet Loving Friendship*

If you look out from some high, high window,
You will see the sun set beyond the town;
You will see the rooks to the tree-tops screaming
And the wing of evening come folding down.

Between the morning and the evening,
Between the springtime and the winter drear,
There comes a time of new beginnings
When sweet loving friendship drives away all fear.

There's many here know nought but sorrow
And like the beasts they live from day to day,
But we can think of a bright tomorrow
Since sweet loving friendship drives all grief away.

All hope in prison it soon will smother
If none will with you your sorrow share,
But we cling fast to one each other
And sweet loving friendship banishes despair.

Just like the sailor when his ship makes harbour,
Just like the traveller who finds an inn,
What care they if the wind blow harder
When they be safe and warm within?

PETER BELLAMY

No lonely convict can resist the darkness,
Just as no sailor can the driving rain;
But find a comrade to share your fastness
And sweet loving friendship will ease your pain.

So if you look out from some high, high window
And see the sun set beyond the sky,
You need not mourn at the coming shadow
If some loving friend is standing nigh.

ERIC BOGLE

293. *Now I'm Easy*

For nearly fifty years I've been a cocky,
Of droughts and fires and floods I've lived through plenty;
This country's dust and mud have seen my tears and blood,
But it's nearly over now, and now I'm easy.

I married a fine girl when I was twenty,
But she died giving birth when she was thirty;
No flying doctor then, just a gentle old black gin,
But it's nearly over now, and now I'm easy.

She left me with two sons and a daughter,
And a bone-dry farm whose soil cried out for water;
So my care was rough and ready, but they grew up fine and steady,
But it's nearly over now, and now I'm easy.

My daughter married young and went her own way,
My sons lie buried by the Burma Railway;
So on this land I've made my own, I've carried on alone,
But it's nearly over now, and now I'm easy.

cocky] Australian word for a small farmer   gin] aborigine

294. *No Man's Land*

Well, how d'ye do, Private William McBride,
D'ye mind if I sit here down by your graveside?
I'll rest for a while in the warm summer sun,
I've been walking all day, and I'm nearly done.
And I see by your gravestone you were only nineteen
When you joined the 'glorious fallen' in Nineteen-sixteen.
Well, I hope you died quick and I hope you died clean,
Or, Willie McBride, was it slow and obscene?

> *Did they beat the drum slowly, did they play the fife lowly,*
> *Did the rifles fire o'er ye as they lowered you down,*
> *Did the bugles sing the 'Last Post' in chorus,*
> *Did the pipes play 'The Floo'ers o' the Forest'?*

And did you leave a wife or a sweetheart behind,
In some faithful heart is your memory enshrined,
And though you died back in Nineteen-sixteen,
To some faithful heart, are you forever nineteen?
Or are you a stranger without ever a name,
Enshrined for ever behind a glass pane,
In an old photograph torn and tattered and stained,
Fast fading to yellow in a leather-bound frame?

The sun's shining now on these green fields of France,
The warm wind blows gently and the red poppies dance,
The trenches have vanished under the plough,
No gas and no barbed-wire, no guns firing now.
But here in the graveyard it's still No Man's Land,
The countless white crosses in mute witness stand
To man's blind indifference to his fellow man,
To a whole generation who were butchered and damned.

And I can't help but wonder, Private William McBride,
Do all those who lie here know why they died?
Did you really believe them when they told you the cause,
Did you really believe that this war would end wars?
Well, the suffering, the sorrow, the glory, the shame,
The killing, the dying, it was all done in vain.
For, William McBride, it all happened again
And again and again and again and again.

ERIC BOGLE

295. *The Band Played Waltzing Matilda*

When I was a young man I carried a pack,
I lived the free life of a rover;
From the Murray's green basin to the dusty outback,
I waltzed my Matilda all over.
Then in Nineteen-fifteen, the country said, 'Son,
It's time you stopped roving, there's work to be done.'
So they gave me a tin hat and they gave me a gun,
And sent me away to the war.

> *And the band played Waltzing Matilda,*
> *As the ship pulled away from the quay,*
> *And midst all the cheers, flag-waving and tears,*
> *We sailed off to Gallipoli.*

How well I remember that terrible day,
How our blood stained the sand and the water.
And how in that hell that they called Suvla Bay,
We were butchered like lambs at the slaughter.
Johnny Turk he was ready, he'd primed himself well,
He showered us with bullets and he rained us with shell,
And in five minutes flat he'd blown us all to hell,
Nearly blew us right back to Australia.

> *And the band played Waltzing Matilda,*
> *When we stopped to bury the slain;*
> *We buried ours, the Turks buried theirs,*
> *Then we started all over again.*

And those that were left, we tried to survive,
In a sad world of blood, death and fire.
And for ten weary weeks I kept myself alive,
Though around me the corpses piled higher.
Then a big Turkish shell knocked me arse over head,
And when I woke up in my hospital bed,
I saw what it had done and I wished I was dead,
Never knew there were worse things than dying.

> *For I'll go no more Waltzing Matilda,*
> *All round the green bush far and free.*
> *To hump tent and pegs, a man needs both legs,*
> *No more Waltzing Matilda for me.*

So they gathered the crippled and wounded and maimed,
And they shipped us back home to Australia.
The legless, the armless, the blind and insane,
The brave wounded heroes of Suvla.
And when our ship pulled into Circular Quay,
I looked at the place where my legs used to be,
And thanked Christ there was nobody waiting for me,
To grieve, to mourn and to pity.

But the band played Waltzing Matilda
As they carried us down the gangway,
But nobody cared, they just stood and stared,
And they turned their faces away.

So now every April I sit on my porch,
And I watch the parade pass before me.
And I see my old comrades, how proudly they march
Reviving old dreams and past glory.
The old men march slowly, old bones stiff and sore,
Tired old men from a forgotten war,
And the young people ask, 'What are they marching for?'
I ask myself the same question.

But the band plays Waltzing Matilda
And the old men they answer the call.
But as year follows year, they get fewer and fewer,
Someday no-one will march there at all.

SYDNEY CARTER

296. *The First of My Lovers*

To the first of my lovers
On a high and holy hill
And the last of my lovers
I light a candle still.

And the bells will be ringing
On a high and holy hill
For the first of my lovers
And the last.

On the hill that was holy
For the pagan long ago
In the house of Our Lady now
I praise the name I know.

Oh my loves have been many
But the loving was for One
For the same light can shine in
A candle or a sun.

To the end and beginning
Of the loving that I know
To the end and beginning
My candlelight will go.

To the first of my lovers
On a high and holy hill
And the last of my lovers
I'll light a candle still.

297. *Lord of the Dance*

I danced in the morning
When the world was begun,
And I danced on the moon
And the stars and the sun,
And I came down from heaven
And I danced on the earth,
At Bethlehem
I had my birth.

> *Dance then, wherever you may be,*
> *I am the Lord of the Dance, said he,*
> *And I'll lead you all wherever you may be,*
> *And I'll lead you all in the dance, said he.*

I danced for the scribe
And the pharisee,
They would not dance
And they would not follow me.

I danced for the fishermen,
For James and John,
They came with me
And the dance went on.

I danced on a Friday
When the sky turned black—
It's hard to dance
With the devil on your back.
They buried my body
And they thought I'd gone,
But I am the dance
And I still go on.

They cut me down
And I leap up high;
I am the life
That'll never, never die;
I'll live in you
If you'll live in me—
I am the Lord
Of the Dance, said he.

PETER COE

298. *The Wizard of Alderley Edge*

From Mobberley on a bright morning, on a snow-white pure-bred
  mare,
A farmer rode to Macclesfield for to sell her at the fair.
Over Alderley Edge he took his path where the day is endless night,
But the mare did halt in a shroud of mist, for a man all clad in white.

> *From Macclesfield to Mobberley if you have wares to sell,*
> *Don't leave the path at the Wizard's Inn, or drink at the Wizard's*
> *Well.*

'Well met,' said the man as he stood in the path. 'Won't you sell to me
  your mare?'
But the farmer said, 'She's not for sale till I get to Macclesfield
  Fair.'
'Well, you can stand all day at the fair, but no bidding you will hear,
I'll await you in this very same place as the evening does draw near.'

Now this farmer was a puzzled man as he rode into Macclesfield
town,
For admiring glances all that day could never fill his purse with
crowns.
So he returned a bitter man as the sun fell in the sky,
And just as he had said that morn, this wizard did draw nigh.

'Now you must sell to me your mare for silver and bright gold,'
And he led the farmer and his mare down a path both dark and cold.
And they passed through some Iron Gates and through a great rock
wall,
Like moles they went, nigh double-bent, till they came to the
Sleepers' Hall.

With fear this farmer wide did gaze, and loudly did he moan,
For full-dressed knights each with one mount except for one alone.
'These are King Arthur's gallant men, who wait on England's need,
So fill your purse and leave your mare, and leave the Edge with
speed.'

Though he left the Edge a very rich man, his story caused him pain,
And those who would search for the Iron Gates will search the Edge
in vain.
But some do say that Old Nell Beck did find the Iron Gates,
But most say that she stricken was, with the March Hare as her mate.

PHIL and JUNE COLCLOUGH

299. *Song for Ireland*

Walking all the day
Near tall towers where falcons build their nests,
Silver-winged they fly,
They know the call of freedom in their breasts.
Saw Black Head against the sky,
Where twisted rocks they run to the sea.

Living on your western shore,
Saw summer sunsets, asked for more,
I stood by your Atlantic Sea
And sang a song for Ireland.

349

Drinking all the day
In old pubs where fiddlers love to play,
Saw one touch the bow,
He played a reel which seemed so grand and gay.
Stood on Dingle Beach and cast,
In wild foam we found Atlantic bass.

Talking all the day
With true friends who try to make you stay,
Telling jokes and news,
Singing songs to pass the time away.
Watched the Galway salmon run,
Like silver dancing, darting in the sun.

Dreaming in the night
I saw a land where no-one had to fight;
Waking in your dawn
I saw you crying in the morning light.
Sleeping where the falcons fly,
They twist and turn all in your air-blue sky.

300. *Blood on the Sails*

May the harpoon rust, may the cold steel be gone,
May the seas all be clear where the whale fishes run,
May the hook, knife, dart and line all be lost in the brine,
May the blood on the sails all be fishermen's tales.

May the whaleman's breath no more hang like the mist,
May he never face danger nor take any risk,
May the boat, gun, oar and mast all be lost in the frost,
May the blood on the sails all be fishermen's tales.

May the girls on the shore never have any fears,
May smiles touch the cheeks which once ran with tears,
May the ship, deck, rope and bells all grow cockle shells,
May the blood on the sails all be fishermen's tales.

May the seas ne'er be red where the whale fishes bled,
Nor shine like the wine when the whale fish is dead.
May the fleets, flags, sheds and quays all freeze in the seas,
May the blood on the sails all be fishermen's tales.

301. *Grey October*

Grey October in Glamorgan,
High pit heaps where the houses stand,
Fog in the valley, back shift ending,
Children awake in Aberfan.

Warm October in Thi Binh Province,
Huts of bamboo and rattan.
Sun comes up, repair gangs stop,
And children awaken in Thuy Dan.

Pithead hooter sounds from Merthyr,
Load the coal in the waiting trams,
Shoot the slag down the high pitheap
While children eat in Aberfan.

Oxcarts rattle down Thi Binh highway,
Work begins on the broken land.
Night's work ended, the roadway's mended,
Children eat in Thuy Dan.

School bell ringing, children running,
Down by the river and across the dam.
Hot sun burning, time for learning,
Time for school in Thuy Dan.

Lessons start in Pantglas Junior,
Through the fog a black wave ran;
Under the weight of the man-made mountain
Children die in Aberfan.

Lessons start in the Thi Binh schoolhouse
And another day began.
Bombs fly in the morning sky
And children die in Thuy Dan.

Tears are shed for Glamorgan children
And the world mourns Aberfan.
But who will weep for the murdered children
Under the rubble of Thuy Dan?

Grey October in Glamorgan,
Warm October in Vietnam,
Where children die while we stand by
And shake the killer by the hand.

VIN GARBUTT

302. *Mr Gunman*

Through years of Irish history
You've died and you've been named;
By British troops with British guns
Your families have been maimed.
I'm the first man to admit this—
My gran was Irish too—
And in my youth I learned the truth
Of what you have been through.

> *But Mr Gunman, I am saddened*
> *When I hear what you have done,*
> *And what you'll do tomorrow*
> *To another mother's son.*
> *Though your counterparts in office*
> *Are as guilty as the gun,*
> *With a thousand women weeping,*
> *Who will claim the battle won?*

My mother was born in England,
She married an Englishman,
They brought me up a Catholic
Though me Dad was a Protestant.
As man and wife for thirty years
They have lived in harmony,
So I've never had to understand
The world of bigotry.

I have sung about your heroes
And it was plain to see
That Irish songs would always stir
The Irish blood in me.
But heroes that I sang about
Were champions of the free,

Not trigger-happy hooligans
With patriot's disease.

The world is looking on now
In sympathy and rage
As Ulster's pagan bloodbath
Stares out from each new page.
And the hearts of folk around the world
Condemn your heartless crew
For the murder of the innocent
Whose face you never knew.

Your deeds the world should not condone
But neither close the door,
For British troops are now the pawns
Of a regime's ancient law.
And while the sniper's bullet brings
A tear into my eye,
My English blood condemns the cause
In which our soldiers die.

ALEX GLASGOW

303. *The Escalator*

Slowly upwards past the girdles,
Slowly upwards past revealing bras,
She floated slowly on the escalator
Slowly, slowly up to me.
And I descending to the underground,
Playing my familiar game,
Was captivated on the escalator,
Making downwards to another train.

But suddenly she smiled, smiled at me,
And such a smile it was, the kind you only see
In adolescent dreams.

And as we passed and shared the smiling,
Escalated briefly to a pair,
I rushed headlong down the escalator,
Joined the upward-rising stair.

And I raced to catch the moment,
Jostling sluggards, cursing loud,
Breathless through the barrier flying.
She had vanished in the crowd.

Slowly downwards past the girdles,
Slowly downwards past revealing bras,
Floating slowly down the escalator,
Slowly, lonely, to another train.

304. *Little Tommy Yesterday*

Little Tommy Yesterday, canny little man,
Little Tommy Yesterday, thinking of his mam.
Those roly-poly puddings and that crusty home-made bread,
And that feather-cushioned bosom always there to soothe his head.
Little Tommy Yesterday, canny little man,
Picks a bunch of daisies as a present for his mam.

Little Tommy Nowadays, canny little thing,
Gets his independence with a key upon a string,
Learns to fry fish-fingers at a very early age
And loves his absent mammy when she's out to earn a wage.
Little Tommy Nowadays, canny little man,
Buys some plastic roses as a present for his mam.

305. *Hands*

The notice at the factory gate
Announces they want hands.
I've seen the message many's the time
And now I understand.
It's hands they want and none beside,
Not hands with dignity or pride.
Just hands, hands, hands, lad,
Hands, hands, hands.

It's hands they want, just hands, lad,
And damn-all else beside.

ALEX GLASGOW

These hands seen through the master's eyes
Are simple horny hands.
They've got no bellies or brains attached,
They're merely horny hands.
These hands have got no hope, no fear,
No mouths to feed, no bairns to rear,
Just hands, hands, hands, lad,
Hands, hands, hands.

The master wants his hands as cheap
As dirt upon his floor,
And when they're old and weak
He'll hoy them careless out the door.
So remember as you make your plans,
Your life and his are in your hands.
Just hands, hands, hands, lad,
Hands, hands, hands.

DAVE GOULDER

306. *January Man*

Oh the January man he walks abroad in woollen coat and boots of
    leather,
The February man still wipes the snow from off his hair and blows his
    hand;
The man of March he sees the Spring and wonders what the year will
    bring,
And hopes for better weather.

Through April rain the man goes down to watch the birds come in to
    share the summer;
The man of May stands very still watching the children dance away
    the day.
In June the man inside the man is young and wants to lend a hand
And grins at each new comer.

And in July the man in cotton shirts he sits and thinks on being idle,
The August man in thousands take the road and watch the sea and
    find the sun.
September man is standing near to saddle up and lead the year
And Autumn is his bridle.

The man of new October takes the reins and early frost is on his
    shoulder,
The poor November man sees fire and wind and mist and rain and
    winter air.
December man looks through the snow to let eleven brothers know
They're all a little older.

And the January man comes round again in woollen coat and boots of
    leather
To take another turn and walk along the icy road he knows so well.
The January man is here for starting each and every year
Along the way for ever.

307. *The Long and Lonely Winter*

Summer comes October, the green becomes the brown,
The leaves will all be red and gold before they reach the ground.
Before they reach the ground, my dear, before they reach the ground,
The long and lonely winter will be here.

The early autumn evening was once the afternoon
And now the chill and frosty night it always comes too soon.
It always comes too soon, my dear, it always comes too soon,
The long and lonely winter will be here.

The whitethroat and the swallow are nowhere to be found,
And the redwing is upon the land before you turn around.
Before you turn around, my dear, before you turn around,
The long and lonely winter will be here.

The travellers have left the road so very long and still,
The sun will wait the winter through before he leaves the hill.
Before he leaves the hill, my dear, before he leaves the hill,
The long and lonely winter will be here.

Summer comes October, a season here and gone
And very little time to lose before the day is gone.
Before the day is done, my dear, before the day is done,
The long and lonely winter will be here.

MIKE HARDING

308. *Christmas 1914*

Christmas Eve in Nineteen-fourteen,
Stars were burning, burning bright,
And all along the Western Front
Guns were lying still and quiet.
Men lay dozing in the trenches
In the cold wind, in the dark,
And far away behind the lines
A village dog began to bark.

Some lay thinking of their families,
Some sang songs while others were quiet,
Rolling fags and playing brag
To pass away this Christmas night.
As they watched the German trenches,
Something moved in No Man's Land,
And through the dark there came a soldier
Carrying a white flag in his hands.

Then from both sides men came running,
Crossing into No Man's Land,
Through the barbed wire, mud and shell holes,
Shyly stood there shaking hands.
Fritz brought out cigars and brandy,
Tommy brought some Christmas pudding,
Stood there talking, shyly laughing,
As the moon shone down on No Man's Land.

Christmas Day we all played football
In the mud of No Man's Land.
Tommy brought some Christmas pudding,
Fritz brought out a German band.
When they beat us at the football,
We shared out all the grub and drink,
And Fritz showed me a faded photo
Of a brown-haired girl back in Berlin.

For four days after no-one fired,
Not one shell disturbed the night,
For old Fritz and Tommy Atkins
They'd both lost the will to fight.
So they withdrew us from the trenches,
Sent us far behind the lines,
Sent fresh troops to take our places,
Told the guns, 'Prepare to fire.'

And next night in Nineteen-fourteen,
Flares were burning, burning bright.
The message came, 'Prepare offensive,
Over the top we're going tonight.'
And men stood waiting in the trenches,
Looked out across our football park,
And all along the Western Front
The Christmas guns began to bark.

EWAN MacCOLL

309. *Freeborn Man*

I'm a freeborn man of the travelling people,
Got no fixed address, with nomads I am numbered.
Country lanes and byways were always my ways,
Never fancied being lumbered.

Oh we knew the woods, all the resting-places,
And the small birds sang when wintertime was over.
Then we'd pack our load and be on the road,
They were good old times for a rover.

There was open ground where a man could linger,
Stay a week or two, for time was not your master.
Then away you'd jog with your horse and dog,
Nice and easy! No need to go faster.

Now and then you'd meet up with other travellers,
Hear the news or else swap family information.
At the country fairs we'd be meeting there
All the people of the travelling nation.

EWAN MacCOLL

All your freeborn men of the travelling people,
Every tinker, rolling stone and gypsy rover,
Winds of change are blowing, old ways are going,
Your travelling days will soon be over.

310. *The Dove*

The dove it is a pretty bird, she sings as she flies,
She brings us glad tidings, she tells us no lies.
She sucks the spring waters to keep her voice clear,
When her nest she is building then summer is near.

Come all you young fellows, take a warning by me,
Don't go for a soldier, don't join no army.
For the dove she will leave you, the raven will come,
And death will come marching at the sound of a drum.

The dove it is a pretty bird, she sings as she flies,
She brings us glad tidings, she tells us no lies.
She flies in the mountains and the village so low,
And if you live peaceful she never will go.

Come all you pretty young girls, come walk in the sun,
And don't let your young man ever carry a gun.
For a gun it will scare her and she'll fly away
And then there'll be weeping by night and by day.

The dove it is a pretty bird, she sings as she flies,
And if you don't harm her she'll tell you no lies.

RALPH McTELL

311. *First and Last Man*

I am your noble savage
But to me I am a man,
The father of my sons
And the server of my woman.

And I have made my bow,
I take only what I need.
I am the maker of fire
And the planter of seed.

And I have learned an order in things
And I teach my children:
For each seed a star
To each son a generation.

I have no time for freedom,
Barefoot I run on the forest leaves.
There is pain in birth
But for the dead I do not grieve.

I have cut marks on my body;
There is beauty in pain
And a sadness in joy
Like death and the sunset.

I am the willing heathen,
I worship everything.
I will add new words to my language
But write them on the wind.

I am the maker of music
And the reader of the heavens;
I am the worker of magic
And the fearer of storms.

I am the writer in sand,
I am the first and last man;
And if I could read the future
I would ask you not to come.

AUSTIN JOHN MARSHALL

312. *Dancing at Whitsun*

It's fifty-one springtimes since she was a bride,
And still you may see her at each Whitsuntide
In dress of white linen and ribbons of green,
As green as her memories of loving.

The feet that were nimble tread carefully now,
As gentle a measure as age do allow,
Through groves of white blossom by fields of young corn,
Where once she was pledged to her true love.

The fields they stand empty and the hedges grow free,
No young men to tend them or pastures go see.
They have gone where the forests of oak trees before
Had gone to be wasted in battle.

Down from their green farmlands and from their loved ones
Marched husbands and lovers and fathers and sons.
There's a fine roll of honour where the maypole once stood,
And the ladies go dancing at Whitsun.

There's a row of straight houses in these latter days
Are covering the downs where the sheep used to graze.
There's a field of red poppies and a wreath from the Queen,
But the ladies remember at Whitsun
And the ladies go dancing at Whitsun.

LEON ROSSELSON

313. *Palaces of Gold*

If the sons of company directors and judges' private daughters
Had to go to school in a slum school,
Dumped by some joker in a damp back alley,
Had to herd into classrooms cramped with worry,
With a view on to slagheaps and stagnant pools,
Had to file through corridors grey with age
And play in a crackpot concrete cage,

361

Buttons would be pressed,
Rules would be broken,
Strings would be pulled
And magic words spoken.
Invisible fingers would mould
Palaces of gold.

If prime ministers and advertising executives,
Royal personages and bank managers' wives
Had to live out their lives in dank rooms,
Blinded by smoke and the foul air of sewers,
Rot on the walls and rats in the cellars,
In rows of dumb houses like mouldering tombs,
Had to bring up their children and watch them grow
In a waste land of dead streets where nothing will grow,
 Buttons would be pressed,
 Rules would be broken,
 Strings would be pulled
 And magic words spoken.
 Invisible fingers would mould
 Palaces of gold.

I'm not suggesting any sort of plot,
Everyone knows there's not,
But you unborn millions might like to be warned
That if you don't want to be buried alive by slagheaps,
Pitfalls and damp walls and rat-traps and dead streets,
Arrange to be democratically born
The son of a company director,
Or a judge's fine and private daughter.
 Buttons will be pressed,
 Rules will be broken,
 Strings will be pulled
 And magic words spoken.
 Invisible fingers will mould
 Palaces of gold.

CYRIL TAWNEY

314. *Sally Free and Easy*

Sally free and easy,
That should be her name.
Sally free and easy
That should be her name.
Took a sailor's loving
For a nursery game.

Well, the heart she gave me
Wasn't made of stone,
It was sweet and hollow
Like a honeycomb.

Think I'll wait till sunset,
See the ensign down.
Then I'll take the tideway
To my burying ground.

Sally free and easy
That should be her name.
When my body's landed,
Hope she dies of shame.

315. *On a Monday Morning*

Too soon to be out of me bed,
Too soon to be back at this bus-queue caper
Or fumbling for change for me picture paper
On a Monday morning.

Wrong end of the week for a smile,
Wrong end of the day for being civil,
There's many a saint would be a devil
On a Monday morning.

Where is the weekend now?
Where is the whisky and beer I tasted?
Gone the same way as the pay I've wasted
On a Monday morning.

If only the birds would booze,
If only the sun were a party-giver,
If I could just lend someone else me liver
On a Monday morning.

My lover she lies asleep,
My lover is warm and her heart is mellow,
I'd trade you the world just to share her pillow
On a Monday morning.

316. *The Grey Funnel Line*

Don't mind the rain or the rollin' sea,
The weary night never worries me,
But the hardest time in a sailor's day
Is to watch the sun as it dies away.

It's one more day on the Grey Funnel Line.

The finest ship that sailed the sea
Is still a prison for the likes of me,
But give me wings like Noah's dove
I'd fly up harbour to the girl I love.

There was a time my heart was free
Like a floating spar on an open sea.
But now the spar is washed ashore,
It comes to rest at my real love's door.

Every time I gaze behind the screws
Makes me long for old Peter's shoes,
I'd walk right down that silver lane
And take my love in my arms again.

O Lord, if dreams were only real,
I'd have my hands on that wooden wheel,
And with all my heart I'd turn her round
And tell the boys we're homeward bound.

CYRIL TAWNEY

I'll pass the time like some machine
Until the blue water turns to green.
Then I'll dance on down that walk ashore
And sail the Grey Funnel Line no more.

317. *Reunion*

Sorrow is my stock in trade
And sadness is my style,
And if you're looking for a smile from me
You'll need to wait a long, long while.

Because I'm not the man you used to see
In smoky taverns years ago,
When heads were reeling in the easy days
And Youth knew all there was to know.

You knew a lady then and so did I.
Did I say 'lady'? That's a laugh.
I tried to tame her off and on for years,
She proved too smart for me by half.

How come she always stayed so young, my friend,
While we grew older by the day?
It brings to mind the way that people smile
To see December chasing May.

There's more to drinking than a glass of wine,
There's more to dying than 'Goodbye'.
I know it's hard to toss the glass away,
But comes a time you have to try.

And that means goodbye Jack and goodbye Joe,
Farewell companions everywhere.
If I could draw the line at one or two,
Next time they gathered I'd be there.

And what price revelry without the ale?
The bonhomie becomes a bore,
The roaring laughter rings so hollow then,
The jokes aren't funny any more.

So spare a thought for this old sobersides
Next time you're standing jar in hand.
If I don't celebrate our meeting here
I'm sure by now you'll understand.

Yes, that's why sorrow is my stock in trade
And sadness is my style,
And if you're looking for a smile from me
Wait on, wait on, wait on, old pal of mine,
You'll need to wait a long, long while.

ALLAN TAYLOR

318. *Time*

Time will not be mastered, he will do just as he please,
He will watch you when you stumble, watch you fall upon your knees.
He will place upon your breaking back a weight you cannot hold,
And as you stand there broken he will watch you growing old.

> *But while there's time take a chance,*
> *Join the laughter, join the dance,*
> *And just sing along with the lovers who walk hand in hand.*
> *Life is grand but too short for the learning;*
> *Try not to hear, but the wheel is still turning.*

In your youth you'll want to laugh at him, you're too young to feel
    afraid,
And you'll keep him from your company and you'll turn your gaze
    away;
But as the years lie heavy, and you turn and he's still there
You may try to treat him gently, but he's grown too old to care.

You will reach out with your shaking hands, he will welcome you with
    grace,
But as you move to touch him you will see he has no face,
For he hides behind a shadow like a thief hides out of sight,
And like a thief he waits for you as your day approaches night.

319. *Ballad for the Unknown Soldier*

I was running back when I heard him call
And as I turned I saw him fall,
His body frozen in disbelief,
And fell to earth like a fallen leaf.

> *Strike the flag, bring it down,*
> *Bury it with the sad unknown.*

I laid a hand upon his brow,
It felt cold and I wondered how.
He stared at me through faded eyes;
So this is how a young man dies.

There's no glory when it comes to this,
No grand farewell, no final kiss.
The taste is bitter and fouls the mouth
And never fades for fallen youth.

One man dies and I survive,
It leaves me empty, just alive.
Another number is all it means
To those who watch behind the scenes.

Who lies forgotten, far away,
Who really died on that cold day?
Was it someone you thought you knew
Was it me or was it you?

320. *Still He Sings*

After night there comes the day
And so the dark will pass away;
Through the dawn a wondrous thing is born,
Comes the day.

When the minstrel sings his song
And the people wonder on,
Still he sings for the pleasure music brings,
Still he sings.

When the words begin to rhyme,
And then flow as rich as wine,
Then you've heard the poet's spoken word,
Rich as wine.

When the colours seem to fade,
Perhaps you're standing in the shade;
Just for you the colours filter through,
Just for you.

ACKNOWLEDGEMENTS

I am indebted to the following for freely-given assistance and constructive comments: Peter Bellamy, Harry Boardman, Professor Alan Gemmell, Paul Graney, Michael Kennedy, S. A. Mathews, Michael Grosvenor Myer, Jon Raven, Cyril Tawney, Malcolm Taylor, and Brian Turner.

That prince of folk-song researchers, Roy Palmer, has given me unstinting encouragement and smoothed my path on many occasions; I have also availed myself of some of his edited texts, since it would be difficult to improve on them.

Mrs Ursula Vaughan Williams has been, as in all things, the soul of warmth and generosity in the matter of her late husband's manuscripts: to her my very special thanks.

I also wish to thank the following for their permission to reproduce copyright lyrics in this book:

Harvey Andrews: 'Unacompanied'. Reprinted by permission of Westminster Music Ltd.

Peter Bellamy: 'Sweet Loving Friendship'. Reprinted by permission of Free Reed Music.

Eric Bogle: 'Now I'm Easy', 'No Man's Land', 'The Band Played Waltzing Matilda'. Reprinted by permission of Island Music Ltd.

Sydney Carter: 'The First of My Lovers,' 'Lord of the Dance'. Reprinted by permission of Stainer and Bell Ltd.

Peter Coe: 'The Wizard of Alderley Edge'. Reprinted by permision of Highway Music.

Phil and June Colclough: 'Song for Ireland.' Reprinted by permission of Mole Music Ltd. 'Blood on the Sails.' Reprinted by permission of the authors.

The Critics: 'Grey October'. Reprinted by permission of Ewan MacColl Ltd.

Vin Garbutt: 'Mr Gunman'. Reprinted by permission of the author.

Alex Glasgow: 'The Escalator', 'Little Tommy Yesterday', 'Hands'. Reprinted by permission of the author.

Dave Goulder: 'January Man', 'The Long and Lonely Winter'. Published by Robbins Music Corporation Ltd. and reprinted by permission of EMI Music Publishing Ltd.

Mike Harding: 'Christmas 1914'. Published by Francis Day and Hunter Ltd. and reprinted by permission of EMI Music Publishing Ltd.

Ewan MacColl: 'Freeborn Man', 'The Dove'. Reprinted by permission of Harmony Music Ltd.

Ralph McTell: 'First and Last Man'. Reprinted by permission of Westminster Music Ltd.

Austin John Marshall: 'Dancing at Whitsun'. Published by Shapiro Bernstein Ltd. and reprinted by permission of the author.

ACKNOWLEDGEMENTS

Leon Rosselson: 'Palaces of Gold'. Reprinted by permission of Essex Music Ltd.

Cyril Tawney: 'Sally Free and Easy', 'On a Monday Morning', 'The Grey Funnel Line', 'Reunion'. Published by Gwyneth Music Ltd. and reprinted by permission of Dick James Music Ltd.

Allan Taylor: 'Time', 'Ballad for the Unknown Soldier'. Reprinted by permission of Chrysalis Music Ltd. 'Still He Sings'. Reprinted by permission of the author.

Traditional: 'The Shepherd and the Shepherdess' (No. 79). Reprinted by permission of Stainer and Bell Ltd. 'When Adam was first created', 'Softly the Night' (Nos. 86 and 200). Reprinted by permission of Coppersongs.

NOTES AND REFERENCES

Most of the lyrics in this collection have been handed down through generations of traditional singers. It is only just that acknowledgement should be given to such devoted care, and I have therefore given the names of the singers who allowed their words to be taken down, together with their location, the date of collection, and the initials of the collector (in brackets).

Abbreviations

SB-G	Revd Sabine Baring-Gould
LB	Lucy Broadwood
GBG	George B. Gardiner
PG	Percy Grainger
FH	Fred Hamer
HEDH	H. E. D. Hammond
ALL	A. L. Lloyd
EM	Ewan MacColl
RP	Roy Palmer
CS	Cecil Sharp
AW	Alfred Williams
RVW	Ralph Vaughan Williams

'Child' in the Notes that follow refers to F. J. Child, *The English and Scottish Popular Ballads* (1882–98), 5 vols. See Introduction, p. ix.
For details of lyrics still in copyright, see also the Acknowledgements.

1. Child 156A.
2. Child 139.
3. Child 120B.
4. Child 162B. Chevy Chase was called by the Scots the Battle of Otterbourne, and there is a separate Scottish ballad of that title. The engagement took place on 15 August 1388 and the facts—as distinct from the ballad's embroideries—are that Douglas raided Northumberland and defeated Henry Percy (Harry Hotspur). Percy struck back with a night attack but was defeated and captured, even though Douglas was killed.
5. Child 164. A story of doubtful validity, though some early historians (e.g. Otterbourne) mention it. In similar vein, Darius wrote to the young Alexander patronizingly, and sent him a ball to play with.
6. Printed in Chappell, *Popular Music of the Olden Time*. Henry V forbade the making of ballads on his victory, but this one seems to have been accepted, perhaps because of its religious refrain.
7. George Gouldthorpe, Brigg, Lincs, 1906 (PG). Lucy Broadwood has suggested that this song refers to William de la Pole, 1st Duke of Suffolk, whose body was thrown into the sea at Dover after his murder by political enemies in 1450. See also *Henry IV, Part 2*, Act 4.

8. Mrs Russell, Upwey, Dorset, 1907 (HEDH).

9. Child 288A, from a broadside published by John White of Newcastle upon Tyne. The text is almost certainly eighteenth century.

10. Child 287. Ward became a pirate in 1604 and was referred to as 'late' in 1609. The 'jewels' mentioned in the last verse are George Clifford, Earl of Cumberland (d. 1605), Charles Blount, Lord Mountjoy (d. 1606) and Robert Devereux, Earl of Essex (d. 1601). The *Rainbow* was the name of one of Drake's four ships in the Cadiz expedition of 1587.

11. Text taken from Nettel, *Sing a Song of England* (Phoenix House, 1954). The song is a product of the Gloucestershire Society, founded in 1657 and comprising many old Catholic families and a number of Dissenters— an unlikely mingling united by opposition to Cromwell. It is a code song, with a political meaning buried below its apparently innocuous surface. For an explanation I can do no better than quote Reginald Nettel (op. cit.):

> 'George Ridler' was Charles I, whose 'oven' was the Cavalier Party; the stones with which the oven was built, and which 'came out of the Blakeney Quaar' were the followers of the Marquis of Worcester, who held out to the last at Raglan Castle, not surrendering until August 1646. George Ridler's head grew above his hair because the head of the State was the Crown, which the King wore. The King's boast before he died was that the British Constitution would recover, despite his adversity, in its true form of King, Lords, and Commons (the three sons who sang in harmony—treble, mean, and bass). 'Mine hostess' was the Queen, and her maid the Catholic Church of which she was a member. The 'dog' was a faithful adherent to the society; he would visit the 'sick', meaning desponding members, and prevent them from 'dying', or losing faith in the cause; he would also seek out any likely recruits to the society, whatever their opinions (hen, duck, or goose), providing they honestly wished the return of Charles II. 'The good ale tap' was supposed by reason of a pun on 'ale' and 'aisle' to refer to the Church of England, and the final warning is about the timid, who gather round when things look prosperous (three sixpences under the thumb) but drop away when things look ill (poverty). The singer therefore wishes in the end to be buried with his loyal companions in the church.

It should perhaps be added that the present editor shares Mr Nettel's caution as to the accuracy of this interpretation, intriguing though it is.

12. From an unimprinted broadside *c.* 1722.

13. Sam Gregory, Beaminster, Dorset, *c.* 1907 (HEDH).

14. Broadside text printed in Kidson's *Songs of Britain*. One of the pro-Napoleonic songs of the period.

15. Broadside from H. Such, London, 1815.

16. Harry Cox, Catield, Norfolk, 1953 (Peter Kennedy). Recorded.

17. Broadside from J. Harkness, Preston, 1852.

18–19. Walter Pardon, Knapton, Norfolk, 1977 (Bill Leader). Recorded.

20. Jack Barnard, Bridgwater, Somerset, 1906 (CS).

21. Child 63A.

22. Collated from versions by Mrs Emily Cockran, Meshaw, Devon, 1904 and Sister Emma, Clewer, Berks, 1909 (both CS).

23. James Parsons, n.p., n.d. (SB-G). Baring-Gould originally printed the song in two (obvious) parts. Parsons, however, sang the song right through as printed here. This was the only time, apparently, that the first part has been collected, and it has the merit of suggesting a reason for the lady's later capricious behaviour. Child found this version unacceptable, but Parsons was illiterate and got the song orally from his grandfather. Child also maintained that the song was Scottish but, as Baring-Gould observed, 'The Scotch are wont to take an old ballad, give it local habitation and name, and so make it out to be purely Scottish.'

24. Child 74B.

25. Child 295B (originally collected by SB–G).

26–7. Walter Pardon, Knapton, Norfolk, 1975 (Bill Leader). Recorded.

28–9. Cecilia Costello, Birmingham, 1951 (Marie Slocombe and Patrick Shuldham-Shaw). Recorded.

30. Recalled by Mrs Gibbons as sung to her by her nurse Elizabeth Doidge, *c.* 1828, and sent to SB-G. Vv. 5, 6, 10 and 11 supplied by SB-G from another, unknown source. St John's Wort exudes a milky fluid when cut; no other plant has so many medicinal uses.

31. From *Four Excellent Songs: Licensed and Entered According to Order*, n.d. BM 11621.b.6[12].

32. Mr Barrett, Puddletown, n.d. (HEDH).

33. May Bradley, Shropshire, *c.* 1965 (FH).

34. J. Watts, Thrushleton, Devon, *c.* 1890 (SB-G).

35. Jesse Eldridge, Highworth, Wilts. *c.* 1914 (AW).

36–7. From broadside texts in the Madden Collection, University Library, Cambridge.

38. Jack Barnard, Bridgwater, Somerset, 1907 (CS).

39. Walter Locock, Martock, Somerset, 1906 (CS).

40. Joseph Alcock, Sibford Gower, Warwicks, 1922 (CS).

41. George Radford, Bridgwater, Somerset, 1905 (CS).

42. Miss Wilson, Lancs, *c.* 1965 (FH).

43. Broadside from Pitts, Seven Dials, London.

44. Mrs Powell, nr. Weobley, Herefordshire, 1909 (RVW).

45. Lucy Stewart, Fetterangus, Aberdeenshire, *c.* 1965.

46. James Hill, Dunmow, Essex, 1912 (CS).

47. Unknown singer at Bishopstone, Wilts, *c.* 1914 (AW).

48. Mr Seers or Shears, Winterslow, Wilts, 1904 (RVW).

49. Text in Bruce and Stokoe, *A Northumbrian Minstrelsy* (1882).

50. Broadside by Wood of Birmingham. Birmingham Reference Library 119932, p. 77.

51. Harry Green, Essex, *c.* 1965 (FH).

52. Charlie Wills, Ryall, Dorset, 1972 (Bill Leader). Recorded.

53. Henry Larcombe, Haselbury Plucknett, Somerset, 1905 (CS).

54. Child 106.

55. Mrs Sweet, Somerton, Somerset, 1907 (CS).

56. Mrs Slade, Minehead, Somerset, 1904 (CS).

57. David Sawyer, Ogbourne, *c.* 1915 (AW).

58. George Dowden, Lackington, Dorset, 1905 (HEDH). An obscure song. Although it has been more frequently encountered in Sussex, Lucy Broadwood postulated a Cornish origin, with the 'little streamers' being young tin-miners who 'stream' or wash the ore. Mis A. G. Gilchrist suggested that the song might be 'an unrecognised relic of a hymn to Mary'. Baring-Gould, however, collected a West Country version called 'The Streams of Nantsian', and pointed out that 'Nant' means a falling stream or a valley in Cornish. By the same token, the suffix '-sian' or '-zion' is also to be met in Cornwall. 'Lovely Nancy' could therefore be merely a corruption of a Cornish place-name. None of which really makes the text any clearer, but it remains a quite hypnotic lyric.

59. The King family, Castle Eaton, *c.* 1915 (AW).

60. Ephraim Head, South Marston, Wilts, *c.* 1914 (AW).

61. Alfred Oliver, Axford, Hampshire, 1907 (GBG).

62. Mrs Elizabeth Webb, Alvescot, Oxfordshire, *c.* 1915 (AW).

63. Text in Pinto and Rodway, *The Common Muse.* Nottingham Library 118/B2.

64. William Briffett, Bridgwater, Somerset, 1905 (CS).

65. Mrs Jane Gulliford, Combe Florey, Somerset, 1908 (CS).

66. Mrs Louie Hooper and Mrs Lucy White, Hambridge, Somerset, 1903 (CS).

67. Captain Lewis, Minehead, Somerset, 1906 (CS).

68. (a) William Stokes, Chew Stoke, Somerset, 1908 (CS). (b) Singer not noted, Hambridge, Somerset, 1904 (CS).

69. Walter Pardon, Knapton, Norfolk, 1978 (RP). One verse has been added by Mr Palmer, from a broadside by Such of London.

70. Mrs Pike, Somerton, Somerset, 1906 (CS).

71. John Briffett, Bridgwater, Somerset, 1905 (CS).

72. Mrs Susan Clarke, Bridgwater, Somerset, 1907 (CS).

73. Mrs Laurence, Somerton, Somerset, 1906 (CS).

74. Mrs Lizzie Welch, Hambridge, Somerset, 1904 (CS).

75. Text collated by James Reeves from versions from William Morley, Bincombe, 1907; James Beale, Wareham, Kent, 1908; Lucy White and Louis Hooper, Hambridge, Somerset, 1903; Alfred Emery, Othery, 1908 (all CS).

76. Mrs Pike, Somerton, Somerset, 1907 (CS).

77. Mrs J. Masters, Bradstone, n.d. (SB–G).

78. Text from the Firth Collection, Bodleian b. 26.220.

79. Mrs Johnstone, Goldrington, Bedfordshire, 1966 (Martin Webber).

80. Taken from O'Keefe: *First Book of Irish Ballads* (Mercier Press, 1955). Traditional Irish, but thoroughly assimilated into the English tradition.

81. Walter Pardon, Knapton, Norfolk, 1975 (Bill Leader). Recorded.

82. Child 105.

83. Unnamed workman at Burra Tor Reservoir, Devon, *c.* 1890 (SB–G).

84. Child 26.

85. James Harris, Southleigh, Oxfordshire, c. 1914 (AW).

86. The Copper family, Peacehaven, Sussex, 1970 (Bill Leader). Recorded.

87. Elijah Iles, Inglesham, Wilts, c. 1914 (AW).

88. Broadside by Bebbington of Manchester, 1800.

89. Unnamed lady in Clanfield, Oxfordshire, c. 1915 (AW).

90. Luther Stanley, Lincolnshire, c. 1956 (FH).

91. Sister Emma, Clewer, Berkshire, 1909 (CS).

92. Child 81A.

93. Thomas Bowers, Titchfield, Hampshire, 1907 (SB-G).

94. J. Paddon, Holcombe Burnell, 1889 (SB-G).

95. Broadside from T. Bloomer of Birmingham.

96. Mrs Lucy Woodall, Cradley Heath, Worcestershire, 1979 (RP).

97. Shepherd Hayden, Bampton, Oxfordshire, 1909 (CS).

98. Cecilia Costello, Birmingham, 1951 (Marie Slocombe and Patrick Shuldham-Shaw). Recorded.

99. William Briffett, Bridgwater, Somerset, 1907 (CS).

100. James Beale, Warehorne, Kent, 1908 (CS).

101. Text from Nettel, op. cit.

102. Broadside from Harkness of Preson, no. 386.

103. (a) Broadside in the Madden Collection. (b) J. Curtis, Lyme Regis, Dorset, 1906 (HEDH). Two of a particularly interesting chain of transmission, ending up with the American 'Streets of Laredo', in which the cowboy dies not of syphilis but of a clean gunshot wound.

104. William Bartlett, Wimborne, Dorset, 1905 (SB-G).

105. (a) Mrs Overd, Langport, Somerset, 1904 (CS). (b) Mrs Goodyear, Axford, Hampshire, 1907 (SB-G).

106. Mrs Gulliver, 1905 (HEDH).

107. Baring-Gould suppressed the 'objectionable' words he took down and rewrote the text for inclusion in *English Minstrelsie*. I have used the text restored by RP from a typescript copy in Shrewsbury City Library, entitled 'Mow the Meadows Down'.

108. James Masters, Broadstone, Devon, 1891 (SB-G).

109. (a) Mrs Jarrett, Bridgwater, Somerset, 1908 (CS). (b) Mrs Elizabeth Smitherd, Tewkesbury, Gloucestershire, 1908 (CS). A good example of a song consisting entirely of 'floaters' (i.e. general purpose verses in wide circulation.) See also No. 210 and, for a contemporary pacifist pastiche, No. 310.

110. Henry Thomas, Chipping Sodbury, Gloucestershire, 1907 (CS).

111. William Tucker, Ashcott, Somerset, 1907 (CS).

112. Jack Barnard, Bridgwater, Somerset, 1906 (CS).

113. Mrs Overd, Langport, Somerset, 1904 (CS).

114. Text taken from Pinto and Rodway, op. cit.

115. Eileen Hannoran, Brownhills, Staffordshire, 1967 (collected by the Birmingham and Midland Folk Centre).

116–17. Broadsides in the Madden Collection.

118. George Dowden, Lackington, Dorset, 1905 (HEDH).

119. Collated from various versions collected by CS.
120. Broadside from Harkness of Preston, no. 211.
121. Child 286C.
122. Henry Burstow, Horsham, Sussex, 1894 (LB).
123. James Thomas, Cannington, Somerset, 1906 (CS).
124. Mrs Elizabeth Smitherd, Tewkesbury, Gloucestershire, 1908 (CS).
125. Henry Thomas, Chipping Sodbury, Gloucestershire, 1907 (CS).
126. Mrs Esther Williams, London, 1908 (CS).
127. Captain Lewis, Minehead, Somerset, 1906 (CS).
128. Harry Richards, Curry Rivel, Somerset, 1904 (CS).
129. Collected by HEDH from unknown singer.
130. Collated from versions from Mrs Betsy Pike, Somerton, Somerset, 1906 and Frederick Crossman, Huish Episcopi, Somerset, 1904 (both CS).
131. John Vincent, Priddy, Somerset, 1905 (CS).
132. Tom Sprachlan, Hambridge, Somerset, 1903 (CS).
133. Stan Hugill, self-collected and published in *Sea Shanties* (Barrie and Jenkins, 1977).
134. Broadside from Russell of Birmingham.
135. R. Gregory, Two Bridges, 1890 (SB-G). Some versions of this song cynically give priority to the whale in v. 11.
136. William Lawrence, Ely, Cambridgeshire, 1911 (CS).
137. Text taken from Ashton, *Real Sailor Songs* (1891).
138. As 137. The lyric has the distinct air of a Stanley Holloway monologue!
139. As 133.
140. Originally printed in *Ben Brierley's Journal*, 20 October 1888—five years before the canal opened! The initials RSK are the only signature.
141. David Parrott, Bedford, Bedfordshire, 1960s (FH).
142. William Briffett, Bridgwater, Somerset, 1907 (CS).
143. Mrs Goodyear, Axford, Hampshire, 1907 (GBG).
144. W. H. C. Bartlett, Wimborne, Dorset, 1905 (HEDH).
145. W. Crossing, Dartmoor, 1878, with vv. 8 and 9 from Richard Cleave, Buckley Bridge, 1892 (both SB-G).
146. Mrs Poole, Beaminster, Dorset, 1906 (SB-G).
147. Mrs Overd, Langport, Somerset, 1906 (CS).
148. Printed in Chappell, op. cit. There is a tradition that General Wolfe wrote this song on the eve of the Battle of Quebec, but it was in fact written for an opera performed in London in 1729.
149. Text taken from P. W. Joyce, *Old Irish Folk Music and Songs*.
150. Text taken from a handbill distributed c. 1800 (AW).
151. Broadside from J. Whiting of Birmingham c. 1817.
152. As 148.
153. Collated from versions from Isla Cameron, London, and Sidney Richards, Curry Rivel, Somerset; the latter collected by Peter Kennedy. The collation is by Karl Dallas.
154. O. J. Abbott, Quebec, Canada, 1957 (Edith Fowke).
155. J. T. Huxtable, Workington (ALL).

156. Walter Wilcock, London, 1908 (CS).

157. A soldiers' song from the First World War.

158. J. Ree, Hambridge, Somerset, 1905 (CS).

159. May Bradley, Shropshire, 1960s (FH).

160. Charles Neville, East Coker, Somerset, 1908 (CS).

161. Mrs Hopkins, Axford, Hampshire, 1907 (RVW and Charles Gamblin).

162. Henry Larcombe, Haselbury Plucknett, Somerset, 1905 (CS). V. 6 added from version from Mrs Elizabeth Edbrook, Withycombe, Somerset, 1908 (CS).

163. Mrs Jane Gulliford, Combe Florey, Somerset, 1908 (CS).

164. Henry Burstow, Horsham, Sussex, 1893 (LB).

165. Alexander Crawford, Leck, Ballymoney (Sam Henry). Sam Henry Collection no. 735.

166. Mrs Bowring, Cerne Abbas, Dorset, 1907 (HEDH).

167. (a) Mrs Holden, Worcestershire, 1960s (FH). **(b)** Tony Seymour, Kidderminster, 1960s (RP). A music hall parody of (a). See also Child 12.

168. Version of Child 10, collated by RP.

169. Broadside by Thomas Millington, London, 1598. 'A tract by Luke Hutton, of which there were two editions, the first without date, and the last in 1638, is very well known, and an account of it may be found in the Bridgewater Collection (privately printed for Lord Francis Egerton), p. 149. Hence it appears also that Hutton was the author of an earlier production, called his "Repentance". He seems to have been a highwayman and housebreaker who, being condemned and pardoned, dedicated an affected piece of contrition to Lord Chief Justice Popham; and on subsequent liberation, returned to his old courses, and was hanged at York in 1598. Whether what follows, or indeed anything that goes under his name, were really written by him is very questionable.' J. Payne Collier, *Old Ballads* (Percy Society).

170. G. Giles, Blunsdon Hill, Oxfordshire, *c.* 1914 (AW).

171. William Nott, Meshaw, Devon, 1904 (CS).

172. Jack Barnard, Bridgwater, Somerset, 1908 (CS).

173. Charles Ash, Crowcombe, Somerset, 1908 (CS).

174. James Brooman, Upper Faringdon, Hampshire, 1908 (GBG).

175. (a) Walter Pardon, Knapton, Norfolk, 1975 (Bill Leader). Recorded. **(b)** Mr Broomfield, East Hornden, Essex, 1904 (RVW).

176. Broadside by J. Catnach, London, 1828. Corder was hanged at noon, 11 August 1828, at Bury St Edmunds.

177. Broadside from Disley, London, 1865. For once the broadside scribblers got it wrong. Constance Kent was reprieved and served a prison sentence of twenty years. On her release in 1885, she emigrated to Canada, changed her name, and lived out the rest of her life working as a nurse.

178. Text taken from John Ashton, *Modern Street Ballads*.

179. The song exists in several versions with relatively minor variants. For many years there was a tradition in the army that to sing it was a chargeable offence (incitement to mutiny). The present editor first heard it in 1955, sung by a piper of the London Scottish on Salisbury Plain, and it was clear that he at least believed the tradition.

There has been much confusion about the facts that gave rise to the ballad, though they are now beyond dispute. On 14 September 1861, Private Patrick McCaffery of the 32nd (Cornwall) Regiment of Foot (Light Infantry), stationed at Fulwood Barracks, Preston, shot and killed his Depot Commander, Colonel Hugh Denis Crofton, and the Depot Adjutant, Captain John Hanham. He was publicly executed on 11 January 1862. Versions of the song have been collected which give the regiment as either the 42nd (Black Watch) or the 47th (Loyal Lancashire Regiment): these errors have arisen through aural confusion. For a detailed account of the background and trial, see *Folk Review*, Vol. 3, no. 8, June 1974.

180. Mrs Reservoir Butler, Armscote, Warwickshire, 1913 (CS).

181. Thomas Taylor, Ross, Herefordshire, 1912 (CS).

182. As 180. The superbly-named lady actually sang 'O God's in France all Sunday'—a quite inspired piece of corruption!

183. (a) Mrs Whatton and Mrs Loveridge, Dilwyn, Herefordshire, 1908 (RVW). **(b)** May Bradley, Shropshire, 1960s (FH).

184. J. Evans Dilwyn, Herefordshire, 1907 (RVW). It would probably take a lengthy theological—and indeed herpetological—debate to determine precisely where a serpent's knee is situated!

185. Attributed to Hugh Bourne of Newcastle under Lyme.

186. Mrs Bond, Quenington, Oxfordshire, *c.* 1914 (AW).

187. Mrs Kilford, Lilleshall, Shropshire, 1911 (CS).

188. Thomas Taylor, Ross, Herefordshire, 1921 (CS).

189. Text in Nettel, op. cit. This well-known song is of Cornish origin and, according to Etonian tradition, was once used to teach the Creed. The key to the symbols goes as follows: 1 = God; 2 = Christ and John the Baptist; 3 = the Magi; 4 = the Evangelists; 5 = possibly the Hebraic pentagon that protected the Israelites from the plagues in Egypt, but possibly also the five wounds of Christ; 6 = those who carried the water-pots at the feast of Cana; 7 = the Great Bear or the planets (an obscure point if the song is to be taken as Christian teaching); 8 = the Archangels; 9 = either the orders of Angels or the joys of Mary; 10 is self-explanatory; 11 and 12 = the Apostles (minus Judas in the first line). See also No. 190.

190. Nettel, op. cit. 'Dial' as in clock-face, with twelve points. The 11,000 virgins seems a touch excessive, and was most probably a misreading of the roman XI.M.V., abbreviating eleven martyr-virgins.

191. Nettel, op. cit. A fascinating mingling of the Christian belief with the Arthurian legend.

192. W. Jenkins, Kings Pyon, Herefordshire, 1909 (RVW).

193. Mrs Gentie Phillips, Birmingham, 1910 (CS).

194. Mr Hirons, Haven, Herefordshire, 1909 (RVW).

195. Child 54B.

196. Henry Thomas, Chipping Sodbury, Gloucestershire, 1907 (CS).

197. Tom Miners, Camborne, Cornwall, 1912 (CS).

198. Collated from versions from Mrs Gentie Phillips, Birmingham, 1910, and Mrs Reservoir Butler, Armscote, Warwickshire, 1913 (both CS).

199. May Bradley, Shropshire, 1960s (FH).

200. The Copper family, Peacehaven, Sussex, 1970 (Bill Leader). Recorded.

201. Samuel Bradley and Seth Vandrell, Lilleshall, Shropshire, 1911 (CS).

202. Mrs Johnstone, Buckworth, Bedfordshire, 1960s (FH).

203. Mr Flack, Fowlmere, Cambridgeshire, 1907 (RVW)

204. 'Wassail' Harvey, Cricklade, and E. Smart, Oaksey, Wiltshire, c. 1915 (AW).

205. Unnamed singer in Pembridge, Gloucestershire, 1909 (RVW).

206. The Drayton Wassailers, Somerset, 1908 (CS).

207–8. Collected by Miss M. E. Durham, Duncton, Sussex, c. 1890.

209. Text in C. S. Burne, *Shropshire Folk-Lore.*

210. Elijah Iles, Inglesham, Wiltshire, c. 1915 (AW).

211. Shepherd Haden, Bampton, Oxfordshire, 1909 (CS). Appropriately enough, this is usually sung to the tone of 'We plough the fields and scatter' ('Wir Pflügen').

212. J. Wright, Coombe Bisset, Wiltshire, 1904 (RVW).

213. William Henry Watts, Tewkesbury, Gloucestershire, 1908 (CS).

214. Text in Clayre, *100 Folk Songs and New Songs.*

215. F. C. Crowsley, Bedford, Bedfordshire, c. 1965 (FH).

216. David Sawyer, Ogbourne, Wiltshire, c. 1915 (AW).

217. Mrs Tilley, Clutton, Somerset, 1908 (CS).

218. Robert Baxter, Eastleach, Gloucestershire, c. 1915 (AW).

219. James Midwinter, Aldsworth, Gloucestershire, c. 1915 (AW).

220. Robert Parish, Exford, Somerset, 1907 (CS).

221. W. Mills, South Cerney, c. 1915 (AW).

222. Broadside by H. Disley, London, c. 1870.

223. George Barrett, Marston Meysey, c. 1915 (AW).

224. Broadside by Kendrew of York. Mops and statutes were hiring fairs, at which farm-workers were taken on, usually for a year at a time. The fairs died out during the First World War.

225. Broadside from Clun, Shropshire, in Shrewsbury Library Collection. For a less good-tempered approach to the same situation, see No. 244.

226. Arthur Lane, Corvedale, Shropshire, 1974 (Philip Donnellan).

227. Jesse Baggaley (RP). The lyric features an ancient numbering system still in use in relatively recent times. This Lincolnshire version goes (from one to twenty): yan, tan, tethera, pethera, pimp, sethera, methera, hovera, covera, dik, yan a dik, tan a dik, tethera dik, pethera dik, bumfits, yan a bumfits, tan a bumfits, tethera bumfits, pethera bumfits, figgits. 'And figgits have a notch': i.e. a notch is cut on the shepherd's stick. See Palmer, *The Everyman Book of English Country Songs.*

228. Mrs Dommett, Staplehay, Somerset, 1907 (CS).

229. James Lovell, Ball's Cover, Somerset, 1908 (CS).

230. Shepherd Haden, Bampton, Oxfordshire, 1909 (CS).

231. William Mantel, Bridgwater, Somerset, 1906 (CS).

232. Henry Thomas, Chipping Sodbury, Gloucestershire, 1907 (CS).

233. J. Whitby, Tilney All Saints, Norfolk, 1905 (RVW).

234. Walter Pardon, Knapton, Norfolk, 1975 (Bill Leader). Recorded.

235. C. Shire, Langport, Somerset, 1904 (CS).

236. Edwin Thomas, Dulverton, Somerset, 1914 (CS).

237. Jack Beeforth, Wragly, Yorkshire, 1974 (David Hillery). The song was written for the North Warwickshire Hunt by W. Wilson.

238. George Dunn, Quarry Bank, Staffordshire, 1971 (Charles Parker).

239. Text in E. J. Homeshaw, *The Story of Bloxwich* and quoted in Jon Raven, *The Urban and Industrial Songs of the Black Country and Birmingham*.

240. Text in *Songs of the Fell Packs* (Hunt Show Committee of the Melbreak Hunt, Cumbria, n.d.).

241. As 240. Master McGrath won the Waterloo Cup three times, in 1868, 1869, and 1871.

242. Text in Chamber's *Book of Days*, Vol. 2, 1863, and quoted in Palmer, *Touch on the Times*. Tradition says that the bull-running at Stamford, Lincolnshire, began in the reign of King John. It took place on 13 November every year until the late 1830s, when it was finally suppressed after a five-year campaign by the SPCA (as it was then). See R. W. Malcolmson, *Popular Recreation in English Society 1700–1850*.

243. Broadside by Wright of Birmingham. The song was probably based on Martin Parker's 'Time's Alteration' (*c.* 1630).

244. First four lines and chorus from John Denny, Newington, Essex, 1904 (RVW). Remainder supplied by RP from a broadside in the Cecil Sharp Collection.

245. Written in 1778 by John Freeth, and included in his *Modern Songs on Various Subjects* (Birmingham, 1782).

246. Text in W. Henderson, *Victorian Street Ballads*. Joseph Arch formed the first agricultural union in 1872.

247. Broadside by Hanson of Northampton in the Madden Collection.

248. Mr Sparks, Dunsfield, Surrey, 1898 (LB).

249. Thomas Mitchell, Merriott, Somerset, 1905 (CS).

250. Walter Pardon, Knapton, Norfolk, 1978 (RP). Sung, of course, to the tune of 'My Grandfather's Clock'.

251. Collated from versions from Mrs Lock, Muchelney Ham, Somerset, 1904 and Charles Ash, Crowcombe, Somerset, 1908 (both CS).

252. Nettel, op. cit.

253. James Stagg, Winchester, Hampshire, 1907 (GBG). The agricultural machine-smashing took place in 1830, under the leadership of the mythical Captain Swing. 644 men were subsequently hanged and about 500 transported. After the disturbances in Owlesbury (pron. Ullsbury), Hampshire, 2 were hanged, 171 transported and 65 sentenced to hard labour.

254. Broadside by Henry Gosson, London, 1630. I have used the abridged text by RP.

255. Tom Daniel, Batley, Yorkshire, 1965 (A. E. Green).

256. Broadside from Bebbington, Manchester, 1860. The song dates from *c.* 1820.

257. Broadside by J. Bromley, Kidderminster, *c.* 1828. The employers were seeking a seventeen per cent reduction in wages to meet competition from Scotland and north England. The strike, which paralysed the town's trade, lasted from March to August.

258. Broadside by Harkness, Preston, *c.* 1830.

259. Mary Brookbank, Dundee, n. d. (EM).

260. MS in Kidderminster Library. Text in Raven, *Victoria's Inferno*.

261. Public Record Office H42.119 dated 27 January 1812. 'Colting and cutting and squaring'—a practice that arose in or around 1811. Pantaloons and fancy stockings called 'twills' were made on wide looms, but the war and changing fashions had severely damaged trade in both commodities. Some owners had cloth made up on the idle wide looms and cut the pieces into the shape of gloves, stockings, etc. These 'cut-up' items fell to pieces quickly, and the shoddy goods were ruining the market. In 1811 a Luddite campaign started in Nottinghamshire and many wide frames were smashed.

262. Text in J. Horsfall Turner, *Yorkshire Anthology*.

263. Written by Richard Pomfret. Text supplied by Paul Graney via Harry Boardman.

264. Broadside from W. and T. Fordyce, Newcastle upon Tyne, n.d.

265. Broadside from Pratt, Birmingham, *c.* 1848. 'Tommy shops' were owned by the employers, who compelled their workers to use them by giving part of the wages in the form of credits ('tommy notes') that could only to be used in their shops. Needless to say, prices in the tommy shops were high.

266. From a collection of broadsides made by John Bell in the late eighteenth century.

267. John Gowland, Middleton-in-Teesdale, 1960s (EM) and Joan Littlewood. Ascribed to Thomas Raine.

268. Written by Tommy Armstrong, 1885. The actual events occurred during a stoppage in that year. The song was written by Armstrong for a 'song duel' with another miner-songwriter called William Maguire. Maguire's song is now lost.

269. R. Greening, Glasgow, and Mrs Cosgrove, Newtongrange, Midlothian, 1951 (ALL). The explosion occurred at William Dixon's Colliery, High Blantyre, on 22 October 1877. 207 men and boys were killed.

270. Written by Tommy Armstrong, 1882. The disaster occurred on 16 February 1882, and seventy-four miners were lost, six of them in the neighbouring East Hetton colliery due to the seeping through of afterdamp. The song was written within a few days of the tragedy to raise funds for the dependents.

271. From a young miner named Ford, Sheffield, *c.* 1961 (EM). The explosion took place on 22 September 1934. Actually, 262 miners and 3 rescue-workers were killed. In spite of a highly critical report, the colliery company was only fined £15 for negligence.

272. Written by an unknown Durham miner and collected by John Moreton in the early 1960s.

273. Text in Joe Wilson's *Tyneside Songs and Drolleries* (1872).

274. Written by John Freeth and printed in his *Political Songster* (1970). The phrase 'Oh the brave Dudley boys, O' is a quotation from the refrain of another contemporary song about a food riot.

275. Originally printed in Ritson's *Northumberland Garland* and quoted in Raven, *Victoria's Inferno*. There was a common superstition among miners that the devil lived underground. The refrain refers to the fact that the ponies could find their way out of the mines in the dark.

276. Unnamed singer in Aberaman, *c.* 1960 (ALL).

277. Henry Nattress, Low Fell, Gateshead (Walter Toyn).

278. Unnamed singer in Bishop Auckland, 1959 (ALL).

279. Text in Ashton, *Modern Street Ballads*.

280. Text from *Manchester City News, Notes and Queries*, 12 March 1881. Sung by a music-hall performer called Mr Hammond, *c.* 1826. The canal was eventually opened in 1894!

281. Written by John Freeth and published in his *Warwickshire Medley*, 1780. The reference to the mulberry tree concerns the one supposedly planted by Shakespeare in his garden, and to the fact that Stratford only got full value out of it during Shakespearian anniversaries.

282. Unnamed boatman at Wolverhampton canal basin, 1962 (David Blagrove). The railway was completed in 1854. 'Unbehurried'—what a splendid word that is!

283. Written or collected by Dr Moorman, President of the Yorkshire Dialect Society, *c.* 1900.

284. Broadside from H. Disley, London, *c.* 1867.

285. Broadside by Russell, Birmingham *c.* 1837. Colonel Evans commanded the British forces which fought in Spain on behalf of Queen Christina against Don Carlos, 1835–7. Fieschi was a Corsican who tried to assassinate King Louis Philippe in 1825; he was executed the following year.

286. Text in Fairbairn's *New Dashing Songster* (1822).

287. Broadside by Pratt, Birmingham, 1876.

288. Text in *The Harvest Songster*, printed by Pitts, London, *c.* 1825.

289. Broadside by W. Pratt, Birmingham, 1876.

290. Handbill printed by W. C. Such, London, 1920s.

291. HARVEY ANDREWS (b. 1943) Left teaching to become a professional singer-songwriter in the late Sixties, and has since produced a number of excellent recordings.

292. PETER BELLAMY (b. 1944) After art-school training, turned to folk-song and became the leader of an influential group called The Young Tradition. Has set many of Kipling's poems to music, and is now a Vice President of the Kipling Society. The song printed here is taken from his ballad opera *The Transports* (1977), a work that involves a certain amount of pastiche. Hence the deliberate 'ungrammaticism' in v. 4.

293-5. ERIC BOGLE (b. 1950) Emigrated from his native Scotland to

NOTES AND REFERENCES

Australia during the early Seventies, and has since made a considerable reputation as a songwriter. His Gallipoli song (No. 295) was a remarkable example of the workings of the current oral tradition, in that it was known in folk clubs all over the country long before it was recorded or even broadcast.

296–7. SYDNEY CARTER (b. 1915)   One of the doyens of the Folk Revival, thanks to 'Lord of the Dance'. As both poet and songwriter, he has formed an occasional stage team with Donald Swann and Jeremy Taylor.

298. PETER COE (b. 1946)   Born in Cheshire, he has single-handedly attempted to create a corpus of Cheshire songs (that county being singularly poor in actual traditional songs). The one printed here refers to the well-established legend that King Arthur and his knights lie under Alderley Edge waiting for the time when their country needs them again. Similar legends exist about Owen Glendower, Charlemagne, Holger Danske, Barbarosa, and Don Sebastian.

299–300. PHIL and JUNE COLCLOUGH (b. 1940 and 1941 respectively). Both are now teachers, but Phil Colclough spent a number of years as a navigator with the merchant navy. Both were also members of The Critics (see note 301).

301. THE CRITICS were a group of young folk-singers who formed round Ewan MacColl and Peggy Seeger in the 1960s. The group finally disbanded in the mid-1970s. This song is a communal effort.

302. VIN GARBUTT (b. 1947)   Of Irish extraction, but born in Cleveland. An artist with a rare, surrealistic humour and a forcefully dramatic style of singing.

303–5. ALEX GLASGOW (b. 1935)   Well-known for his television appearances and plays such as *Close the Coalhouse Door*. Now resident in Australia.

306–7. DAVE GOULDER (b. 1939)   Once a railway fireman, now a drystone dyker in the north of Scotland. He is also an experienced mountaineer. 'January Man' is generally recognized as one of the very best songs to emerge from the Folk Revival.

308. MIKE HARDING (b. 1944)   Best known nowadays as a stage and television comedian. An ex-teacher, he has always had his serious side, and his talent for songwriting has perhaps been overshadowed by his popular image.

309–10. EWAN MacCOLL (b. 1915)   One of the driving forces behind the Folk Revival, and writer of some of the best songs of the post-war era in that field. His career has been too diversified to describe adequately here but, in the folk context, he is probably best known for his development of the radio ballad (eg. 'Singing the Fishing,' 'The Ballad of John Axon', 'The Fight Game', etc.)

311. RALPH McTELL (b. 1944)   Commercially the most successful of all the singer-songwriters to develop during the Folk Revival. His early hit 'The Streets of London' is a contemporary folk-song *par excellence.*

312. AUSTIN JOHN MARSHALL   Record producer and writer during the 1960s. The song refers to the fact that, following the First World War,

383

women took up morris dancing in an effort to keep alive a tradition that was in danger of being lost along with the men whose exclusive domain it had previously been. Women's morris teams are now fairly common in England, and there are even some mixed teams, so that the strictly male function of fertility, originally associated with the dances, has been totally eroded.

313. LEON ROSSELSON (b. 1934) One of the first of the British protest songwriters, writing usually from a fairly extreme left-wing position.

314–17. CYRIL TAWNEY (b. 1930) An ex-submariner, now a professional singer of both his own and traditional songs. His output is not as large as his admirers (the present writer included) would like, but he is certainly one of the outstanding writers in his field.

318–20. ALLAN TAYLOR (b. 1945) An English writer with strong American influences, who nevertheless manages to retain an essentially English voice. His songs have been recorded by singers on both sides of the Atlantic.

INDEX OF TITLES AND FIRST LINES

The references are to the numbers of the poems

INDEX OF TITLES AND FIRST LINES

INDEX OF TITLES AND FIRST LINES

INDEX OF TITLES AND FIRST LINES

INDEX OF TITLES AND FIRST LINES

INDEX OF TITLES AND FIRST LINES

INDEX OF TITLES AND FIRST LINES